THE KNIGHTS TE

THE KNIGHTS TEMPLAR

Influences from the past and impulses for the future

Developed from the conference '*Confronting the Future: Templar Influences in the 21st Century*', held at Emerson College, East Sussex, August 2009

Compiled and edited by Gil McHattie

TEMPLE LODGE

Temple Lodge Publishing
Hillside House, The Square
Forest Row, RH18 5ES

www.templelodge.com

Published by Temple Lodge 2011

A catalogue record for this book is available from the British Library

ISBN 978 1 906999 26 1

Cover by Andrew Morgan Design
Typeset by DP Photosetting, Neath, West Glamorgan
Printed and bound by Gutenberg Press, Malta

Dedicated to the memory of Friedwart Bock (1928–2010) who was connected strongly to the spiritual social impulse of the Templars

Contents

Preface

The beginning of the Templar Order is shrouded in mystery as very little is known of its foundation or the inner workings of the Order. This gives rise to all sorts of speculation and, sometimes, bizarre theories to account for the growth of the organization. This book hopes to provide some clarity as to why the Order was formed, the aims and intentions of this group of men and to redeem the picture that many now hold of the Templar Knight. It is not an exhaustive contribution but its broad scope will hopefully encourage the reader into further enquiries. It explores the spiritual and historical background and the esoteric significance of the Knights Templar, and how their spiritual impulse has continued, and still continues, to evolve and work further.

During its time the Order was regarded as possessing the highest principles and integrity. The Knights Templar lived so intensely with the reality described by St Paul 'Not I, but Christ in me', uniting themselves profoundly and inwardly with the Mystery of Golgotha, that many underwent true Christian initiation. This took place not only personally but also on behalf of the whole of humanity. The Templar Order was violently eradicated and many knights underwent terrible tortures before being burned at the stake. Nevertheless the true spiritual fruit of their work remains as an impulse—now and for future centuries. It is becoming more and more important to add truth to the plethora of distortion that surrounds the order. The Templars' spiritual legacy therefore needs voices that make conscious the impulse they carried and to show how these impulses have reappeared and metamorphosed in later times, and how they continue to be of pressing relevance today in all spheres of life from spirituality and the arts, to politics and the worlds of banking, commerce and business.

The articles were developed from a conference held on the theme at Emerson College, East Sussex, UK, in August 2009, along with extra contributions. It was an international conference with people attending from 16 countries and three continents. It was inspired by a similar conference held in Hamburg, 2007. The British conference was held through the auspices of the Humanities Section of the School of Spiritual Science (UK group), Goetheanum, Dornach, Switzerland.

I would like to thank the contributors for their work and also my colleagues, Angela Lord, Steve Roberts and Peter Snow for their assistance and encouragement.

Gil McHattie

THE PAST

The Templars as Knights of Christ, and the Opposing Forces

Peter Tradowsky

We can pose the questions 'Why are the Templars the Knights of Christ?' and 'What actually were their tasks?' A great deal can be learnt about the Templars when studying the second Mystery Drama written by Rudolf Steiner.[1] The seventh scene is a review of all the characters in their medieval incarnation. There one finds the brotherhood to whom the Grand Master says:

> You have become companions to me
> in search of humanity's future goals.
> We are directed by our Order's precepts
> to bring these aims from the spiritual world
> into the realm of activity on earth.

So there is a clear aim to be fulfilled, and underlying this one can sense what stands behind the Order of the Knights Templar.

We have yet another hint of what lived in the Knights Templar in their maxim 'Non nobis, Domine, non nobis, sed nomine tuo da gloriam', which translates as 'Not to us, Lord, not to us, but to your name give glory'. The 'Gloria' is actually untranslatable in modern times because what the Knights Templar sensed from the meaning of the word is something of the brilliance of the spiritual world beyond the threshold. The 'Gloria' is something that we can sense that descends from heaven to earth but also, in the words of Rudolf Steiner, ascends from earth to heaven. Here, Rudolf Steiner in his Mystery Drama spoke, in the scene quoted, of the tasks of the Templars but in a different way. This is therefore not a full translation of 'Non nobis, Domine, non nobis, sed nomine tuo da gloriam'.

It is important to be aware that we are talking about a brotherhood, that it is an order and a spiritual community. From the beginning the emphasis did not lie on the 'I' or the individual. There was no emphasis on 'I' as we can understand it today in this fifth cultural epoch.

In the scene that Rudolf Steiner created spiritual laws are mentioned and this spiritual law or impulse pulsates or radiates towards the Grand Master from the hearts of the younger knights.

The separate life and being must be sacrificed
by him who would set eyes on spiritual goals
through revelations of the sense-world;
who would dare with courage
to pour the spirit's power of will
into his individual will.

The major motifs or impulses of the Knights Templar are seen in this. Then comes the surprise which we can try to understand in the following text: '... who would set eyes on spiritual goals through *revelations of the sense-world*'—not through heavenly revelation, not through spiritual revelation but through revelation of the senses—'who would dare with courage to pour the spirit's power of will into his individual will'. Spiritual will lives in the tasks which come to us from our surroundings and which can be sensed from the outer world and which wait to be taken up. But to do this one's own will has to be sacrificed. The perception and taking up of a spiritual task is brought about out of the revelation of the senses, that is to say, in a way that has never happened previously and that can only be understood because the Spirit of the Sun has incarnated into the earthly realm as Christ.

Now we can observe that the nature of Intuition, in the sense found in *The Philosophy of Spiritual Activity: A Philosophy of Freedom*[2] (which is the basis for free thinking) is mentioned here in a medieval form. For within intuitive action are deeds deriving from the intuitively sensed being whose task serves aims for the future of humanity. In *The Philosophy of Spiritual Activity: A Philosophy of Freedom*, the chapter 'The Idea of Freedom', Rudolf Steiner shows us this in a form which corresponds to our time.

If we ask ourselves what made the Knights Templar the Knights of Christ (one of their many titles) then we need to consider something which we haven't described so far, namely the fact that we all go through different earthly lives. The fruits of work and also events undergone in one life will ripen in a next life or a further life. This is a process whereby we connect ourselves with what we take up in the course of an incarnation.

If we ask ourselves what makes the Knights Templar different we are led to the fact that these were human beings whose destiny in a previous incarnation was such that they had met with Jesus Christ or had contact with those still able to have a connection to Christ, through the Apostles and scholars of the Apostles. They still had this intimate contact. This is something that we can only follow with difficulty, today, because of our modern consciousness. Rudolf Steiner said that once a human being when led by their destiny had looked into the eyes of Christ, then through the impulse of their heart they would be Christian in their next incarnation.

And so we have in the first one or two centuries a process that cannot happen now and therefore cannot be understood by today's thought or feeling, or only in extreme cases. It is surely a very special destiny to have lived in Palestine at the time of Christ. Something could happen there which we could call a deeper spiritual connection to Christ Jesus who lived there for three years. And one who is open to this, through their destiny and as a human being, could sense something of this very deep contact in a manner equivalent to the fine sensitivity through which the soul of the human being knew 'Christ is risen'. This was a fundamental experience that had nothing whatsoever to do with intellect, with understanding, but was purely an act of feeling. A little later something like this was still possible through eye contact or touch.

This had a special meaning and we can still see it today in the ritual of confirmation where the priest holds the confirmand's head with both hands. Something spiritual radiates from the hands of the priest. What actually happens is an awakening of the heart which means that the human individual has taken into the consciousness of his heart a connection that is based on one important fact—the revelation of Christ. The human being has then taken something in, which for him is a physical reality. People at that time were so completely different to us today; they didn't have the intellectual life that we have now. The events described were not something that could be understood through the intellect; they sit much deeper within the person.

It is also not something that today we call belief. It is the culture of the heart that belongs to the consciousness of the fourth epoch (until 1413). Different forces were active during that time than those at work today. Therefore a situation like that is not possible today.

Such a human being then goes through death and life after death and into a new incarnation, be it the next life or one after, and this element lives on, according to the very important law that is still valid for us today. That which we have worked with spiritually, that which we have absorbed spiritually ripens or matures in the life after death and, in the following life, is brought back as an ability, almost a natural inheritance, as something that happens naturally. One has achieved this through a development and maturing process and one can recognize it as a reality.

We can notice abilities in us which surprise us at first but which can be explained by understanding this in a spiritual sense. The human being that has reincarnated in the second or third incarnation after these events has therefore a totally different connection to the life of Christ on earth and to the Resurrection.

In a certain sense one can observe this in the two festivals with which the Knights Templar were especially connected and that were celebrated in a special way. The Jesus child, who is connected to us especially during Advent and Christmas, did not play a special role at that time and also not during the time of the origins of Christianity. This has only developed in the form we know now (which is very beautiful) in the last century and began during the Middle Ages.

The two festivals that the Templars found most meaningful were Epiphany, which is connected with *et incarnatus est*. They celebrated the appearance of God's spirit, as the spirit of Christ in the Jesus that we know from the Baptism in the River Jordan. And the other festival was of course the Resurrection. The event of the Crucifixion disappeared into the background. It was the Resurrection that connected them to Palestine. These two festivals were the two pillars of the Templar Order: Epiphany and the Resurrection. The other things clearly moved into the background.

What did the Knights of Christ achieve? One is the opening of the path to Palestine, and the principle of the sword plays a significant role here. That meant there was a problem already at the time and also later. This was a soldier's order; it was also a monk's order but ordered in a military way. The Order had this military, fighting impulse—to fight against the heathens of the Orient. Because of this the Holy Land was, more or less, a Christian realm for almost 200 years.

We always find this a little difficult because now we have a different consciousness, a different viewpoint. But then it was a completely different time. The change in connection to this question of the sword was in 1604. It was then possible, through the mission of Buddha to Mars, to affect a change in the development of humanity.[3] Quite rightly today we have an impulse towards pacifism, an impulse of peacefulness to overcome warlike elements. That was not there at the time of the Templars. We must try to understand a time out of itself instead of from our own time.

If one opens any literature about the Templars one always finds a picture of the seal of the Grand Master. This seal has two sides. On one side there is a depiction of a horse on which there are two riders. Historians have put great stress on finding an explanation for this and we find fantastic interpretations. The most facile explanation is to say that the Templars were so poor that two knights had to share one horse. In fact each knight had two or three horses, or more, each and needed them for battle so it does not make any sense to share a horse. The individual knights were poor but the Order collected funds precisely to equip them for battle.

Even the most conscientious and well-meaning historian cannot make sense of this so what does it mean? Now, dear friends, it is simple. The explanation is that each of us has a 'day' aspect and a 'night' aspect within us. These day and night consciousnesses are normally separated from one another by a threshold (sleep) but not in reality. The Grand Master wanted to say with this seal that he had the ability to unite these consciousnesses. The Grand Master had the ability to unite this life on earth with that of the hereafter (penetration into the spiritual world) and which are both within us. With his deeds he had the ability to bring these together, so two aspects were united in one person and this is depicted on the seal. A very simple explanation, but that is definitely how it was.

In the second Mystery Drama (seventh scene) this is described by the Grand Master from the Rule of the Order:

> You have become companions to me
> in search of humanity's future goals.
> We are directed by our Order's precepts
> to bring these aims from the spiritual world
> into the realm of earth activity.'[4]

In this the unity is stated, in so far that the aims for the future from the realms of the spirit are carried into the deeds of the earthly realm. There the bridge is built across the threshold to the spiritual world. It was the core of the work of the Templars to create this unity between the spiritual world and the earthly world and the seal of the Grand Master is an indication of this. It was the early Templars who had this possibility and the ability to do this. The seal of the Grand Master expresses this in the scene succinctly—what the truth was inwardly and the relationship between the life on earth and the life after death. This relationship was often tested in battle by the knights finding the courage to sacrifice their lives. The fighting forces of the Templars were feared by the enemy and admired by friends. No Templar was allowed to retreat even if there were as many as three times the number of foe. Today it is, of course, much more difficult to do such a thing as there are so many different types of conflict.

On the reverse side of the seal one can see something that looks like a church which is believed to be the Holy Sepulchre in Jerusalem. But one does wonder what it does depict.

Another maxim of the Templars was 'The Grave is empty'. This was very significant. The Grave is empty. Here we also question the meaning. When we connect to Easter Sunday we look into the story of the Resurrection. The Grave is empty means that there is nothing material in the grave with which to refer to or connect with. There is not even a corpse we can refer to because the women and the Apostles who come to the grave really do find an empty grave. The Resurrection has nothing to do with what we can physically touch. We refer to something purely spiritual.

The Templars, as the Knights of Christ, understood their service as sacrificial service. They were of the view that their blood was not theirs but was blood to be sacrificed for Christ. In a higher sense the blood was not their own.

We can also ask the question 'How did the Templars deal with their opponents?' This starts with an exercise that one can describe as follows. The first challenge is a purely inner one and this challenge is to be able to say, 'I could betray the Lord just as well as Judas, I could deny the Lord just as well as Peter, I could disbelieve in the Lord just as well as Thomas.' One has to imagine this as a religious practice which plays its role in the most inner part of the soul that somehow one doesn't bring to outer life.

This process happens in the most secret parts of the soul. What we have tried to look at here the Templars meant in a most radical form and that is what they endured as an inner process. A human being, in general, tries to reach the realm of truth and honesty, which is necessary for any spiritual work. Can one make a confession to oneself influencing the footprints that Lucifer leaves in one's soul? It is important that a person enters an honest and truthful state in relation to him/herself. This is a radical act of self-perception when one ceases to pretend to oneself and which is one of the most difficult tasks we can carry out as human beings.

Goethe felt this similarly and each and every one of us can do this in our own individual way. Goethe said of himself, 'If I am honest then I have to admit that I would be capable of all crimes which are known to me in world history.'[5] We know that Goethe didn't commit any crimes but the secret of this matter is that by exercising in this way one can find a possibility to fight against Lucifer. We also find hints of this in Rudolf Steiner's writings. He once said that if we were ever in the position to be able to fight all the aggressive and destructive impulses in our souls, in our astral bodies, then we wouldn't need to fight wars any longer. If we could carry out this battle within ourselves then we would fight against the negative and aggressive forces within us. And this we can do for ourselves. It is a type of cleansing process when one tries this but we find out after a while that it has to be repeated again and again because the dross within our soul grows again and again like weeds grow in a garden. This is not a unique story but the process of life. The challenge of what is left in the human soul from the realm of Lucifer (and in a certain sense is a necessary opposition) is what exercised the Templars in their own way.

A further step is to challenge or deal with the ahrimanic spirit. We cannot of course look at all the facets of such things; we will just deal with that which is in outer life. The Templars gained more and more land and property for themselves in these 200 years. When a young man of the nobility entered the Order it was common that the family gave it an estate. Due to this about half the area in Berlin, from Tempelhof to Teltow, more or less belonged to the Templars. Now a highly important point is that then they knew what to do with land. It was so that everything belonged to the Order and nothing to the individual. The individual was just a caretaker of the lands that were given him and he had to use these in a responsible way. Land was in that sense a mere tool. The Knights Templar and the other ranks, sergeants, squires, servants, were part of this service. We have the harvest of this now in a certain relationship towards land.

The way these men matured in one or two incarnations in respect to the Christ impulse also led to a change in how they felt: there is not only the Sun soul and the Sun Spirit but also the Sun body and, for them, this was the Earth. Land was always holy ground, so one couldn't just say something was private property because it was felt that Christ was a part of this property. The transformation of the Earth to the Sun had begun in the moment of the Mystery of Golgotha. This process determined their deeds even though it was a secret, invisible process.

In Russia this still resounds a little today. Even the Soviet bloc kept this attitude, feeling that one cannot *buy* land. When a real Russian stands in front of one one realizes there is still this attitude about him. 'We cannot just sell off the living, fertile Mother Earth; it cannot be bought with money.' This was elementary to them and was deeply rooted in their souls.

It was just this way of thinking in regard to having land that allowed the Templars to become immensely wealthy. This selflessness is a method by which enterprises become rich very fast because all profits always flow back into the whole. This is how this amazing, vast wealth was created which was so often envied.

The second thing that has to be mentioned is closely connected: the relationship of the Templars towards gold and towards money. During that time money was a mere metal currency, while gold was of course most important and most valuable. Here one also has to try to understand the consciousness, the way of thinking living at that time. Gold is connected to the Sun body, the gold that was first in the Earth when the Earth and gold were still molten. The whole of the Earth was not yet densified into matter as it is today; then gold was really Sun gold or gold of the Sun. This connection with the Sun gold was something holy and went so far that only in special circumstances was the Templar Knight allowed to have even a penny in his pocket and therefore was without money. There was much treasure in the preceptories, especially in the Temple in Paris, but nothing in the pockets of the individual. In the course of time the Order became much like European central banks, although it spent a great deal of this wealth on building and equipping its castles and maintaining its fleet which connected England and the south of France with Palestine across the Mediterranean Sea. Therefore large expenses were incurred by the Order and of course the largest expenditure was for military campaigns.

One can quite rightly say that the Templars were actually the inventors of the credit card system, though of course money was a direct counterpart, a real equivalent, to goods or services. Here is how this credit worked. Let us say, for example, that the preceptor from the Tempelhof in Berlin would receive an amount from a crusading knight and in exchange would give the knight a letter confirming the transaction, which could be handed in at another preceptory to gain funds on the journey. This was, for that time, an incredible procedure. This invention shows us the trust felt towards the Templars and also the military competence that something like this could be guaranteed. It also shows the strength and the great influence they attained, and this continued for several centuries and should be noted.

The maxim above should be emphasized once more: 'The Grave is empty. Christ is risen'. There is a singular spiritual connection to this, which is the secret of the Resurrection and the secret to Christ generally, and all of this was given to them. Due to this the Templars were more or less protected from ahrimanic attacks. There was the highest protection around them especially from the principle of having no personal possessions.

I would like to refer here to a book by Rudolf Steiner, *Die Kernpunkte der Sozialen Frage*.[6] This is a true Templar book. It is quite easy to read and one can feel it is about the Templar Knights because it exactly echoes these Templar thoughts, impulses and attitudes. Of course, Rudolf Steiner transposes this into the machine age of modern times, of divisions of work, of connection to possessions and land ownership and to money, but one can quite easily see from this that this relationship to money is continued into our present time.

The time of the change to a different consciousness (from the fourth cultural epoch to the fifth cultural epoch—from about 1413) is thought out clearly. The Order of the Knights Templar (not the individual) amassed wealth that could almost compete with that possessed by the Emperor. In the aforementioned book one finds a new concept in regard to owning land and also in regard to production, which is an activity connected to the ego or the individual self. One has the possibility of owning something correlating to working with a tool as long as one's ego is able to carry out the activity and take on the responsibility towards everything with which it is connected. From the brotherhood of the Knights the fruits of this way of working together are then given over to the individual ego or to a small group of human egos but at any rate to the principle of the ego. This is the difference from a medieval situation; in those times it would not have been possible. There the Grand Master would have had a higher ranking function, especially in the spiritual sense. But even the Grand Master had no personal right to possession, that is, to ownership of land and gold.

Today, the new ego comes in with its individual capabilities in con- nection to using land. But accordingly the ego has to be able and willing to work with this issue of land. This has to be understood as being connected to the will and so taking on a definite concrete relationship to it in full responsibility. This responsibility cannot be shifted onto someone else as happens so often. It becomes a focused ego situation.

We can say that we can admire the Templars, but they were working up to the end of the fourth cultural epoch and hence we cannot transfer these past impulses directly to the present time. Everything has to go through metamorphosis, as Rudolf Steiner achieved with his vision of the social organism of the present and of the future. Of course today we neither have the old metal currency nor do we have the horses, just horsepower. Even if we portray the Templars and their Order with a certain enthusiasm, that doesn't mean that we can copy or re-enact something like this again.

But there is an inner connection between the Knights of Christ and the impulse of their social threefoldness. Rudolf Steiner has indicated, without mentioning the Templars by name, that this impulse of three-foldness has emerged from the Christ who lives among us today. At one point he says:

> These things, which are also being made known in another form today through our proposals concerning a 'threefold social ordering', are the Christianity of today; they are spiritual revelations clothed in external forms.[7]

Just as the Templars wanted to act in the sense of the Sun Spirit that had become Earth Spirit, Rudolf Steiner put himself in the service of the Christ impulse after the First World War, or to be more precise from 1917. This impulse was not only not accepted but actually denied.

Without doubt the tragedy and the dissolution of the Order of Templars was connected to this theme of gold. The possession of gold and the use of it planted in one man's soul a seed of unimaginable jealousy. This was Philip the Fair of France. Apparently he was seen as the most handsome man in the Occident. But he was also the man having the most greed for gold in the whole of history. He was obsessed with gold to an extreme extent, for him all was about gold and without the aura of aurum the only meaning left for him was wealth. He was obviously a man who was led by lust, by his desires, which activated an immense energy to find this substance. He was also a highly intelligent man and a very modern leader because he had debts and more debts; he was completely debt ridden. This is also, in a certain way, a phenomenon which contrasts with the behaviour of the Templars.

It is said that he deflated the currency of the time—Brakteaten[8]—by reducing the amount of gold. But Philip overdid this to such an extent that the coins were almost pure iron with only a very little gold. What he did was to illegally debase the coinage, and because of this there was the famous uproar in Paris where the citizens protested so fiercely at the state of their coinage that Philip had to be rescued by Templar Knights. The Templars left the Temple in Paris in their white cloaks with the red cross and calmed the citizens. This fired Philip's jealously of the Knights to an even more extreme level and he became obsessed with the need to possess their treasure for himself. Philip was able to lure Pope Clement V into his plans. This was necessary because in the statutes of the Order of the Knights Templar it states that only the Pope had the authority to command them as the Order stood outside the legislature of the country. Philip did not pay much attention to the rights of his nobles or to the laws of the land.

On 13 October 1307, a date of world importance, the king was able with the help of his henchman William de Nogaret, in an underhand and very secret way, to capture all the Templars in France. All the preceptories were occupied at dawn that day and once that decision was taken there was no way back. Philip wanted the gold and he got it (or some of it). The Templars, though, were spiritually aware of something of this and it was then possible for them to give back the esoteric cultus to the spiritual world from whence it came.

They were probably also able to get part of this gold treasure away secretly and this was used in building the great cathedrals. Philip was disappointed that his booty was smaller than expected.

Philip and Clement now faced an immense question as the truth was, and is, that seen from the outside the Order could not be destroyed. All the accusations, the blasphemies arising from torture and insults towards the Christ, were actually not true and Rudolf Steiner emphasizes this. It was about the fact of how a real spiritual truth can be changed into a lie and so distortion occurs.

It was all about how one could distort the truth. This was clearly done by torturing the Templars in an unimaginable way and there one can witness something that goes beyond ahrimanic or satanic forces. The torturers of Philip understood themselves as creatures of Philip and fulfilled themselves in a most inhuman way. They tortured the Templars in a most unimaginable way to force them to give up their secrets. In principle this can be said more simply. If one thinks of the exercises or spiritual practices given earlier, for example, 'I could betray Christ just as Judas did', then when one of the Templars was tortured into near unconsciousness and was asked a question such as 'Have you betrayed Christ in your life?' the tortured Knight would reply 'yes', and this would be documented as follows, 'He has admitted that he has betrayed Christ.'

It is a gruesome story. Anything can be obtained from the practice of torture and we accept this today. It shows that when any human being is tortured for long enough they will admit to anything, they will talk at the end and whether it is truth or lie is irrelevant to them. If any knight really managed to withstand the torture the torture would continue until he died and this happened to many. If they resisted too much they were burned at the stake.

None of the Templars admitted to any of the accusations when not under torture but the statements made under duress did, of course, affect public opinion and to a certain extent this happened. Just as the proverb says, 'There is no smoke without fire.'

There were other situations where this wasn't the case. A scene from the *Grandes Chroniques de France* where the last Grand Master, Jacques de Molay, was shown to the people outside Notre Dame and said to the crowd that the accusations against the Templar Order were true,

> 'Sirs, everything that the Council of France has told you, that I and all the Templar Brothers who are here, and yet others, have confessed is true.' Next he opens his cloak and strips off his clothing, 'You see, Sirs, how we were made to say what they wished,' at which point he reveals his arms, emaciated to the bone, and the traces of the torture he has undergone. Then he retracts his admissions.[9]

They made sure that such a scene was not repeated as they could not be sure whether another Templar would not disclose the facts as happened here. The torture described here of Jacques de Molay, showing flesh stripped from the bone, was one of the lesser tortures used on the knights.

If one wants to penetrate this in a spiritual way, we can understand that this evil goes into the asuric element. One can gain a clearer picture of the difference between ahrimanic thoughts, which Philip and his henchmen followed, when they were under the influence of Ahriman (Satan), and the torturers who were under the influence of the asuric element. Here one doesn't just have ahrimanic thoughts but those thoughts have been transferred into brutal deeds. Here the most inhuman impulses are practised. They cross into life because the will makes them happen.

This is the important difference between ahrimanic thoughts and asuric will. The thoughts prepare, without a doubt, that which one has within oneself, but it is still held back and then in an enormous step this changes into the deed. There one reaches the point made earlier when truth is degraded into lie and the lie appears as truth. This became an impulse in European history from this time onward.

When tortures like this happen, and Rudolf Steiner has tried to clarify this for us, something occurs that was even worse for the Templars to endure. One can say it was a satanic intelligence that possessed Philip. When the confessions were made under torture it was as if a bacterium or virus was set free and the blasphemies made under this torture were released into the space around like viruses or bacteria. What was released went into the history of Europe and what happened was something quite horrific.

We can only console ourselves with the clear fact that another stream was working throughout the last 700 years. The Templars lose gold as metal, but gold will become completely spiritualized, completely etheric and completely weightless in the future. It turns into the actual Sun quality of wisdom and enters humanity by permeating such individuals as Goethe. Rudolf Steiner once said, 'Goethe knew the secrets of the Templars.'[10] One can see this through his fairy tale *The Green Snake and the Beautiful Lily*.[11] The Mystery Dramas were written after the fairy tale which is very interesting. There were many people who absorbed, maybe without completely realizing it, this gold of wisdom, this spiritualized gold.

Now to continue, the Order was disbanded due to the pressure of the King and Pope in 1312. The statutes of the Order were destroyed, which was illegal and a classical breach of law. And this is also something modern, since who bothers now whether something is lawful or not? One just carries out the deed. With this act the Order of the Knights Templar was destroyed.

Some of the leading Templars had been imprisoned since 1307. Neither the Pope, who in reality would not have been held responsible, nor anyone else wanted to address the question 'What should now happen to these people?' Finally on 18 March 1314 a world historical event happens. The Pope was not present as he never appeared in public or intervened personally in the issue. Instead three cardinals were sent in his place to visit the imprisoned Templars. They were sent to bring the mercy of the Pope to the men, or all that existed of the mercy of the Pope, and to give absolution to the men for the sins they had seemingly committed. The 'merciful' sentence of lifelong entombment was given which means lifelong imprisonment. This led to a kind of awakening in Jacques de Molay. After seven years of imprisonment plus the accompanying torture he suddenly said that it was all blackmail. 'The Order is innocent. We are good Christians; I know by saying this I sentence us to death. We will all be burned like our brothers have been burned. But honour to the truth. All these accusations are lies and do not reflect the reality.'

This countered Philip's intentions; the cardinals were helpless even though in later accounts it was always the cardinals who took the blame for the burnings. Historically this is not correct. Philip went into a furious rage and immediately issued orders for the burnings that were carried out the same afternoon with him watching everything. His plan was now seen—the scheme to become the 'saviour' of Christianity was finished, with the whole charade showing something quite different. It cannot be assumed that the Templars knew something of the forces working against them in the spiritual sense but it was present in their lives and was what they endured. What happened at the end—in March 1314—goes beyond the Asuras into the forces of the Antichrist, Sorat.

Rudolf Steiner has given an insight into this event with the lecture cycle to the Priests.[12] This cycle was only published in 1995 and therefore has hardly been penetrated by the consciousness of anthroposophists and others. Only the Vatican has acknowledged and reacted to this event in 2007. Those who objectively observe these things have to admit that the Pope or Vatican have tried to portray Pope Clement V as a figure who gave Jacques de Molay and his brother absolution in 1308 instead of which Clement was actually a servant of the Antichrist. Pope Clement V had not intended to give the two men justice and the Vatican has tried in a very clever way, by focusing on side issues, to divert public attention from understanding what really happened. Rudolf Steiner indicated decisively that Sorat was active as the Antichrist on this day. So we are not speaking about Ahriman or the Asuras but about the being of Sorat who is the Sun Demon and the actual opponent of Christ.

Rudolf Steiner said:

> But in the hearts and souls of those who could not rest until the Order had been destroyed in 1312 and until Jacques de Molay had met his death in 1314, in the hearts of those who were the adversaries of the Christ who looked to the cosmos, in these hearts Sorat lived again, not least by making use of the Roman Church's attitude of mind at that time to bring about the death of the Templars. The appearance of Sorat was more visible than it had been the previous time, and the demise of the Templars is shrouded in a stupendous secret.[13]

As has already been said, Rudolf Steiner explained what happened during these tortures. But in one particular place, in the lecture of 12 September, he broadens and changes his findings. He takes the events of this day and goes much further than previously in saying the following:

> When you can see into what went on in the souls of the Templars while they were being tortured you can gain some idea of how what lived in their visions was instigated by Sorat. As a result they slandered themselves, providing their enemies with a cheap indictment through

what they themselves uttered. People were confronted with the terrible spectacle of seeing individuals being unable to speak about what they genuinely represented, while different spirits from among the cohorts of Sorat spoke through them instead, accusing the Order of the most disgusting things out of the mouths of its own adherents.'[14]

This is something completely new from Rudolf Steiner. In earlier descriptions he says that while overcoming temptations it were these temptations that surfaced during torture. But now it is explained here that the intention of the Antichrist, Sorat, was to destroy the Order of Knights Templar within European history. It was like a poisoning which went through European history and which acts right up to the present time.

Rudolf Steiner explained further and said it was the second attack of Sorat towards mankind. The first attack was around the year 666 with the impulses of the Academy of Gondishapur. The second attack was 666 years later in 1332. (These dates are approximate.) The third attack connected with this rhythm was 666 years later (approximately) in 1998.

This is the relevance of the entire process that their suffering then spreads out in our present time, in the twenty-first century, in a powerful way. These impulses of the Antichrist are present now, and it is possible today through spiritual science to name the connections and the workings of the different adversarial powers. What the Templars suffered and what has not been penetrated or understood can now be used by these adversarial powers. With the Templars it was still within the element that belonged to their own lives, their own inner experiences, and so was not so much knowledge but their own life wisdom.

Today it is possible, through the aid of spiritual science, to follow the steps that pass from the luciferic through the ahrimanic to the asuric element of the tortures right to the kernel which sits in the impulse of the Antichrist, Sorat. The Templars were pursued because they were Knights of Christ; they really tried to work across the threshold of the spiritual world to create an order based on the Christ.

To continue this path Rudolf Steiner called the threefoldness of the social organism the Christlike appropriate form of society. Today we are far away from the substance of this in any depth. We have something that only corresponds to the beginning of events 700 years ago. This step is only important in so far as it might be able to transform the spiritual knowledge from anthroposophy into insight so that we can resist these forces and must resist these forces from the work of our own egos or selves.

We have to be clear that the anti-forces of Sorat focus on the central part of the human being, the 'I' or ego forces. Rudolf Steiner says in respect to the Asuras:

> In our time we are approaching the era in which other beings can get hold of the human being and which intervene more and more into human development and into the future of humanity which lies before us. It is the same way that the luciferic spirits intervened in the Lemurian era, the ahrimanic spirits in the Atlantean era and so now they will also intervene in our era.[15]

One has to become clear that the asuric powers have different intentions to those of Lucifer and Ahriman. There is a distinct division between these beings and this division becomes obvious when we observe that the sculpture *The Representative of Humanity*[16] survived the fire that destroyed the first Goetheanum and we meet Lucifer and Ahriman in this happening. Only if we see the connection between Christ, Lucifer and Ahriman, which means when the necessary balance can be created, does one have the possibility to fight against the asuric and soratic impulses that aim to damage the ego, the 'I' of the human being, and to break it into pieces.

The difficult challenges of our present time are something that we have to take seriously. One has to be absolutely clear about the fact that the Asuras and especially Sorat are not ahrimanic. The Templars were the first people to experience this. There are the lesser sins, one may say that lesser human frailties can be excused and these are the ones found through luciferic or ahrimanic entanglements. There one has the impression that all is still in the realm of the human being. But then there is a clear division where things enter from a completely different dimension and this became really evident in the twentieth century. Soratic impulses want to take over our time through using untamed will impulses of men and women and to actually wrest the Earth away from the Christ-being. Whether they will succeed or not depends solely on the human being's ego forces and it will depend on humanity and how we will act in these situations.

The task of the spiritual science of anthroposophy is to bring strength to our ego forces so that we can live through this. The principle of the Resurrection has to root deeply within human ego forces so that he/she can meet these attacks. We cannot rely solely on God's will. This now depends on the consciousness soul and on the development of the human being's path towards freedom. We are now in a time of change where the human ego is in the centre of activity as co-worker, as participant. This is an immense test for humanity.

Today Sorat has a mighty helper—Mammon. Mammon is a spiritual being in the sub-physical world. When one thinks about this one comes to the conclusion that Mammon, unlike the Templars, has no interest in the Earth. This is not a friendly being that would serve humanity but a being that serves Sorat. It is an important helper of Sorat, one that pushes the whole of development of humanity into the direction of a social order which is opposite to that of the Templars and to that of the Christ-being.

Finally I want to bring a Whitsun verse that shows us the threshold where we meet Lucifer and Ahriman in exactly the same way that the Templars experienced. At this threshold we can gain the consciousness in order to sustain being on both sides of the threshold with stability. This also appears in a very simple way on the Templar seal of two riders on one horse. Every individual also has two riders on one horse!

Where outer senses' knowledge ends,
There and there only is the gateway
That leads to the realities of life.
The soul of man himself/herself forges the key
When he/she grows strong in the battle
Which cosmic powers with human powers wage
Upon the soul's deep ground,
And by her/his own free will dispels the sleep
Which at the senses' frontiers
Plunges in spiritual night
Her/his faculties of knowledge.[17]

Peter Tradowsky was born in Berlin in 1934 and taught at the Berlin Rudolf Steiner School between 1962 and 1972. He is co-founder of the Berlin Waldorf Teacher Training course and a lecturer and writer. Some of his published works include Kaspar Hauser, Ere the Century Closes *and* Christ and Antichrist.

His relationship to the Templar Order became consciously alive in him through studying the second Mystery Drama—The Soul's Probation. * *In the seventh scene the destruction of the order on the physical plane can slowly be perceived and also the abyss of misunderstanding through the involvement of the Dominican Order. This has occupied him again and again as a conflict that has not been solved to this day.*

Peter was also very impressed by the books The Trial against the Templars *by*

---

* Rudolf Steiner, *Four Mystery Dramas*, Hans & Ruth Pusch (Rudolf Steiner Press, London 1997) (GA 14). The second drama, *The Soul's Probation*, Scene 7.

*Krück von Poturzyn** and Schiller's dramatic fragment* The Knight of Malta.[†] *The latter was intended to have been a tragedy about the destruction of the Order of the Knights Templar but was never finished.*

Notes

1. Rudolf Steiner, *Four Mystery Dramas*, Hans & Ruth Pusch (Rudolf Steiner Press, London 1997) (GA 14). The second drama *The Soul's Probation*, Scene 7.
2. Rudolf Steiner, *The Philosophy of Spiritual Activity: A Philosophy of Freedom*. tr. R. Stebbing (Rudolf Steiner Press, Forest Row, Sussex, 1992) (GA 4).
3. Rudolf Steiner. *From Buddha to Christ*. trs. D.S. Osmond et al. others (Anthroposophic Press, New York, 1978) (GA 109; 58; 60; 130).
4. Rudolf Steiner, *Four Mystery Dramas*, op. cit.
5. *Conversations of Goethe with Johann Peter Eckermann*. Conversation of 2 March 1831, ed. J. Moorhead (Da Capo Press, 1998).
6. Rudolf Steiner, *The Threefold Social Order*, tr. F.C. Heckel. 1st ed. (Anthroposophic Press, New York 1966). (GA 23) 2nd ed. 1972. Formerly *The Threefold Commonwealth/The Threefold State*. Now published as *Towards Social Renewal*.
7. Rudolf Steiner, *The Meaning of Life* (Rudolf Steiner Press, London 1999). Lecture of 12.06.1919.
8. 'Between the 12th and the 15th century in Europe a money system was used called "Brakteaten". This is a process that was undertaken by the respective towns, bishops and sovereigns and not only helped the exchange of goods and services but also provided the means of collecting taxes. Every year the thin coins made from gold and silver were "recalled", re-minted one to three times and devalued on an average about 25% in the process. Since nobody wanted to keep this money, people instead invested in furniture, solidly built houses, artwork and anything else that promised to keep or increase its value. During that time, some of the most beautiful sacred and profane works of art and architecture came into existence. For while monied wealth could not accumulate, real wealth was created.' Dr Margrit Kennedy, www.margritkennedy,de
9. Alain Demurger, *The Last Templar* (Profile Books, 2009).
10. Rudolf Steiner, *Inner Impulses of Evolution*, trs. Church, Kozlik, Easton (Anthroposophic Press, New York 1984) (GA 171). Lecture of 25.9.1916. Lecture also in Rudolf Steiner, *The Knights Templar*, ed. Margaret Jonas (Rudolf Steiner Press, 2007).
11. P.M. & J. Allen, *The Time is at Hand—The Rosicrucian Nature of Goethe's Fairy Tale of the Green Snake and the Beautiful Lily and The Mystery Dramas of Rudolf Steiner* (Anthroposophic Press, New York 1995).
12. Rudolf Steiner, *The Book of Revelation and the Work of the Priest* (Rudolf Steiner Press, London 1998) (GA 346).
13. Ibid.

---

[*] M.J. Krück von Poturzyn, *Der Prozess gegen die Templer* (Ogham Verlag, Stuttgart 1982).
[†] English Translation of the whole text of Friedrich Schiller's fragment *Die Malteser.* in *The Maltese Cross*, ed. Toni Cortis (Malta University Publishers, Malta 1995).

14. Ibid.

15. Rudolf Steiner, *The Deed of Christ and the Opposing Spiritual Powers*, tr. D.S. Osmond (Steiner Book Centre, Vancouver 1976) (GA 107). Lecture of 22.03.1909.

16. *The Representative of Man* is a wooden sculpture carved by Rudolf Steiner, assisted by Edith Maryon, that shows the figure of Christ surrounded by the adversary spiritual powers. See Peter Selg, *The Figure of Christ* (Temple Lodge Publishing, 2009).

17. Rudolf Steiner, *Festivals of the Seasons* (Anthroposophical Pub. Co. and Anthroposophic Press, London 1928) (GA 96). Lecture of 22.05.1915.

The Link Between the Order of the Knights Templar and the Early Cistercian Order

Gil McHattie

When looking at personalities and events from the past that have influenced world history, it is valuable to attempt to penetrate the historical facts in such a way as to reveal the underlying spiritual impulses that give rise to the facts or the outer picture. Rudolf Steiner calls this activity 'symptomatology' and other writers in this volume have also referred to this.

It is not easy to glimpse these spiritual impulses, which readily slip through the net of historical research leaving only the outer facts. Facts can often have as many different interpretations as there are researchers, and the further back in time one goes the more difficult the interpretation. This article will attempt to gather events and personalities from two Orders, the Knights Templar and the Cistercians, from approximately 1050 to 1150 and create an overview that can alert the reader to traces of spiritual impulses at work which can lead to further research. When undertaking research the more questions one can leave open the more the content can reveal itself, and when focusing on specific topics it is helpful to widen the area and time and resist the temptation to narrow the focus.

The political and geographical background

Earlier centuries in Europe were turbulent times in which to live and the eighth and ninth centuries in particular were difficult and dangerous periods.

> ... the conditions of the eighth or ninth centuries ... were times of bloodshed. Men were accustomed to live among bloodshed ... there were wild forests everywhere and there men fought. They still shed blood in their sacrifices.[1]

From the ninth to the eleventh centuries the turbulence continued with Vikings repeatedly attacking from the north, making violent inroads far into the continent. Hungarian Magyar tribes were attacking from the east and Saracens and Seljuk Turks from the south.

Europe was immersed in violent migrations of non-Christian or Aryan Germanic tribes, and in the tenth century Carolingian Europe seemed to be assailed from all sides—Vikings in the north, Hungarians in the east, Muslims in southern Italy and Spain and along the Mediterranean shore. There were few distinctions made in the common man's mind between Scandinavian and Muslim—both were non-Christian and both were the origins of violent and deadly raids and long martial contests. Such a long history of struggle and conflict could hardly have failed to leave an indelible mark on the minds of Europeans. There was a constant tension between the order of Roman law behind walls and the frightening wilderness just beyond.[2]

There were no stable countries (cultural groups) as we know them now, with the exception of England after 1066 when William of Normandy invaded. England has sea boundaries that make defensive control and a cultural grouping somewhat easier. In the years before his death in 1087, William began a firm rule initiating a national census (excepting Cumberland and Northumberland)—the Domesday Book, which gave any ruler an overview of all that had been conquered. He set in motion tight control of his new country, using his followers who were given land, and began to oversee all parts of England from north to south.

On the Continent it was different. Boundaries shifted continually according to who owned what, and there was an enormous number of varying sized feudal domains within vast tracts of landscapes that were heavily wooded. Centuries earlier, the occupying Romans called Gaul (France) 'hairy' due to the immense areas of forest. Charlemagne (*c.* 745–814) has been called the father of Europe, for during his reign the separate states of France, Germany and Italy gradually formed although not in as unified a way as they are today. His death in 814 was followed by family infighting and this first semblance of political stability waned. (Manfred Schmidt-Brabant says that after death Charlemagne 'becomes the protector of the Camino and the Grail Mysteries'.[3] (Those individualities who were especially connected to the Grail and its Mysteries will be referred to later.)

In the late tenth century Hugh Capet began a new dynasty of Capetian kings, but he was only able to control Paris and a small outlying area around the city. His vassals included some extremely wealthy and powerful noblemen such as the Duke of Burgundy. Bernard of Clairvaux was born in Burgundy and it was through his impulse that the Cistercian Order increased phenomenally fast in a short space of time. Hughes de

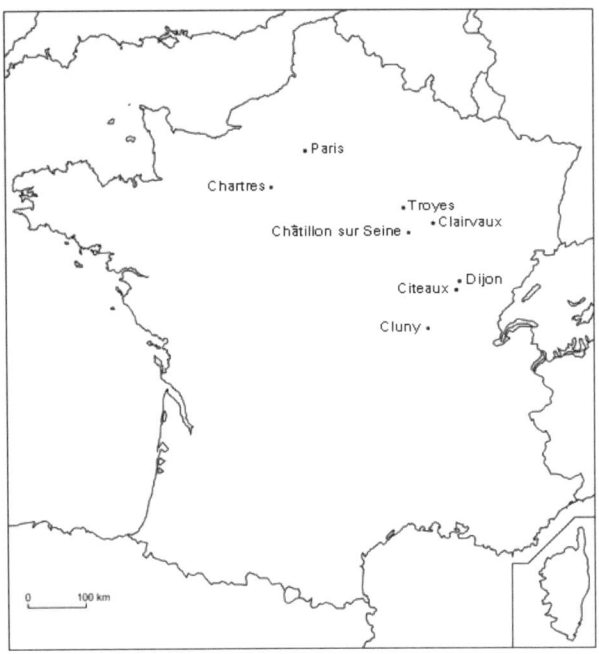

Payens, the first Grand Master of the Order of the Knights Templar, was born very near Clairvaux in Champagne, the province adjoining Burgundy. This was the seat of another powerful vassal of the king and one of the richest feudal nobles in France, Hughes, Count of Champagne. He was a great friend to Bernard and was overlord and possibly a relative of Hughes de Payens.

The time up to the end of the eleventh century was a period of turmoil. During these dangerous times, where life expectancy was below 40 years, the numbers of free peasants owning their own land became fewer as more and more put themselves under the protection of the local lord and so sacrificed their free status for a somewhat uncertain safety. Those peasants who were dispossessed and could not find a new living had either to join the large numbers trying to survive in the forests or to travel up and down the country in search of safe places in which to live. Travelling was dangerous unless in groups.

Lords and knights were occupied with hunting, war and a little agriculture; they could seldom read or write. The clergy were mostly uneducated, often making profit out of their feudal tenants. Bishops were usually as uneducated as the knights and peasants, but it was different in the monasteries where there was much profound learning by both men and women. The education of the time came entirely from the monasteries and it was a real schooling path of spiritual training.

The religious background

Due to the disorder following Charlemagne's death in 814, the monasteries and churches lost their former ties to Rome and, as with the peasants, began to rely on the local lords for protection with the resultant loss of control over their own affairs. The papacy now had freedom from the control of Charlemagne and looked to

> take the place of the bankrupt empire at the head of western Christendom ... in particular, the pontificate of Nicholas I (858–67) saw a rapid development of the papal theory of the empire [and] the firmness with which he asserted his right to intervene against unjust rulers made a lasting impression.[4]

But during the early tenth century dynastic Roman families, competing to select popes from their own families, were corruptly controlling the papacy. Marozia became the mistress of Pope Sergius (904–11). Pope John X (914–28) became involved with Marozia's mother who had the Pope deposed and installed her illegitimate son (as Pope John XI, 931–35) fathered by Pope Sergius. She saw one of her grandsons become Pope John XII.

A counter-movement grew from the concerns and piety of a few great noblemen, one of whom was Duke William of Aquitaine who founded Cluny in Burgundy in 910. This was a conservative reform movement based on aristocratic principles repeating forms used previously. Other establishments were also founded, arising from the great concerns to counter the anarchy resulting from marauding invaders and to defend the life of the Church, but Cluny became the largest. Duke William streamlined ecclesiastical organization and he ended the practice of simony and investiture where local lords elected their own relations and men to positions of authority within the Church. Cluny became a major power in Europe in the tenth and the eleventh centuries.

> It became the light of its time by taking up the path of Augustine that was then continued by Benedict. This was a path of rhythmically spiritualizing the daily flow of time but almost exclusively with the emphasis on the liturgy, the Opus Dei.[5]

The monks of Cluny followed the rule of Benedict of Aniane (*c.* 745–

c. 821), which emphasized the importance of liturgy to the extent that the holy offices took up most of the day. By the eleventh century it came under criticism for its immense acquisition of wealth and excessive liturgical practice.

In 1046 Heinrich III, the German Holy Roman Emperor, arrived in Rome with an army to suppress the political factions and to promote his own German popes, some of whom began real papal reform. Heinrich III died in 1057 and was succeeded by his young son, Heinrich IV. By the time his son came of age the balance of power between the papacy and the royal court had shifted. The arch-reformer Hildebrand, the later Pope Gregory VII, was now a leading figure at the papal court. He became Pope in 1073 and this was a turning point in the history of medieval papacy. He created the College of Cardinals, which was really a declaration of independence from the Holy Roman Emperor as it abolished the imperial right to choose the pope, giving this right to the new College of Cardinals. But he went much further and claimed the right to dismiss political officials from the Emperor down if they were not good Christians. From then on there was conflict between Empire and papacy until he died in 1085.

> He set the papacy on the road to universal dominion and absolute theocratic power—with the attempt to bring the state into sub-ordination to the Church.[6]

Bernard of Clairvaux was later outspokenly critical of this direction of papal policy.

Notwithstanding all this activity, the majority of people at this time, from serf to lord, possessed a deeply religious trait without dogma. Rudolf Steiner tells us that souls lived in a different atmosphere to that of the present time. The power of faith was intensely strong, far less superficial than it is in the different age of today.

> It is not easy now to understand the incredible forces of belief present in man in the High Middle Ages.[7]

This was a time belonging to a different consciousness from that of today and one term for it is the consciousness of the intellectual and mind soul ('mind' is better understood as 'the soul state that carries the heart forces').

Within the turmoil between state and Church, the monasteries stood like beacons of light in the community.

> If we look for the heart of the Church in the days before it was transformed by the impact of heresy, Islam and its own reforming

movements, we shall find it in the cloister. This is a fact of quite exceptional importance: up to the middle of the twelfth century the leadership of Christendom was largely in the hands not of popes, canon lawyers and university trained theologians, but of monks. The half-century before 1122 was dominated by a series of monastic popes; and Bernard of Clairvaux was the uncrowned pope of his time ... The monks lived in the midst of the people and shared their joys and sorrows; it was to the monasteries that peasants fled for refuge, to escape the pangs of hunger and the feuds of their aristocratic overlords ... it was the most deeply held conviction of medieval Christianity that it was impossible to live in the world and be wholly and entirely a Christian. Yet there must be people capable of leading a perfect Christian life in some place apart, and the monks in their cloister were called on to do this. It is surely significant that the cloister was called the 'gate of Paradise', or simply Paradise itself. All the hopes, prayers and demands the medieval Christian set on the monks and the monasteries were centred on one expectation: that they would achieve the complete sanctity of a perfect Christian life. The world was full of violence, steeped in mortal sin and depravity; amid such confusion only a monk could achieve personal perfection.[8]

Great and minor lords encouraged the new monastic settlements and supported them with the knowledge that with their donation prayers would be said for the souls of their person and their family in perpetuity. The poor brought what they could and many a new establishment, especially the new reforming movements, survived their early years through the auspices of the surrounding poor.

The spiritual reasons for the origin of the Orders

It was from this background that one could say that the time was right for the impulse, carried by the Knights Templar and the Cistercians, to seed in Europe. Within this seed was the aim to tame the wildernesses of Europe so that Christianity could grow. If people need to expend most of their energy just to survive, spiritual development will not be as strong as it might given better soil.

It is the Cistercian order that actually cultivated the ground of Europe. They went where it was inhospitable, where there were swamps and primeval forests. The swamps were drained, lakes were established, fields were drained, and cattle breeding, fruit farming and fisheries were begun. We owe the fact that we live in a civilized Europe to the Cistercians and their esotericism, their secrets.[9]

The wealth of later medieval England came from the sale of wool to the Flemish weaving industry. This was due to the sheep farming enterprises started by the Cistercian Abbeys in Yorkshire and other northern counties. And their brother's ...

the Templars laid down roads, took care that markets were developed in certain places, secured the roads; they were, so to speak, the social, legal aspect of the whole process.[10]

The individualities

Walter Johannes Stein tells us:

It is of estimable value to study how the destiny of peoples, indeed of whole spheres of culture, is formed through individuals and through links between their destinies.[11]

So who were the individuals who prepared the ground for the birth of the two great medieval Orders that changed the face of Europe—the Cistercian Order and the Order of the Poor Knights of Christ and of the Temple of Solomon (the Knights Templar)?

Manfred Schmidt-Brabant makes the following point:

Historians cannot understand the most important aspect of this Order [of the Knights Templar] and this was its mighty expansion from 1128 to 1138. Young men joined an order that seemed as though it had been established long ago. This is because of a wise spiritual leadership of mankind, a leadership that extends over one millennium. A White Lodge comprised of Masters, like the circle of the Bodhisattva, had prepared for this long ago and *the souls were present and incarnated when they were needed*. A secret physical connection made the Templars' sudden land ownership possible.[12]

The astonishing growth of the Cistercian Order can also be pointed out.

There were many unknown individuals connected to these two Orders but some names are more prominent. Those who merit special attention are *Godfrey de Bouillon, Hughes de Payens, Hughes, Count de Champagne, André de Montbard, Robert de Molesme, Stephen Harding, Bernard of Clairvaux and King David of Scotland*. They will all be introduced in the following pages.

The first to examine is **Godfrey of Bouillon** (*c.* 1060–1100). His name is synonymous with the First Crusade, but otherwise details of his life are sparse. He was reputed to have been born in Boulogne and his father was Eustach II, Count of Boulogne. More interestingly, his mother was Ida, daughter of Godfrey the Bearded, Duke of Lower Lorraine. This immediately gives a connection to the family of the Grail stream. Stein comments:

> ... those connected with the history of the Grail are linked together in a family relationship. One sees, for instance, that Godfrey of Bouillon, whose companions in arms founded the Order of the Knights Templar, stands in a relationship with the family of Odilie. Charibert of Laon, Charlemagne, Hugo of Tours, Charles III, Richardis, Dietrich of Alsace and Philip of Alsace are all within this connection. Philip of Alsace was the Master of Chrétien de Troyes ... The Grail race has the mission of expanding to cosmopolitan proportions all that belongs to the narrow group, of enlarging separate interests to world interests.[13]

Godfrey was one of the leaders of the First Crusade. Hughes de Payens very probably took part in this venture and it is also very likely that Bernard's father, a knight from Fontaines-lés-Dijon, also took part. Godfrey was one of the first knights to enter the city of Jerusalem after its capture in 1099. He stripped off his armour and walked barefoot around the ramparts, then offered prayers in the Church of the Holy Sepulchre (where he was later buried in 1100). Two days later at a council he was elected King of Jerusalem and he accepted 'for the love of Christ' but refused to wear a crown 'through respect for Him who had been crowned in that place with the Crown of Thorns'. He accepted the title 'Defender of the Holy Sepulchre'. The trouvères made him a hero of *chansons de geste*, calling him a descendant of the legendary Knight of the Swan—and here we pick up the Grail connection again.

Stein again comments:

> The legend of Godfrey of Bouillon, who is supposed to be descended from the Swan Knight, that is Lohengrin, is also well known ... The saga of the Swan Knight, however, does not, as some would have us believe, derive its origin from Brabant, Holland or Cleve, but in the English province of Holland in the vicinity of Peterborough. But in this case it is no longer saga—it is history. The time has now arrived, after the passage of a thousand years, when history should be retrieved from the mists of legend.[14]

Key figures in the Cistercian Order

To seek the preparatory ground to understand the unfolding of the spiritual tasks Bernard of Clairvaux undertook within the Cistercian Order one should first view the figure of **Robert of Molesme**. He was born around 1028, in the vicinity of Troyes, to Theodoric and Ermengard. His cousin was reputed to be the Viscount of Beaune. He entered the Benedictine monastery of Montier-la-Celle near Troyes at the age of 15 and became prior of this abbey in 1053. His deep spirituality and religious life became recognized outside his monastery and he was asked to become the new Abbot of Saint-Michel at Tonnerre in 1069. He was becoming known for his ascetic way of life and desire to live according to the principles based on those of the rule of St Benedict of Nursia (*c.* 480–*c.* 547).

It seems, however, that his new community did not follow his desire for a strict, ascetic regime. He resigned his post in 1072 and moved to the dependent priory of Montier-la-Celle, St Ayoul, as prior. He then was asked to join a group of monks who had started a reform venture, as hermits, in the forest of Colan. From 1073 this group looked upon him as their spiritual leader and guide. They had an ascetic and rigorous way of life and also adopted manual work as an important part of their life, so returning to the original rule of St Benedict of Nursia. This venture culminated in their moving to a new abbey at Molesme.

Robert also encouraged a German monk to follow his vocation as a hermit in the forest and this man, Bruno of Cologne, went on to found the rigorous monastic order of the Carthusians. (Another pupil was Odo of Lagery who later became Pope Urban II and preached the First Crusade.) All these new reforming ventures were closely watched and the more spiritual the venture the more people wanted a part of it—by giving donations or becoming novices. The new establishments would attract wealth and novices, which of course could destabilize the sought-for aims of poverty and simplicity.

The Englishman, **Stephen Harding**, was a monk at Molesme at this time. Robert tried to reinstigate the original reforming principles in the abbey but there was disagreement and so he left, accompanied by 21 of his monks. They then started anew in the marshy forest of Citeaux. Alberic, the prior, and Stephen Harding accompanied him. Robert managed to obtain recognition from the papal legate for the new abbey in 1098. But he had actually committed a canonical sin by abandoning his flock at Molesme! They complained and he was forced to return to them but he was given two years in which to establish the monastery of Citeaux.

Alberic became the new Abbot of Citeaux after Robert left, but he brought in an excessively rigorous ascetic way of life with the result that no new novices sought admittance and no donations were given. The numbers of monks dropped from 21 to 12, dying through privation and old age. But when studying biographies of those who have carried out great tasks for the world one can observe that times of trial and hardship fire and shape the will and often precede the task. The birth of the Cistercian Order came through this time of trial into the hands of Stephen Harding who became abbot after the death of Alberic in 1109.

There are few extant details of Stephen Harding's early life. He was most likely born near Sherborne, Dorset around 1060, becoming a monk at the Benedictine community of Sherborne Abbey. The Anglo Saxon Chronicle mentions that King Aethelbald was buried at the abbey in 860 and King Aethelbert in 866. It started to follow the rule of St Benedict of Nursia from 998. In 1075 the episcopal see was removed from Sherborne and taken up by Old Sarum (Salisbury), which would have had some effect on the community at Sherborne although their land holding from before and after the Norman Conquest remained the same.

How much this affected Stephen Harding is not known, but he is reputed to have travelled to Scotland and Paris after leaving Sherborne. Ekkehard Meffert states that he visited the Isle of Iona and the school of Celtic Druidic monks at Lismore, Ireland. Meffert also states that Stephen Harding studied at the School of Chartres before finding his mentor, Robert of Molesme.[15] It is known that he travelled to Rome before meeting Robert.

Stephen, perhaps using his English pragmatism, continued the reform principles of Robert of Molesme but eased the extremely rigorous life that Alberic had introduced. Donations started to flow into Citeaux; it attracted 50 major offerings between 1109 and 1119. He also continued the policy of manual work and its importance for the life of the community. One effect of this was that lay brothers and hired workers were introduced into the rule and welcomed to Cistercian abbeys. They were able to manage land that was some distance from the abbey, enabling the monks to carry out work nearer to hand and thus to observe the liturgy. This practice greatly increased the area of land that could be farmed. Granges were used as agricultural centres serving a multitude of farming practices to sustain the abbeys, providing grain, wood, poultry, animals etc. They were fundamental to the expansion of the Order and were

A Grange at Clairvaux

subject to the same Cistercian regulations. Early statutes stipulated that granges were to be sited no more than a day's walk from the abbey so the lay brothers could return on Sundays and Feast days. Later abbeys increased the distances between Abbey and granges. Underlying this practicality was the important spiritual precept of *Ora et Labora*—'Prayer and Work'. The monks prayed to the spiritual world above but their manual labour below was just as important so that the earth was worked and cultivated and, in a way, sanctified.

The 'Charter of Charity' (*Carta Caritatis*) was written and approved by the first official General Chapter of the Order in 1119 and was then approved by the Pope. This confirmation of the charter's validity can be seen as the beginning of the Cistercian Order. (Bernard of Clairvaux had been in the Order six years by this time.) This extraordinary document formulated a rule that is very modern. It eliminated the feudal 'pyramid' system used by other religious houses, including Cluny, and introduced a system whereby each Cistercian Abbey was autonomous both financially and in the election of its own officers. But the Abbot of Citeaux would visit each daughter-house every year (La Ferté, Pontigny, Clairvaux and Morimond were abbeys that had been founded by Citeaux) and the abbots of each daughter-house would also visit their foundations annually. All abbots would come together in a General Chapter each year to decide policy matters for the coming year, functioning as a sort of annual parliament. The Abbot of Citeaux would have the final say in debates that were not unanimous. Also a single community was never allowed to become too large. When a foundation was fully established it would send out twelve monks who were specialists in their own areas to found another abbey.

The twelfth century, in the main, was a time of tolerance and light, with Jewish and Muslim scholars assisting with translations within many scriptoriums. Stephen Harding initiated a new translation of the Bible with the help of Rabbis, initiated an important reform of the liturgy and made a collection of music to be sung at the offices. The scriptorium at Citeaux became renowned for its high-quality work. Manfred Schmidt-Brabant remarks: 'The twelfth century has an extraordinarily high concentration of events related to the Mysteries.'[16] By the next century, however, a sort of spiritual cramping had set in and there was far less tolerance. The Catholic Church started its crusade against the Cathars and dogma entered the Jewish religion. It seems that on all fronts the light was attacked.

Bernard of Clairvaux

We now focus on the most important individual, Bernard of Fontaines, or Bernard of Clairvaux as he is more widely known. He was born in Fontaines-lés-Dijon in Burgundy in 1090 or 1091. His father, Tescelin le Roux or Tescelin Sorus, was a knight in the service of the Duke of Burgundy and was from the family of the Chevaliers de Châtillon. Fontaines-lés-Dijon is a steeply wooded hill overlooking the road from Paris to Dijon and Bernard's father, Tescelin, with his group of knights was responsible for protecting this pass into Dijon. He married Aleth of Montbard and they had seven children with Bernard being the third child. Aleth of Montbard was related to the ducal family of Burgundy through her father.

Bernard studied the liberal arts at the school of the church of St Vorles run by the secular canons in Châtillon-sur-Seine, which had a reputation for its learning before and after Bernard attended there as a pupil. His family had property in the area. The church is also sited on a steeply wooded hill (there are fewer trees now) and one remembers that Bernard, the mystic Platonist, wrote as an adult: 'Woods and stones will teach you what you can never hear from any master' (Letter 107) and 'that you will have experienced sometimes under the shade of a tree during the heat of midday what you would never have learned in the schools' (Letter 177).[17] He was one of the greatest writers of the Middle Ages. As a boy Bernard, had a revelation of the

'mystery of Bethlehem, Mary and the Holy Child "coming forth as a bridegroom from his chamber—of form more beautiful than the sons of men". .... He believed to the last that it was an experience which confirmed his faith, sowed in him the seeds of mystic contemplation and became the incentive of his works upon the Incarnation.'[18]

Bernard is an immensely interesting figure and not easy to understand with our modern-day thinking, which is based on a consciousness that naturally has changed from that of the attitude and awareness of a thousand years ago. We might say that our time now is one where the consciousness soul or spiritual soul predominates, and this can be seen in how we are much more separate and individual. Large family groupings are from the past and the isolated individual must work to achieve in freedom what was given in the past.

Bernard typifies the soul configuration prevalent at the turn of the first millennium after Christ and this can be characterized as having a twofold quality, one the thinking, the intellect, and the other the feeling part. (This does not mean sentiment but rather 'heart warmth' from the untranslatable German word *Gemüt*). As with most things in life, the key is balance, where one pole does not dominate at the expense of the other. Two great Church fathers can help clarify these two poles or aspects of the soul configuration present then. Bernard of Clairvaux typifies where the 'heart warmth' soul aspect is developed fully and is representative of the early Middle Ages while Thomas Aquinas typifies the intellectual soul aspect and the later move towards scholasticism. This twofold quality meant that the individual of the time was able to carry polarities within themselves in a way we would find extremely difficult now; Bernard was an extremely influential political figure but also an unambitious religious man who always refused advancement within Church hierarchy and remained an abbot all his life.

Rudolf Steiner helps us further:

> Saint Bernard, perhaps the most outstanding personality of the twelfth century, manifested a structure of soul which after the fifteenth century was no longer possible in Europe. Nowadays it is very hard to describe this, because the preconditions for forming the right conceptions are altogether lacking ... In this personality there was an amazing devotion to the spiritual world, an absolute absorption in it. If anyone today undertakes something and it fails, he naturally begins to doubt whether he was right to embark on it. A personality such as St Bernard was never doubtful because he had always taken counsel with his God in the spiritual worlds before he undertook or advised anything.[19]

Bernard's mother had a reputation for piety as did his father, and although this might be part of Catholic hagiography it seems reasonable to suppose that this spiritual attitude was present in his childhood. Aleth of Montbard had close ties with the Benedictine community of St Benigne in Dijon and was buried in their abbey when she died in 1106/7. At *c.* 1111/12 Bernard started a monastic community of sorts in the parental home (possibly in Châtillon-sur-Seine) and in 1113 at 22/23 years of age he entered Citeaux accompanied by 29 relatives and companions. Instead of choosing a wealthy foundation he chose a poor and relatively obscure community, that of Citeaux. (Hughes de Payens was closely linked, through his family, to the Abbey of Molesme which was founded by St Robert who also founded Citeaux.[20])

> In the way (Bernard) induced so many of his noble companions to undertake with him such a hard and rough manner of life, we encounter for the first time an indication of that extraordinary power of moving others which is characteristic of him throughout his life. His aura radiated far and wide. This means working out into many regions. A person could sense Bernard even if he were 60 miles away. He simply worked through his etheric aura.[21]

I consider it a possibility that Bernard may have been one of the group of individuals who possessed part of the etheric body of Christ.

> We sow a grain of wheat in the earth; it germinates: the stalk and ears of wheat grow and the many, many grains are facsimiles of the one grain of wheat we sowed in the earth. It is exactly the same in the spiritual world, for 'all things transitory are but symbols' (as below, so above). When the Event of Golgotha had taken place something happened to the etheric body and the astral body of Jesus of Nazareth: through the power of Christ they became *multiplied* and in the spiritual world there have been since that time many, many reproductions of this astral body and this etheric body, and these worked on. When a spiritual individuality descended, it clothed itself with an etheric body and an astral body; and when an individual's karma allowed it, an image of the etheric body of Jesus of Nazareth was woven into him. This was the case, for example, with St Augustine in the early centuries of our era: into his etheric body was woven a reproduction of the etheric body of Jesus of Nazareth, but his astral body and 'I' were his own.[22]

In 1113 Bernard was sent to found the third daughter-house of Citeaux, that of the Abbey of Clairvaux. These new sites for Cistercian foundations were in the most inhospitable places, always near water, often in waterlogged wooded valleys. Clairvaux was in the Vale of Absinthe (wormwood), a wild valley of a tributary of the Aube, near Troyes. The area is still wooded today; when I stayed at the one small hotel in the village overlooking the abbey, a party of hunters arrived to hunt boar. Clairvaux is now a top-security prison and has been a prison since being sold during Napoleonic times. The Temple in Paris also became a state prison at this time.

The group of monks accompanying Bernard would have lived in wooden huts whilst clearing the ground for future buildings. These first few years nearly broke his health and he was never a well man from this time on. His meditative and spiritual life gave rise to a large output of writing. His sermons on the Song of Solomon, begun during his illness, make up the greater part of these.

The theme of his sermons is that the presence of God is within the soul of man. The sermons pulse with love; with the awareness of the frailty of man and of himself. His devotion to Mary shines through most of them.

> St Bernard was among the first to call Mary *Domina Nostra*—'Our Lady'. But we see her true position in the plan of Salvation, in the mystery of Christ, in the dramatic passage on the Annunciation when Bernard describes how not only the Angel waits for her reply, but the whole of creation—right back to Adam. The whole world awaits her answer.[23]

All Cistercian abbeys were placed under the protection of Our Lady as were the churches of the Templars. The *Salve Regina* became the last devotion of the day in all Cistercian communities. Both Orders were devoted to the feminine, to Mary, to the Sophia, i.e. the divine wisdom.

> One could easily show how the mystic Bernard in his preaching, especially in his interpretations of the Song of Solomon reaches an artistic imaginative reality, which has an immediate relationship to the Platonism of the School of Chartres. This mysticism of the Cistercian Order is the reason why the Platonism of the School of Chartres could fully connect to the Christian spirituality of the Cistercian Order. The mystic Platonism of the School of Chartres could then stream on as an undercurrent within the Cistercian Order with the connection of Alanus ab Insulis (1115–1202) to the Order after the death of Bernard (1153).[24]

Bernard's many letters (over 400) show a warm sense of humour and the ability to write to the individual rather than the 'king' or a 'woman'. He always addresses the concerns of the individual, neither being afraid of high position nor of the female sex! His formal treatises are also extant and the first, 'On the Degrees of Humility', was written in 1119.

> It is a formal declaration that the Cistercians, or at least St Bernard, interpreted the Rule of St Benedict as a preparation for the mystical life, for, says St Bernard, 'when the monk has ascended the twelve degrees of humility, he passes through the degrees of truth, the last of which is contemplation, or the transient experience of God in the *raptus* of divine love'.[25]

In 1125 he wrote his famous 'Apologia ad Guillelmum', but again like so many of his works, which sometimes incur criticism, he writes for wider publication when asked by another. The most quoted parts of this work are his comments on the lifestyle of other religious orders.

> The church shines with splendour on all sides, but the poor are hungry... The walls of the church are covered with gold, but the children of the church go naked ... Ah Lord! If the folly of it all does not shame us, surely the expense might stick in our throats?... You will seal my lips saying that it is not for a monk to judge, please God that you seal my eyes also that I may not see. But if I held my peace, the poor, the naked and the starving would rise up and cry out ...[26]

And further, in 'On Free Will and Grace' written in 1126/7:

> In order to love God with disinterested charity (man) must first be free. His whole ascent to divine union is a progress in liberty. Our basic freedom, *liberum arbitrium* or *freedom of choice*, is only the beginning of the ascent. The capacity to choose between good and evil is only the shadow of true liberty. Genuine freedom is the work of grace.[27]

Feudal ties at this time were strong and we can examine this intermeshed group during the 1100s. Bernard was related through his mother's family of Montbard to the Dukes of Burgundy. His younger step-uncle, **Andrew of Montbard**, was one of the original group of Templar Knights and became Grand Master of the Order in 1153. His maternal family also gave land for new Cistercian foundations and some of them were most probably part of the large group that entered Citeaux with Bernard. There is recent research which shows that Hughes de Payens, the first Grand Master of the original group of knights, was a cousin of

Bernard's, again through his mother's family by marriage.[28] Hughes married the demoiselle of Touillon, a family linked to that of Montbard. Bernard's uncle was the knight Gaufried of Touillon. This was at a time when family ties carried considerable importance. The overlord (and possibly relative) of Hughes de Payens was **Hughes, Count of Champagne** who also became a Templar Knight in 1124. But before this the Count had a firm friendship with Bernard and also gave land for the foundation of Clairvaux among others. All these people knew each other well. Bernard's father would have been one of this group and might well have been in Jerusalem with them. Bernard was 8 or 9 years old at the fall of Jerusalem but 14 years elapse before he enters Citeaux. This is a time of which little is known of Bernard, of Hughes de Payens, of Andrew de Montbard or others from the original group of Templars.

The beginnings of the Templar Order

There are three main sources for most of the accepted information about the historical beginnings of the Templars. However, none of these sources were alive at the start of the Templar Order or without bias. William of Tyre (c. 1130–1186) was known for actively disliking the Templars, believing that they were given too many benefits at the expense of Church livings. He also disliked the Cistercians, so he can be said to have had a bias against both groups. Walter Map, Archdeacon of Oxford (c. 1140–1208/10) is described by Malcolm Barber as liking a good story rather than historical facts and he also did not like the Cistercians. Michael the Syrian, Jacobite Patriarch of Antioch (died 1199) is considered less reliable than William of Tyre. Barber also makes the point that there is a definite silence about the beginning of the Order.[29] We can wonder why this should be so.

Hughes de Payens was born some time before 1070 presumably in Payns (modern spelling), 12 km north-west of Troyes. He is part of the family or one of the officers of Hughes, Count of Champagne, and is known to have been at the court as he witnessed several documents between 1085 and 1113. He married Elisabeth some time between 1108 and 1114 and had a son, Thibaud. His wife must have retired into a convent or died for Hughes to enrol in the new Order. Thibaud is mentioned in the annals of the Abbey, of St Colombe of Sens as 'the son of the first master of the Temple of Jerusalem'. He became the abbot in 1139 before joining the Second Crusade (which left his monks without an abbot!).

It could be that Hughes de Payens took part in the First Crusade and he is thought to have accompanied the Count on visits to the Holy Land in 1104 and again in 1114. His name was recorded in Jerusalem in 1120 and 1123 when he was known to have been living in the Holy Land. William of Tyre said this early group promised to devote themselves to God's service in the manner of regular canons, without possessions, under the vows of chastity and obedience. He said that in 1118 King Baldwin II gave them a dwelling place in the south wing of the palace near the Lord's Temple, and they were also given a square near the palace.

Rudolf Steiner tells us:

> ... the Knights Templar (were) the actual messengers of the Grail. They built a centre of wisdom on the site of Solomon's Temple and after preparation there they became servants of the Holy Grail, were initiated there by the Grail. This happened at the turn from the thirteenth to the fourteenth century and was prepared in the eleventh and twelfth centuries.[30]

He enlarges on this some years later

> ... we see the founding of the Order of the Knights Templar in the year 1119 ... united under the leadership of Hughes de Payens and, at the holy place where the Mystery of Golgotha occurred, they founded an Order dedicated entirely to the Mystery of Golgotha. Its first important home was close to the place where Solomon's Temple once stood, so that the holy wisdom from most ancient times and the wisdom of Solomon could work together for Christianity in this spot with all the feelings and sentiments that have arisen from entire and holy devotion towards the Mystery of Golgotha and its Bearer. In addition to the religious vows of duty to their spiritual superiors usual at that time, the first Knights Templar pledged themselves to work together in the most intensive manner to bring under European control the place where the events of the Mystery of Golgotha had occurred.[31]

We might ask what the Grail is, this elusive but evocative symbol in so very many legends and stories. Manfred Schmidt-Brabant describes it thus:

> ... the Grail is always experienced as the human ego that then recedes, creating of itself a vessel for the Christ Spirit to fill. It is clear that this is an earthly aspiration; it is an image of evolution, an image of the plan for salvation.[32]

The fast and great expansion of the Order of the Knights Templar is not explained by the reason, usually given, for their founding which is to protect pilgrims on the route to Jerusalem. But viewed esoterically it begins to become more understandable. The so-called treasure, which many believe was buried somewhere in this ancient place in Jerusalem and therefore was the reason for the Order to request the site, was spiritual, not physical treasure.[33] Any physical treasure had been removed centuries earlier.

> And he [Nebuchadnezzar] carried out thence all the treasures of the house of the Lord, and the treasures of the King's house, and cut in pieces all the vessels of gold which Solomon, King of Israel had made in the temple of the Lord, as the Lord had said [2 Kings 24:13].

We can return to Manfred Schmidt-Brabant who said that the Templars' spiritual impulse was to Christianize Europe. Somewhere deep within the psyche of people there was a recognition and connection to the integrity of this Order and to its aims. This connection is still present today.

Likewise, it is difficult to understand the underlying impulses in the urge to crusade. Within the consciousness of today battle is rightly considered as an evil. But at the time of the Crusades one needs to take into account the centuries of violent incursions into Europe by Muslim and other forces and the occupation of Jerusalem, making it unsafe for Christian pilgrims to worship at the holy sites. There was also a relatively hidden impulse to develop a free spiritual life away from the strictures of Rome and this was centred on liberating Jerusalem. One could say that this impulse was far ahead of its time but that seeds were planted for the future.

> Resounding in the tone and tenor of the sermons of Bernard of Clairvaux, not in what he actually says but in the artistic grandeur and majesty of his utterances, are those mysteries which the etheric cosmos would fain reveal to man and can no longer reveal and, on the other side, all that strives from out of the Earth to work in man's own etheric body. That is what drives men over to Asia seeking for what they had lost in the West.[34]

The rules of the monk were Obedience, Poverty and Chastity; the knight's rules incorporated the qualities of Courage, Fidelity and Justice. Michael Frensch points to the Christmas portal of Chartres and says:

The knightly virtue [is] to protect the birth of the Logos and the monastic art [is] of giving birth to the Logos in the soul and of reading and understanding the incarnated Logos—the book of Wisdom.[35]

The aim of the Templars in battle was to defeat the enemy. But in contrast to the blood lust manifested by considerable numbers of the crusader knights, there were very strict rules of conduct for the Templars. They lived with the strongly held belief that their blood belonged to Christ.

The blood of the Templars belonged to Christ Jesus—each one of them knew this. Their blood belonged to nothing else on Earth than to Christ Jesus. Every moment of their life was to be filled with the perpetual consciousness of how in their own soul there dwelt—in the words of St Paul—'not I, but Christ in me'! … [they] were never allowed to flee, even if a force three times their strength confronted them on the physical plane, but had calmly to await death, the death that they were ready to endure in order to establish more firmly in Earth existence the impulse which came from the Mystery of Golgotha.[36]

The Templars were feared and respected by the Saracen and they also respected integrity and bravery when finding it in their foe.

Hughes de Payens travelled Europe, including England and Scotland, collecting funds and men. There was a unique welcome from and relationship to **King David of Scotland**; Hughes and his knights were recognized spiritually by him. It has been recorded that David greeted Hughes and his men with the words 'You are now the guardian of my morals by day and by night.' David also favoured the Cistercian Order, personally inviting the Order to Scotland from the establishment at Rievaulx in Yorkshire. Aelred, later abbot of Rievaulx, Yorkshire, spent part of his youth at the court of David. It would be interesting to know what contact David had with Bernard, as there is no extant correspondence.

In 1128 or early 1129 there was an ecclesiastic Council in Troyes attended by most of the important French prelates, including Bernard of Clairvaux and Stephen Harding plus Hughes de Payens and a group of his knights. Here the rules of the Order, written by Bernard and based on the rules of St Benedict of Nursia, were presented and accepted (they were to be confirmed later by Pope Honorius II).

Liber ad milites Templi: De laude novae militiae—'In Praise of the New

Knighthood'—was written by Bernard after the Council, at the request of Hughes de Payens. This letter became a turning point in the rise of the Order. In 1139 Pope Innocent II issued a Papal bull, *Omne datum optimum,* which gave them autonomy in their affairs, bypassing local Church officials and making them answerable to the Pope alone. One result of this is that they did not need to pay tithes to the Church which made them unpopular in later years.

The Cistercians and the Templars worked as brothers, and within a short space of time Europe was covered by a network of Templar preceptories and Cistercian abbeys. By the time of Bernard's death in 1153 there were over 350 Cistercian abbeys in Europe, from Ireland to Poland and Scandinavia to Spain and Portugal.

> If the Templars strove for—and, in some measure, founded—a Christianization of the social order of Europe, the Cistercians were responsible for a Christianization of the land... The Templars carried the Grail impulse into the social life; the Cistercians carried it into the cultural life of the land—right down into their manual labour.[37]

Further links

Both orders shared many esoteric secrets, one of which was the ability to work with the cosmic secrets of etheric geography. This can be seen in the sites that they chose. The ancient Celtic-Gallic Mystery Centre of Alesia is very near the early daughter-houses of Citeaux.

> The Cistercian Order is set apart from the other monastic orders through their exceptional connections to space and earth. The other orders were of a sort that rather had the tendency to flee the world. Unlike the Benedictines' and the Abbey of Cluny, all Cistercian Abbeys were consciously built in valleys near water and away from any settlement. They are all places which are encircled by an etheric mystery presence as if the sunken world of Celtic nature religion is still connected like a sort of aftersound.[38]

The elements of our physical world are made up of air, water, earth and warmth and these manifest in the equivalent ethers of light ether, chemical ether, life ether and warmth ether; one of which will usually predominate in any given area.

> Bernard, as a Platonic soul and a mystic, connected the Christianity of the time, which placed emphasis on retreating from the world, saying

no to the world, with that of working with the physical earth. His Platonism is of such a kind that he does not look for Christ in the cosmos (like we still see in the Christian Neoplatonists) but in the etheric sphere of the Earth itself. From this we can understand the intensive connection of the Cistercians to the four etheric secrets of the Earth—space, sound, light and fertility. (Chemical ether, tone ether, light ether and life ether.) This is how the early Cistercians colonized the wildernesses of Europe but they also Christianized and imbued the ground of Europe with soul. This aura is still to be felt today everywhere this Order has worked on the Earth. Magical veils lie over these landscapes.[39]

One can still feel this when travelling to the few unclaimed landscapes on other continents and one can then understand and feel how the European continent has been worked and penetrated by human effort, by soul forces, for millennia.

Rudolf Steiner tells us of an important principle carried by the Knights Templar:

> We believe once more in the elemental forces that are present in the world. We believe that the destinies of human beings are the result of the star constellations and that human beings themselves are born out of these constellations in conformity with the laws of nature.[40]

The knowledge of the cosmos, the starry constellations, the spiritual etheric substance of the Earth and the elemental forces were a shared heritage.

Both Orders took vows of poverty. The Orders themselves were wealthy (the Knights Templar especially had to equip their fighting forces in the East), but the individuals within each Order did not possess anything personally. This was a very important spiritual precept. Gold, to the Templars, was a revelation of the spirit, the Sun metal, the Christ metal. Earthly gold to the Templars was the revelation of spiritual gold; it had to be protected. It was the Sun's body and part of this body was the body of Christ. This is why they could handle it in such a completely selfless way and so were trusted in all their dealings with it. Lust for gold, met in so many people, was something quite alien to them.

Gothic architecture and technology were also part of this occult knowledge, probably adding to the Aristotelian wisdom that was filtering through the Arabic world to the West. Cistercian technology, as used in the granges, was far in advance of its time and was not bettered until the

eighteenth century. Every Templar preceptory harnessed the fruits of
where it was sited. Mining, horse-breeding, viticulture and wine making
were among its activities.

Gothic architecture began to be used in Cathedral building only after
the Council of Troyes. The first four Gothic Cathedrals in France—Sens,
Senlis, Paris and Chartres—all used the same proportional plan which
points to a common source, and this source is thought to have been St
Bernard.[41] The architectural principles of his new churches have been
called 'the Bernadine Plan'—these churches show a purity and simplicity
of line and proportion that is quite specifically Cistercian. Early Cistercian
architecture aimed purely to give a properly designed space for meditation
and prayer in order to come nearer to God, so excessive ornamentation
was seen as distraction. The result is that the whole space with its purity of
line and proportion and with the consciously planned play of light and
shadow is extremely beautiful. The Abbey of Fontenay is possibly one of
the few buildings that have been preserved in its early form showing this
beautiful simplicity. It is sited just outside Montbard, Burgundy, and
building was started in 1139.

The Abbey of Fontenay

Steiner tells us Dante was affiliated to the Templar Order and when
writing his Divine Comedy '. . . used the same symbols as those which find
expression in the Templars, the Christian knights, the Knights of the
Grail, and so on'.[42] He used the same wisdom in his writing that
enlightened the Templars and in Canto 31, after travelling through the
inferno and purgatory and finally reaching Paradise, he meets St Bernard
who representing the direct experience of the Godhead guides him, full
of tenderness, on his last steps. This connection flowed on through the

centuries, Goethe being one such who was spiritually inspired by this Order and taking the Temple Oath to St Bernard.

A last link for consideration is from the life of Bernard himself. When looking at his moon nodes an interesting symmetry can be seen to the Order of the Knights Templar. Every human being incarnates into Earth existence at a specific time and place. The configuration of the starry world, the star wisdom, is such that the tableau of the planetary con-stellations, at the moment of birth, contains an imprint of the destiny ahead. This is then undertaken, or lived, in freedom. Approximately every 18½ years, the moon node returns to the same position it had in the cosmic tableau formed at the time of birth. Rudolf Steiner describes these times of the moon node as having the greatest significance in life where the human being can connect with the destiny aims of his/her life, which are usually difficult to find. It is as though a 'window' opens. 'Our world opens up anew to the astral sphere. Astral streams flow in and out.'[43]

My research indicates that there is a significant period of time leading up to the node which then decreases, so the actual time span is far more than just a few nights. Around the time of his first moon node, Bernard would have been preparing inwardly for his spiritual intentions and future monastic life. The time of his second moon node occurs when the prelates of France gather at the Council of Troyes to confirm the Order of the Knights Templar and where Bernard gave them their Rule. His third moon node occurs when he preaches the Second Crusade at Vézelay. He at first refused to do this but undertook the task at the request of Pope and King.

This alerts us to the deep spiritual connection Bernard of Clairvaux had to the Order of the Poor Knights of Christ and of the Temple of Solomon and to their shared aims.

After attending university Gil McHattie spent many years as a deputy head teacher for special needs children and young people. She then undertook counselling trainings and also training in Facilitation of Biography Group Work at the Centre for Social Development, West Sussex. She gives lectures and workshops on various themes based on the development of the individual and also on the lives of personalities from history. She was responsible, along with Richard Ramsbotham, for the initiative to hold the Knights Templar conference in the UK in 2009.

Gil has had a lifelong interest in ancient and medieval history. She is especially interested in the figure of Bernard of Clairvaux, who has been misunderstood and misinterpreted for centuries. From Bernard it is a very short step to the Order of the Knights Templar. The image of the warrior monk is evocative for many today; it imbues a heroic quality that touches on something very deeply within the psyche of the human being and is connected to the individual striving that is within all of us.

Her article endeavours to bring some clarity towards the understanding of this Order and the link that they have to their brothers in the Cistercian Order.

Notes

1. Rudolf Steiner quoted in Walter Johannes Stein, *The Ninth Century* (Temple Lodge Publishing, London 1991).
2. Castle Duncan Forums—www.castleduncan.com.
3. Virginia Sease and Manfred Schmidt-Brabant, *Paths of the Christian Mysteries* (Temple Lodge Publishing, 2003).
4. Geoffrey Barraclough, *The Medieval Papacy* (Thames and Hudson, London 1968).
5. Ekkehard Meffert, 'Bernhard von Clairvaux—ein Zisterzienser prägt Europa', in *Das Goetheanum*, 35 (2003).
6. Geoffrey Barraclough. op. cit. For further reading on Pope Gregory VII the reader is directed to Virginia Sease and Manfred Schmidt-Brabant, *Thinkers, Saints and Heretics* (Temple Lodge, 2007).
7. Rudolf Steiner, unpublished lecture, 'A Sound Outlook for Today and a Genuine Hope for the Future' (GA 181), 16.7.1918, Berlin. Typescript in library, Rudolf Steiner House, London.
8. Friedrich Heer, *The Medieval World* (Sphere Books, 1974).
9. Virginia Sease and Manfred Schmidt-Brabant, *Paths of the Christian Mysteries*, op. cit.
10. Ibid.
11. Walter Johannes Stein, *The Death of Merlin* (Floris Books, 1989).
12. Unpublished lecture given by Manfred Schmidt-Brabant at Camphill, Aberdeen, 1992.
13. Walter Johannes Stein, *The Ninth Century*, op. cit.
14. Walter Johannes Stein, *The Death of Merlin*, op. cit.
15. Ekkehard Meffert, *Die Zisterzienser und Bernhard von Clairvaux* (Verlag Engel & Co., 2010).
16. Virginia Sease and Manfred Schmidt-Brabant, *Thinkers, Saints and Heretics*, op. cit.
17. Bruno Scott James, tr, *The Letters of St Bernard of Clairvaux* (Henry Regnery Co., Chicago 1953).
18. Watkin Williams, *Saint Bernard of Clairvaux* (The Newman Press, Maryland 1952).
19. Rudolf Steiner, *A Sound Outlook for Today and a Genuine Hope for the Future*, op. cit.
20. Thierry Leroy, *Hugues de Payns, les Templiers* (TheBookEdition.com, 2011). Also his unpublished thesis, 'Les Templiers en Champagne' (University of Reims).
21. Virginia Sease and Manfred Schmidt-Brabant, *Paths of the Christian Mysteries*, op. cit.
22. Rudolf Steiner, *Festivals of the Seasons* (Anthroposophical Publishing Co. and

Anthroposophic Press, London and New York 1928) (GA 109). Lecture of 11.4.1909.

23. Paul Diemer, *Love without Measure* (Darton, Longman and Todd, London 1990).

24. Ekkehard Meffert, 'Zur Spirituellen Bedeutung des Zisterzienserordens', in *Die Drei*, July/August (1998).

25. Thomas Merton, *The Last of the Fathers* (Harcourt Brace & Co., San Diego, New York, London 1982).

26. Jean-François Leroux-Dhuys, *Cistercian Abbeys* (Könemann Verlagsgesellschaft mbH. 1998).

27. Thomas Merton, op. cit.

28. Thierry Leroy, *Hugues de Payns*, op. cit.

29. Malcolm Barber, *The New Knighthood* (O.U.P., 1994).

30. Rudolf Steiner, *The Templars as Initiates of the Grail*. Excerpt 1904 in Rudolf Steiner, *The Knights Templar*, ed. Margaret Jonas (Rudolf Steiner Press, 2007).

31. Rudolf Steiner, *Inner Impulses of Evolution*, tr. Church, Kozlik, Easton (Anthroposophic Press, New York 1984) (GA 171). Lecture of 25.9.1916. Also in Rudolf Steiner, *The Knights Templar*, ed. Margaret Jonas (Rudolf Steiner Press, 2007).

32. Virginia Sease and Manfred Schmidt-Brabant, *The New Mysteries* (Temple Lodge, 2005).

33. Rolf Speckner enlarges on the mystery the Solomonic Temple in the present volume.

34. Rudolf Steiner, *Supersensible Influences in the History of Mankind*, tr. D. Osmond. 1st ed. (Rudolf Steiner Publishing Co., London 1956) (GA 216). Lecture of 01.10.1922. Also in Rudolf Steiner, *The Knights Templar*, ed. Margaret Jonas (Rudolf Steiner Press, 2007).

35. Michael Frensch, *Wie Öffnet sich das Große Portal?* (Novalis Verlag, Schaffhausen 2000). Quote taken from an article in the *Anthroposophical Newsletter*, vol. 77, no 1, Winter (2001).

36. Rudolf Steiner, 'The Templars', unpublished lecture, 02.10.1916 (GA 171), in Rudolf Steiner, *The Knights Templar*, ed. Margaret Jonas (Rudolf Steiner Press, 2007).

37. Virginia Sease and Manfred Schmidt-Brabant, *The New Mysteries*, op. cit.

38. Ekkehard Meffert, 'Zur spirituellen Bedeutung des Zisterzienserordens', op. cit.

39. Ekkehard Meffert, 'Bernhard von Clairvaux. Das religiöse Genie des 12. Jahrhunderts Zum 850', in *Die Drei*, December (2003). For further understanding of the ethers the reader is directed to Günther Wachsmuth, *The Etheric Formative Forces in Cosmos, Earth and Man*, 1932 reprint available from Delta Spectrum Research, 921 Santa Fe Avenue, La Junta, CO 81050. USA.

40. Rudolf Steiner, *The Templars as Initiates of the Grail*. Excerpt 1904 in Rudolf Steiner, *The Knights Templar*, ed. Margaret Jonas (Rudolf Steiner Press, 2007).

41. Gordon Strachan, *Chartres: Sacred Geometry, Sacred Space* (Floris Books, 2003).

42. Rudolf Steiner, *The Temple Legend*, tr. J. Wood (Rudolf Steiner Press, London) (GA 93). Lecture of 22.05.1905.

43. Rudolf Steiner, *The Mystery of the Universe*, tr. Adams (Rudolf Steiner Press, London 1972) (GA 201). Lecture of 16.04.1920.

The Knights Templar in Britain

Horst Biehl

The Templars in England

The First Crusade ended when the crusaders captured the city of Jerusalem in July 1099. King Baldwin II, of the house of Boulogne, welcomed a group of nine knights from France who wanted to protect the pilgrims and defend the borders of the new crusader state. He gave them their quarters on the Temple Mount in Jerusalem and they gave their monastic vows to the Patriarch of Jerusalem. This was the beginning of The Order of the Poor Knights of Christ of the Temple of Solomon in Jerusalem, a new Order of monks who were also warriors.

The group needed the approval of the Pope in order to become a religious order of the Church. This approval was given at the Council of Troyes in Champagne in January 1129 under the influence of the Cistercian abbot, Bernard of Clairvaux. The Templars received their rule and the habit of a white mantle to which the red cross was added later. Their overall commander was the Pope and the Templars owed allegiance only to him. In this way an organization crossing national frontiers was created, which had no obligation to secular lords.

The first Grand Master of the Order was Hugh of Payens from Champagne, France, who came to the British Isles in 1128 looking for support for the newly founded Order. The Anglo-Saxon Chronicle describes his visit thus:

> In this year Hugh of the Knights Templar came to King Henry I in Normandy and the King received him with great ceremony and sent him thereafter into England, where he was welcomed by all good men. He was given treasure by all, and in Scotland too; and by him much wealth, entirely in gold and silver, was sent to Jerusalem. He called for people to go out to Jerusalem. As a result more people went, either with him or after him, than ever before since the First Crusade, which was in the days of Pope Urban.[1]

The reasons for his visit were to attract knights to the new Order, to collect funds and to establish the Order in the British Isles. Donations of land were given immediately. His journey took him as far as Scotland where he was received by King David I, who was impressed by the virtues of this new Order of knights. Aelred of Rievaulx describes the influence exerted by the Templars over David's daily life:

> He committed himself to the counsel of religious men of all kinds and surrounding himself with very fine brothers of the illustrious knighthood of the Temple of Jerusalem made them guardians of his morals by day and night.[2]

Balantrodoch (now Temple, Midlothian) was the earliest possession of the Templars in Scotland. It was their chief preceptory and 'was granted to them by David possibly in 1128 or soon after'.[3]

The chief preceptory of the Templars in England was in London. There is no documentary evidence to show when the preceptory was established but a document dating between 1135 and 1148 confirms a grant of property in London, by King Stephen. The first establishment must then have been before this time. It became known as the Old Temple and was in the parish of St Andrew's Holborn. In 1161, when the Order was growing and needed more space, they built the New Temple with an access through the river gate leading directly to the Templars' pier at the Thames where they could tie up their boats.

Some other early properties were: Temple Cowley, Oxfordshire (1136); Temple Cressing, Essex (1136); Shipley, Sussex (1139).

They established a network of preceptories across the country with the main properties in the south and north east of England. The administrative centre was in London even though most of their properties were in Yorkshire. The London Temple focused on finance whilst in Yorkshire the preceptories concentrated on agriculture. The English Templar Order gained its wealth through finance and agriculture.

Donated land was often marshland or woodland and needed draining or clearing. Much land in Yorkshire was improved in this way and in time it became the county having the most valuable land.

The Order introduced sheep farming and exported fleeces and tanned skins to the Low Countries. They built a harbour for their ships in Faxfleet at the confluence of the rivers Trent and Ouse, on the Humber estuary, which connected the rivers Aire and Wharfe. They used these rivers to transport their goods from the Yorkshire preceptories to Faxfleet harbour and from there onward to the continental markets and to the Holy Land. By 1308 Faxfleet was estimated to be the most valuable Templar preceptory in the British Isles.

Wherever possible they used rivers to transport goods. Templar ships sailed up and down the Thames, and at Hurley upon Thames they built docks to make the river more navigable. Here they established one of their main preceptories in the south, Bisham in Buckinghamshire. Today one can still see the old chapter house fronted with black and white tiles and the old dovecot with over 600 dove holes. The Templars used doves to carry important information across Europe, at speed. All the main preceptories had dovecots.

The Templars as bankers

At the beginning of the fourteenth century the Templars had improved the economic situation of the country by upgrading and cultivating donated land using intensive labour. Most of the land was rented, which meant that their income constantly increased. The aim of the farming activity was mainly to raise money and resources for the Holy Land. Their brethren in Palestine were always in need of manpower, horses, arms, armour, grain and money.

During the time of the Crusades the Templars had established an international organization with a communication network and a network of trade and commerce. They had experience in managing money and in transporting money over long distances. They even developed a system whereby wealth could be transferred between preceptories using paper or little wooden boards instead of coins.

They were trusted by crown and nobility and used their expertise to arrange and pay ransoms. In time they became responsible for collecting and storing taxes and royal revenues through safe-deposit services. They gave loans and credits to kings, nobles and merchants to help finance operations and became financial experts with an international banking system that had the ability to finance projects such as the Crusades or the building of cathedrals. The English contingent of the Third Crusade, under Richard the Lionheart and the Master of England, Robert de Sable, was almost totally financed by the Templars.

They always had a good relationship to the kings of England and became the personal bankers of Edward II. We could ask why the Templars were considered so trustworthy and reliable and the answer lies in their motto:

Non nobis, Domine, non nobis, sed nomine tuo da gloriam.
Not to us, O Lord, not to us, but to your name give the glory.

The Templars were the Poor Knights of Christ. At their acceptance into the Order they had to give the monastic vows of poverty, chastity and obedience. Poverty meant that the individual member of the Order had no personal belongings. Everything belonged to the Order and the Order took care of its members, providing food, clothing, housing, armour and horses although all on a very modest scale. Though the Order acquired great wealth, the individual knight owned nothing personally. By 1307 the Order of the Templars was the wealthiest and most powerful organization in Europe with the status of a state within a state. This made them vulnerable to jealousy and then to political allegations of corruption and violent attack.

King Edward II

By 14 September 1307 King Philip IV of France had sent out the order of arrest to seize, imprison and interrogate all the Templars in France. This order was only to be opened and used on 13 October. The main accusations were heresy, idolatry, sodomy, acquisition of property and the secrecy of proceedings when new knights were accepted into the Order.

Only three days after the arrest Philip wrote to King Edward II of England urging him to deal with the Templars of England the same way as in France. Edward replied that the charges were so incredible that not only he but also his barons and his council could not believe them, and so he rejected them. By the end of November Pope Clement V acted. He was officially responsible for the jurisdiction of the Templars and he issued a Papal Bull, to all the kingdoms of Europe, to arrest and question all Templars on the said accusations. Edward hesitated but capitulated under increasing pressure from the Pope and the French King. On 20 December 1307 Edward decided to arrest all Templars in England and parts of Ireland and Scotland. By allowing a papal inquisition into the land he accepted a court to function within England that was outside his jurisdiction.

Arrests took place on 9 and 10 January 1308. English Templars were imprisoned in the castles of York, Lincoln, Newcastle, Oxford, Warwick, Canterbury and London. The total number of arrested Templars in the British Isles was 170. There were 153 from England, 15 from Ireland and two from southern Scotland. Of those arrested only 15 were knights, the rest were sergeants, chaplains and servants.

The arrest of the Templars in Scotland, and their trial at Holyrood Palace on 17 November 1309 was carried out by the English administration, which was occupying southern Scotland at the time. The situation in the rest of Scotland was different. King Robert Bruce, fighting English occupation in southern Scotland, was excommunicated at the time and therefore the Papal Bull was never read in the greater part of the country.

The papal inquisitors arrived in England in September 1309. The trials in London, Lincoln and York lasted from the end of October 1309 until the beginning of May 1310. Finally the inquisitors sent a long document to the Archbishop of Canterbury and to the Pope, telling of their efforts and their ill success. The Master of the Templars in England, William de la More, and his men would not confess to the accusations. They said they were innocent. In August 1310 Pope Clement wrote to Edward, bitterly reproaching him for not allowing the use of torture and thus hindering the work of the inquisition against heresy. In December he asked Edward to transfer the English Templars to Ponthieu, in France. They would then be on French soil, outside English law, and could be tortured, which would ensure confession.

Edward's reaction to this was to order the Templars to be imprisoned separately and be dealt with 'according to ecclesiastical law'. The question remains whether torture was used to obtain confessions. Only three Templars confessed during the trials. The three knights stated explicitly that they had not been tortured. Helen Nicholson considers that this statement proves that torture was used.[4] The trials in England did not produce much material for the inquisitors and they were disappointed when they departed for France. The trials showed that many Templars did not understand the difference between absolution as a sacrament and absolution for errors against the Order and its Rule. When the preceptor gave them absolution for errors against the Order they assumed it was a sacrament. The Church saw this as a heresy. The Templars were pardoned and sent to different monasteries to do penance and make their peace with the Church. Their Master of England, William de la More, did not confess and remained in custody in the Tower of London.

As King, Edward showed his weakness throughout the process. At the start he was convinced of the innocence of the Templars. He even wrote a letter to the Kings of Aragon, Castille, Portugal and Sicily advising them to ignore the unbelievable charges. But the stronger the demands of the Pope and Philip of France, the more he acquiesced until he finally agreed that the Templars should be treated *according to ecclesiastical law*.

King Philip IV

Rudolf Steiner gives a picture of Philip:

> ... we have a human personality ruling the West who can actually be
> said to have experienced in his soul a kind of inspiration through the
> moral, or the immoral, power of gold ... A highly gifted personality,
> Philip the Fair, who was equipped with an extraordinary degree of
> cunning and the most evil ahrimanic wisdom, had access to this
> inspiration through gold. Philip IV, who reigned in France from 1285
> to 1314, can really be said to have had a genius for avarice. He felt the
> instinctive urge to recognize nothing else in the world but what can be
> paid for with gold, and he was willing to concede power over gold to
> none but himself. He wished to bring forcibly under his control all the
> power that can be exercised through gold. This grew in him to be the
> immense passion that has become famous in history. When Pope
> Boniface forbade the French clergy to pay taxes to the State, this fact, in
> itself not very important, led Philip to make a law forbidding anyone to
> take gold and silver out of France. All of it was to remain there, such
> was his will, and only he was to have control of it.[5]

His will grew even stronger when on a visit to the Temple in Paris; he
could see the financial wealth of the Order with his own eyes. He realized
that the Templars were the richest organization in Europe and that many
kings and nobles depended on them for loans and credits. He knew that
they were a state within his state and only responsible to the Pope. Finally
he began to plan the downfall of the Order. His first thought was to
suggest a union between the Templars and the Knights of St John, the
Hospitallers, with himself as hereditary Grand Master of the new order.
The Templars' refusal to consider this union made him furious and gave
him reason to seek their destruction.

His network of spies were persuaded to report to him that the Templars
were addicted to immorality, that they spat on the cross, denied the
sacraments and worshipped idols and that through secret correspondence
with the infidel they had betrayed the Holy Land. Using this as an excuse
Philip stated that he felt responsible for the protection of Holy Church
and so had to act. He sent out secret orders to the seneschals and baillies of
France, instructing them to arrest every Templar at dawn on Friday, 13
October 1307. He expected that the Grand Master, Jacques de Molay,
and his Templars would be taken by surprise and through using torture
planned to obtain confessions before Pope Clement, or anyone, could act.

The Templars were under the protection of the Pope and by ordering their arrests Philip had flouted Clement's authority.

Pope Clement V

Philip bribed some of the cardinals to vote in favour of his papal candidate, Bertrand de Got, Archbishop of Bordeaux. This succeeded and Bertrand became Pope Clement V, and it was obvious that he was in the hands of the French King from then on. Philip made sure that the new Pope was not allowed to leave France for Rome but forced him to remain in Avignon. It was foreseeable that King and Pope were on a collision course that would become a struggle for power. Philip intervened in Church affairs when he had the Templars arrested, as the Templars were under the protection of the Pope. Philip's action led to a clash between King and Pope.

Clement reacted immediately. His protest was vehement and he could not believe the accusations. Philip responded in a curious way. He declared that his action was from the feeling of responsibility to the Holy Church and the Christian faith. He, as a good Christian and a pious man, could not tolerate the blasphemous and heretical behaviour of the Templars which Clement, as Pope, would surely understand. While the exchange of letters continued, Philip gave the order to torture the imprisoned Templars in a heinous way. Finally he had the confessions he needed in order to confront Clement (even from the Grand Master, Jacques de Molay, and the superiors of the Order). Clement, in his weak way, was looking for an escape from the conflict. He wanted to question some Templars himself to gain his own impression and asked Philip to deliver them to his papal court in Avignon or Poitiers. But Philip held them in Paris as he had something different in mind and the Templars could be useful to him.

A new development had taken place on the European political scene. On 1 May 1308 the German Holy Roman Emperor, Albrecht I, died. Philip had a dream of becoming the new Emperor and uniting France and Germany into one kingdom. He would be the new Charlemagne. He would control European politics with his cousin, Charles, as King of Italy and his daughter, Isabella, as Queen of England. Again, he was seeking absolute power but this time on an even higher level. He realized that he had two problems, firstly, in an election, he needed the support of the German Counts, and secondly, in order to be crowned, he needed the support of the Pope. He asked the Pope for his support and Clement gave this but only on condition that a group of Templars were sent to him, from Paris to Poitiers, for his personal investigation. Philip agreed to the condition and sent 72 Templars to Poitiers.

Meanwhile Clement wrote to the German counts warning them of the unscrupulous and power-hungry King of France and suggested they did not support him but Count Henry of Luxemburg. He feared for the Holy Church if Philip were elected as Emperor.

Philip was aware of Clement's activities, through the work of his spies, and he reacted immediately. He stopped the transfer of the 72 Templar Knights, and imprisoned them in the castle of Chinon, saying they were too weak to travel any further. The Templars became help-less figures on the chessboard of European politics. This development altered the situation for Clement. He wanted to speak to the Templars personally, but he depended on the favour of Philip for this to happen. On 12 August 1308, he issued a Papal Bull to all European kingdoms and ordered an investigation and trial against the Order of the Knights Templar. This Bull was meant to provide the legal background for a trial on behalf of the Church. With this he hoped to come into Philip's favour again.

At the end of November 1308, the German counts elected Henry of Luxemburg as the new Emperor. Philip was furious. All his plans had been destroyed, and he blamed the Pope for the failure. Clement feared reprisals from Philip and on 30 December he wrote to Philip, 'the accusations against the Templars seem to be true. The trial can now begin'. It was at this point that Clement abandoned the Templars.

Up to this time Clement defended the Templars and the Order as a whole, as was his papal duty, and so was in opposition to Philip. But Clement was always a weak pope completely in the hands of the powerful king. Finally he succumbed to Philip's will and used his ecclesiastical power to bring down the Order of the Knights Templar. But Philip became a king with empty hands. He had failed to become the Grand Master of a united order. He had failed to become Emperor. He even failed to gain the treasure of the Templars as after the arrests not a single penny was found. Now he used all his forces to crush the Order of the Knights Templar and the Pope.

Clement obeyed the King's will. On 22 March 1312 he abolished the Order of the Templars at the Council of Vienne 'not by way of con-demnation but by papal provision'. The Order was not found guilty by the bishops and legates but Clement stated 'its reputation had been so blackened that it could not continue'.[6] Its properties were transferred to the Order of the Knights Hospitallers of St John of Jerusalem. On 15 May Clement wrote to King Edward and the clerics and nobles of England with this mandate.

The hidden stream

So far we have looked into the outer history of the Knights Templar depending on the documented historical facts. These give 'a particular version' of events. Now we will try to come closer to the history behind the history, which means to discover the spiritual stream, the hidden stream that lies behind the facts. This makes it possible to view history from a wider context and so gain a deeper understanding of the fate of the Templars.

Rudolf Steiner talked about the mood within which the leaders of the First Crusade acted:

> The ... Order of Knights, the Templars, grew from a mood similar to that which I described as the mood of Godfrey of Bouillon. The Order's real aims were kept secret but through activists working in the background it soon grew very powerful. An anti-Rome outlook dominated it ... The Templars were striving for a purification of Christianity. Taking their cue from John the Baptist, they represented an ascetic tendency. Their acts of worship were so anticlerical as a result of their resistance against the secularization of Rome that it is still not possible to talk publicly about the subject even today. Because of its power, the Order became very awkward for the clergy and the princes so that it suffered severe persecution and was eventually destroyed after the last Grand Master, Jacques de Molay, suffered a martyr's death in 1314 with a number of his fellow Knights.[7]

Godfrey of Bouillon was the leader of the First Crusade. He, as well as many other Christians at this time, was unhappy with the Christianity that was spreading throughout Europe from Rome. Due to the dogma of the Holy Church all spiritual streams were being wiped out or were marked as heretical and not in accordance with the teachings of the Roman Church. The Cathars of southern France were one such group. Godfrey's intention was to found a Church in Jerusalem that was not based on the impulses of Rome, an *ecclesia catholica non Romana*.[8]

The impulse from the Roman Church was to prevent the development of the human 'I' or ego. The leaders of the First Crusade, the group of knights around Godfrey, were opposed to that mission. Rudolf Steiner spoke about the mood out of which these people acted and whom the Roman Church thought heretics.[9]

Godfrey could not carry out his plans as he died in 1100, just a year after the conquest of Jerusalem. The first nine Templars continued his work to develop a spiritual Christianity with its centre in Jerusalem. Here they 'were initiated by the Grail'.[10] They had to keep their real aim secret, and had to play their role as an Order of knights who protected pilgrims and defended the Holy Land. The 'activists in the background' were influential people who supported the Order from the beginning.

First we have to name Bernard of Clairvaux, the great Cistercian abbot, who tried to reform the Church from within. He organized the Council of Troyes in 1128, when the Order was officially founded. He gave the Order its Rule and habit, and sent a letter 'In Praise of the New Knighthood' to the kings in Europe in order to gain support for the Templars. He was in close contact with King Alfonso of Aragon who was so impressed by the Templars that when he died in 1136 he gave his whole kingdom to the Order of the Knights Templar. King David I of Scotland also supported the Order and had close connections to Bernard. He donated the first property, outside the Temple in Jerusalem, to the Templars and 'made them guardians over his morals by day and night'. He was deeply impressed by their spiritual life and their mission.

The Templars were initiated into the Mysteries of Christianity and therefore were striving for a purification of Christian life. They were deeply pious knights and their belief was that the blood in their veins belonged only to Christ. Their motto was: 'Not to us, O Lord, not to us, but to your name give the glory'. This motto was central to their daily life. They lived and worked for Christ. Their intention was to build a new spiritual life in Europe by transforming the power of gold in the name of Christ. This meant a spiritual approach to matter, not using it for personal profit but for the benefit of mankind. In this spirit they would create the new Temple of Jerusalem in the medieval societies of Europe. Their central premise was: 'Not I, but Christ in me'. It was out of this spiritual background that they met the people of their time. They held a totally different view of Christianity, which opposed the power-hungry attitude of the Roman Church of which they were members. The secret of their Christianity was kept within the inner circle of the Order.

The striving of the Templars for a new spirituality must have aroused opposing forces. In the ancient Mysteries, the spiritual force that opposed the development of the human 'I' or ego was known as the Sun Demon. His work was to oppose, in the strongest way, the coming of a free Christianity. This is the force that holds back human beings from developing a higher spirituality and turns them into beings devoid of any humanity. The Sun Demon has a cosmic cycle for his powerful interventions, which are periods of 666 years. These appearances are within approximate periods of time and not exact.

His first intervention became visible in the year 664 when the Synod of Whitby was held. King Oswy of Northumbria called for the Synod because of disagreements between the clerics of the Celtic Church and those of the Roman Church which culminated in a controversy about the calculation of the date of Easter. Each party used a different method of calculation.

Wilfrid, the intellectual scholar and abbot of the monastery of Ripon, presented the position of the 'Roman party' to the Synod. Barbara Yorke said that he 'seems to have continued a campaign against any survival of "Irish errors" and distrusted any communities that remained in contact with Iona or other Irish religious houses, which did not follow the Roman Easter'.[11]

Colman, Bishop of Lindisfarne, presented the Celtic position and stated that their calculation had its origin in the teachings of St Columba who was influenced by the Apostle John.

The Synod, with King Oswy, finally decided in favour of Rome. The discussion did not go into any depths concerning the problem of the date of Easter. The real conflict was the difference between two spiritual streams: the one from the Celtic world was based on the impulse of St John and led to an esoteric Christianity. The one from Rome was based on the impulse of St Peter and led to an exoteric Christianity. Both streams came to a confrontation in Northumbria. The result of the Synod of Whitby was the confirmation of the Roman Church in Northumbria and the rejection of Celtic spirituality. The same process appeared in continental Europe in the eighth century. In this process we can see the work of that spiritual force which is opposed to the development of the human 'I', or ego, in the strongest way. The intention was that mankind should not act out of its own free will towards a higher spirituality but should be kept under the dogma of the Church.

At the beginning of the fourteenth century the Sun Demon rose again. His appearance finally led to the downfall of the Order of the Knights Templar. Rudolf Steiner explained how the Sun Demon was opposed to the cosmic Christianity of the Templars:

It was the time when, out of the deepest depths of soul much more than out of orientalism, the Order of the Knights Templar wanted to found a Sun view of Christianity, a view of Christianity that looked up again to Christ as a Sun Being, as a cosmic being, a view that knew again about the spirits of the planets and stars, a view that knew how in cosmic events Intelligences from worlds that lie far apart from one another work together, not only the beings of one particular planet, a view that knew about the mighty oppositions that are brought about by such obstinate beings as Sorat, the Sun Demon, who is one of the most mighty demons in our system. What is at work in the materialism of human beings is, fundamentally, the demonic work of the Sun Demon.[12]

We can assume that Philip was a tool in the hands of the Sun Demon. He appeared to have no humanity. He ordered the torture of the Templars in a most appalling way and forced them to lie about their Order. By working in this demonic way he incorporated this impulse into the evolution of modern materialism.

The spiritual substance

The last trial of the Templars, in England, ended on 29 July 1311 in York. Although the Order had not been formally dissolved at that time, all the Templars were sent to various monasteries to perform their penance and to be reconciled to the Church. Their property remained in the King's hands and it would be many years before the Hospitallers, as rightful heirs appointed by the Council of Vienne, obtained many of these properties. The Grand Master of England, William de la More, stoutly refused to admit to errors he had never committed. He was kept in the Tower of London, where he died on 20 December 1312. Many of his brothers in France died on the rack during torture. Philip condemned 54 Templars and they were burned at the stake in Paris, May 1310. When Jacques de Molay, the last Grand Master of the Order, was brought before another commission of inquiry in Paris on 18 March 1314 he, and three others, revoked their confessions. Philip gave the order the same day to burn them as heretics.

Spiritual life cannot be rooted out. It lives on and continues to work. Those Templars who died under torture and those who were burned at the stake created a substance in the spiritual world, a spiritual substance out of their impulse of working and living for Christ. This substance is not lost. It can be used as a source of inspiration for bringing spirituality to Earth. The impulses, which were carried into the spiritual world through the destiny of the Templars, flowed into the soul of Johann Wolfgang von Goethe. This spiritual substance inspired him when writing the *Fairy Tale of The Green Snake and the Beautiful Lily*[13] and the poem *The Mysteries*.[14]

> For what the Templars had accomplished by entering in a living spiritual sense into the Mystery of Golgotha was not lost, it lived on. And after their terrible experiences on the rack—the souls of the Templars who had passed through the portal of death under these circumstances were now able to send down from the spiritual world streams of spiritual life for those who lived in the succeeding centuries.[15]

When looking at the Order of the Knights Templar today, we can have in mind, not just the history that had happened 700 years ago, but must be aware of that spiritual substance and the inspiration that can come out of it. It is still here today. We can work for humanity out of this inspiration with the motto of the Templars: 'Not to us, O Lord, not to us, but to your name give the glory'.

Horst Biehl, born in 1953, trained in social work and Waldorf education, and has been a class teacher from 1986 to 2010.

He has a special interest in the Order of the Knights Templar. For many years he has been collecting information about the Order's activities in many European countries. He has focused his research on the agricultural and financial activities of the Order, especially in England and Scotland, and in this way became aware of the transformation of land and the gold.

Every year he goes to the west coast of Scotland, searching for traces of the Templars after the fall of the Order in 1307.

During these visits he became interested in the old Celtic Church and its influence in medieval history.

Today he lectures on the Templar Knights and the Celtic Church.

Notes

1. *Anglo-Saxon Chronicle*, ed. G.N. Garmonsway (Everyman, 1953).
2. Johannis de Fordun, *Chronica gentis Scotorum*, ed. W.F. Skene (Edmonston & Douglas, Edinburgh 1871).
3. Alan Macquarrie, *Scotland and the Crusades* (John Donald Publishers, Edinburgh 1997).
4. Helen Nicholson, *The Knights Templar on Trial* (The History Press, Stroud 2009).
5. Rudolf Steiner, *Inner Impulses in Evolution*, tr. Church, Kozlik, Easton

(Anthroposophic Press, New York 1984) (GA 171). Lecture of 25.9.1916. Also in Rudolf Steiner, *The Knights Templar*, ed. M. Jonas (Rudolf Steiner Press, 2007).

6. M.J. Krück von Poturzyn, *Der Prozess gegen die Templer* (Ogham Verlag, Stuttgart, 1982).

7. Rudolf Steiner, lecture of 28.12.1904 (GA 51) excerpt in *The Knights Templar*, ed. M. Jonas (Rudolf Steiner Press, 2007).

8. Rudolf Steiner, *Cosmosophy*, Vol 2 (Completion Press, Gympie, Australia, 1997) (GA 208). Lecture of 13.11.1921.

9. Rudolf Steiner, *Mysterienwahrheiten und Weihnachtsimpulse* (Rudolf Steiner Verlag, Dornach 1980) (GA 180). Lecture of 17.01.1918.

10. Rudolf Steiner, 'On the Migration of Races', Berlin 1904 in *Gaia Sophia*, Vol. III (Orient-Occident Verlag, Stuttgart 1929). Excerpt in Rudolf Steiner, *The Knights Templar*, ed. M. Jonas (Rudolf Steiner Press, 2007).

11. Barbara Yorke, *The Conversion of Britain* (Pearson/Longman, 2006).

12. Rudolf Steiner, *The Book of Revelation and the Work of the Priest*, tr. Collis (Rudolf Steiner Press, London 1998) (GA 346). Lecture of 12.9.1924. Part of lecture in Rudolf Steiner, *The Knights Templar*, ed. M. Jonas (Rudolf Steiner Press, 2007).

13. Johann Wolfgang von Goethe, *Fairy Tale. The Green Snake and the Beautiful Lily*, tr. J. Heuscher, ed. J deRis Allen (SteinerBooks, 2006).

14. Rudolf Steiner, *A Christmas and Easter Poem by Goethe* (Mercury Press, Spring Valley 1987) (GA 98). Lecture of 25.12.1907.

15. Rudolf Steiner, 'The Templars and the Forces of Evil' (GA 171). Lecture of 2.10.1916, included in Rudolf Steiner, *The Knights Templar*, ed. M. Jonas (Rudolf Steiner Press, 2007).

The Knights Templar and the Grail

Margaret Jonas

A connection between the Templars and the Holy Grail mystery has long been claimed. It usually takes the form of the Templars 'guarding' the Grail in some way, which in more recent times has been extended to include protecting certain bloodlines—a much more dubious interpretation of *San Graal* or *Sang Real* that translates as Holy Grail or Holy Blood. Blood and the Grail are intertwined as the legends indicate that the chalice used at the Last Supper also became the vessel which caught the blood of Christ when his side was pierced by the Roman soldier's lance at the Crucifixion. Joseph of Arimathaea was the first 'guardian' of the cup and its contents, and there are many legends, alternative gospels and visionary experiences of his travels to France and Britain with the sacred treasure. According to some legends the cup was formed from a stone fallen from Lucifer's crown when he was banished from the heavenly world. In other versions this stone itself remains a stone, a sacred object capable of bringing about spiritual nourishment and transformation.

Human blood carries the force of the human 'I' and Christ's blood in the chalice contained the replica of the 'I' of Christ Jesus.[1] Rudolf Steiner has described the forming of the blood from the activity of the human ether or life body,[2] and he says that Christ's blood was, in its etheric component, of a special 'unfallen' nature comprising the ethers withheld from humanity's usage, the forbidden fruit of the 'Tree of Life'.[3] Thus the container and the contained have both a special spiritual quality, a healing, nourishing, regenerating power, and an 'unfallen' aspect that did not suffer the effect of Lucifer's activities and which remained in the care of spiritual beings until the time was right. This blood of Christ, as it worked to transform the Earth, passed through a process of etherization—a return to its etheric, non-physical state but still remaining within the etheric body of the Earth. Our human blood also undergoes transformation back into etheric substance as it streams from the heart to the head.[4] If a person comes truly to understand the Christ and lets this understanding into the heart, this stream can meet and unite with Christ's etherized bloodstream. When Steiner describes the Templars' blood as 'belonging to Christ' we can imagine that this was one important aspect which brought the knights' blood into a 'resonance' with that of Christ's and into which also streamed their strong will forces.

> The blood of the Templars belonged to Christ Jesus—each one of them knew this ... Every moment of their life was to be filled with the perpetual consciousness of how in their own soul there dwelt, in the words of St Paul, '*not I, but Christ in me*'! ... Words are unable to describe what lived in the souls of these men who were never allowed to flee, even if a force three times their strength confronted them on the physical plane, but who had calmly to await death ... It was an intense life of the whole human being in union with the Mystery of Golgotha.[5]

In the light of this we can better understand Rudolf Steiner's words in an early lecture:

> The key thing to emerge from [the Crusades] was the Order of the Knights Templar, the actual messengers of the Grail. They built a centre of wisdom on the site of Solomon's Temple and after preparation there they became servants of the Holy Grail, were initiated there by the Grail.[6]

We are being led deeper into the mystery of the blood, but how might we understand being 'initiated by the Grail'? One key to understanding this comes from beyond the threshold of this world. During the First World War a young German woman began to receive 'messages' from her brother Sigwart who had been killed. These were shown to Steiner who considered them to be genuine communications from beyond the grave. One such message was as follows:

> I was present at the explanation of Parsifal ... The basic thought pertains to Christ's blood, which has *actually transformed* the astral substance of the Earth. Right after this occurrence events took place in the various layers surrounding the Earth. *This* was the transformation of the physical substances. Christ died for us, but *we* also died for Him. In the moment that the drops of His blood touched the Earth the consciousness of humans descended into their 'etheric bodies' and beheld for a short duration of time the greatest event the Earth was ever permitted to experience. Upon returning to their physical bodies they all had become knowing to a high degree. They felt it at first as a strong inner experience; it changed later to an unconscious sentiment of awe and magnificence. This feeling gradually weakened with the passing of

the centuries, but the power of the inner voice remained as a nucleus that rests in *everyone*, becoming especially vocal in times of distress.[7]

It becomes possible for human beings to descend into their own etheric body and experience the effect of Christ's blood. We can imagine that the founding knights especially would have attempted this during their time in Jerusalem.

It was also a task of certain of the dead to become guardians of the Grail. Such souls would work together with those still on Earth, such as, for example, the Order of the Swan which was set up for this purpose.[8] Lohengrin, the son of Parzival, is called the Swan Knight. Manfred Schmidt-Brabant has suggested that the image of two knights riding one horse, as seen on several Templar seals, was not an image of poverty (for, in fact, every knight was allowed three horses) but of the working together of a soul beyond the grave with the brother on earth.[9]

The stories of the search for the Holy Grail form the core of the Arthurian legends of the Middle Ages and have come down to us in various forms. Steiner revealed to W.J. Stein especially that historical personalities were in fact concealed behind some of the familiar names of the Grail legends, and that specific initiations had occurred during the ninth century.[10] The original knights of King Arthur were concerned with understanding the secrets of the cosmos and of nature, and were also working to tame unruly human passions. The Grail knights, however, were the ones carrying the understanding of Christ's deed in their hearts and blood.

During the ninth century the two streams united, although the stories concerning the quests did not appear in writing until the twelfth and thirteenth centuries. The quest of Parzival (Perceval) is probably the best known, and in Wolfram von Eschenbach's epic the knights who guard the Grail castle are called Templars—*Templeisen*. This has led some authorities to question the translation as 'Templars' but other research shows that the Aragonese-Catalan word for Templars was *templés,* and this was rendered by Wolfram as *Templeis/Templeisen.*[11] If the events of the Parzival story do belong to the ninth century then it may be questioned whether the Grail keepers could really be Templars, as outer history tells us that the Order was not founded until 1118 or 1119. Herein lies the mystery of other possible antecedents or orders that may have been behind the setting up of the Order (though we can forget the spurious Priory of Sion, certainly in its present manifestation, now shown to have been founded in 1956![12]). In lectures on Richard Wagner's *Parsifal*, Rudolf Steiner refers to

> an important Mystery centre [which] existed in a region of northern Spain at the time when the Crusades began and *a little before that* [author's emphasis]. The Mysteries of those times were called 'late Gothic Mysteries'. Their initiates were called Tempelisen or Tempeleisen or Knights of the Holy Grail. Lohengrin was one of them.[13]

In the previous year Steiner had also said:

> The Swan Knight therefore appears to us as an emissary of the great White Brotherhood. Thus Lohengrin is the messenger of the Holy Grail.[14]

It may thus be possible to conclude that an earlier, more secret order of some kind did exist which led to the creation of the Order of the Knights Templar somewhat later. We can imagine that the mystery of Christ's blood would have been a significant focus for its esoteric teaching. It appears that these mysteries may have been found in northern Spain especially, for in addition to the reference above there are other allusions to the Grail castle hovering spiritually, so to speak, above this region.[15]

Steiner's emphasis is less on a building of stone or wood and more on a spiritual 'temple' in the same way that the Grail is not to be thought of as a physical vessel. Thus, although the centre of the mystery of Christ's blood was undoubtedly Jerusalem, it did not live on as a Christian centre. Spiritual powers could be active in other regions also and northern Spain, although significant, is not the only Grail Mystery site. It has been suggested by Judith von Halle at the Templar Conferences of 2007 (Hamburg) and 2009 (Forest Row) that these sites arose because Joseph of Arimathaea visited the locations and released a drop of Christ's blood into the ground there. Whether such a physical act took place is less important than that the imagination of a sacred space, a Grail castle, has been imprinted into souls in Europe (and now beyond) from the early Middle Ages onwards, and we can connect with such a 'castle' whenever we read or meditate on the stories and their characters.

In Wolfram's account, dating from the early thirteenth century, a strong emphasis is placed on brotherhood. Parzival is denied the Grail kingship until he learns to ask whom it serves and what ails the sick king. He must develop compassion and empathy. Then he learns of the existence of his half-brother Feirefiz, a Muslim, whom he fights at first but then embraces. Parzival is determined now to lead Feirefiz to the Grail castle. Feirefis begins to love the Grail bearer, Repanse de Schoie, and thus comes to the mystery of Christ through this love. He can see her but not the Grail itself until he recognizes Christ. For the Templars, whose desire was to recognize their brother in the Saracen, this version must have proved especially meaningful. Although the Saracens were deemed the enemy, the knights were often accused of being too fraternal towards them and, indeed, some people even blamed the loss of the Holy Land on a supposed treachery, i.e. consorting with the 'infidel' and even incorporating certain possibly Sufi beliefs. It is hard to imagine how they could have born their destiny without a cult of spiritual love, a more mystical heart-centred practice, and may have added or at least appreciated Sufi ideas together with their Christian practices.

The version of the Parzival story by Chrétien de Troyes, *Perceval*, stresses knighthood as a chivalrous ideal. Chrétien dedicated the work to Philip, Count of Flanders, claiming that Philip had given him the source of it. Philip was the son of Dietrich of Alsace and had inherited a relic, an alleged sample of Christ's blood given to Dietrich by Baldwin III of Jerusalem. Dietrich took part in the Second Crusade, inspired by Louis VII of France and the Cistercian Pope Eugenius III, and promoted by St Bernard of Clairvaux. Hughes, Count of Champagne was the overlord of Hughes de Payen, one of the founding knights of the Templars. He provided the land for St Bernard's Abbey of Clairvaux. André de Montbard, another of the original nine was also his vassal. Thus there were historical links between the transmission of the Grail story and the Templar Order.

It is, however, perhaps the version known as *The Quest of the Holy Grail (Queste del Saint Graal)*[16] that carries a particular relevance. Its author claims to be Walter Map, Archdeacon of Oxford and protégé of Henry II, but as he died in 1209 and scholars have dated this cycle somewhere between 1215 and 1230 this may be untrue. But there is some consensus that this version had a connection to the Cistercian Order and is thought to be part of the 'Vulgate Cycle'. St Bernard died in 1153, but his legacy continued and someone steeped in the mystical theology of St Bernard wrote the Vulgate Queste. Anna Morduch writes:

> St Bernard, the great protector of the Knights Templar ... gave to his spiritual sons much more than the rules of the newly founded militia. He gave them in his book *In Praise of the New Militia* stations of contemplation and inner training, which can be found in vivid pictures and parables in the *Queste del Saint Graal*.[17]

It is within this text that we can find particular references which would have been meaningful to those within or familiar with the Order. On page 97 of the 1975 Penguin edition of the *Queste* there is a reference to the 'Templar' psalm—no. 133, quoted by the aunt of Perceval (a character who takes the place of Sigune in Wolfram's version, and who admonishes him for leaving his mother broken-hearted):

> You are well aware that since the advent of Jesus Christ the world has seen three great fellowships. The first was the table of Jesus Christ, where the apostles broke bread on many occasions. That was the table where the bread of heaven sustained both souls and bodies, while they that sat around it were one in heart and soul, as King David prophesied when he wrote in his book the wonderful words: 'Behold, how good and how pleasant it is for brethren to dwell together in unity.' [Psalm 133] ... Thereafter there was instituted another table in memory of the Holy Grail which, in the days of Joseph of Arimathaea when the Christian faith was first brought to this land, saw the enacting of miracles so great that godly men and unbelievers both should ever hold them in remembrance ... This table was succeeded by the Round Table, devised by Merlin to embody a very subtle meaning. For in its name it mirrors the roundness of the Earth, the concentric spheres of the planets and of the elements in the firmament; and in these heavenly spheres we see the stars and many things besides; whence it follows that the Round Table is a true epitome of the universe. From every land, be it Christian or heathen, where chivalry resides, knights are seen flocking to the Round Table. And when by God's grace they are made companions, they count themselves richer than if they had gained the whole world, and to this end forsake father, mother, wife and children too ... When Merlin had established the Round Table, he announced that the secrets of the Holy Grail, which in his time was covert and withdrawn, would be revealed by knights of that same fellowship.[18]

Thus the Last Supper, the story of Joseph of Arimathaea and the Round Table all become united in an image of brotherhood and Christian mystery.

> There were many in the circle of the Knights Templar who could gain a deep insight into the Mystery of Golgotha and its meaning and into Christian symbolism as it had taken shape through the development of the Last Supper.[19]

At the Grail castle *nine* knights converge to join Galahad, Perceval and

Bors, the three deemed holy enough to perceive the Grail. The twelve partake of a ceremony resembling the Mass during which Christ manifests in the Holy Vessel. Galahad, the virgin son of Lancelot, is the main protagonist of this version, perhaps because he was traditionally celibate. He acquires the shield 'with a red cross on a white ground', which was stated to have been made for none other than him.

Other noteworthy images are the healing power of Perceval's sister's blood, and that the maimed king, when healed finally by the blood from the holy lance with which Galahad anoints his legs, enters a 'monastery of white monks'. The whole tone of this version is more lofty and monastic and perhaps less appealing today than Wolfram's lively tale, but with references to St John's Gospel and also to the Song of Solomon it carries an important esoteric undertone that would very likely have found favour with the Order. Its mystery of the 'holy blood' is strongly emphasized, female characters bear this too—perhaps in honour of the Virgin Mary—and images abound of spiritual states of being, conveying the required mood of those times for penetrating 'through the veil' (Perceval also means 'pierce the veil'). In an image of a ship crossing the sea—entering an 'astral body' state—Galahad, Perceval and Bors journey with the Grail to Sarras, the New Jerusalem, where the Grail displays its miraculous healing powers. Galahad and Perceval die there but Bors returns to this world, to Camelot and King Arthur to relate the tale.

To reach a deeper understanding of these connections we must lay aside the desire for historical proof—documentary evidence which is unlikely to be forthcoming—but by entering into the imaginations of the stories we can come to feel the heart connection which surely was an inspiration to the Knights Templar.

Margaret Jonas has been interested in the Grail and Arthurian legends since childhood. She has been concerned with the Templars for more than 30 years after discovering their significance through anthroposophy. Since retiring from her post as Librarian at Rudolf Steiner House in London she has had the time to pursue her interests, which include history from ancient times until the seventeenth century, religion and the Mystery traditions, stars and planets, psychology and different states of consciousness, as well as continuing research into the spirituality of the Templars. She also undertakes freelance editorial work. She lives in Sussex, finally free to enjoy the countryside, and is involved in anthroposophical life locally and in London.

Notes

1. Rudolf Steiner, *The Festivals and their Meaning* (Rudolf Steiner Press, Forest Row 1996) (GA 109/111). Lecture of 10.04.1909.
2. Rudolf Steiner, *Supersensible Knowledge* (Anthroposophic Press and Rudolf Steiner Press, Hudson and London 1987) (GA 55). Lecture of 25.10.1906.
3. Rudolf Steiner, *The Gospel of St Luke* (Rudolf Steiner Press, 1988) (GA 114). Lecture of 20.09.1909.
4. Rudolf Steiner, *Etherization of the Blood/Reappearance of Christ in the Etheric* (SteinerBooks, 2003) (GA 130). Lecture of 01.10.1911.
5. Rudolf Steiner, *The Knights Templar*, ed. M. Jonas (Rudolf Steiner Press, Forest Row 2007). Lecture of 02.10.1916.
6. Rudolf Steiner, *The Knights Templar*, ed. M. Jonas, op. cit. Undated lecture in *Gäa Sophia*, Vol. III, Berlin 1904.
7. *The Bridge Over the River*, tr. Joseph Wetzl (Anthroposophic Press, 1974).
8. Rudolf Steiner, *The Mystery of the Trinity* (Anthroposophic Press, 1991) (GA 214). Lecture of 23.07.1922.
9. Virginia Sease and Manfred Schmidt-Brabant, *Paths of the Christian Mysteries* (Temple Lodge, 2003).
10. W.J. Stein, *The Ninth Century* (Temple Lodge, 2009).
11. Henry and Renée Kahane, *The Krater and the Grail* (University of Illinois Press, 1965).
12. Lynn Picknett and Clive Prince, *The Sion Revelation* (Touchstone, New York 2006).
13. Rudolf Steiner, *The Christian Mystery* (Completion Press, Gympie 2000) (GA 97). Lecture of 29.07.1906.
14. Rudolf Steiner, *Richard Wagner*. Unpublished lecture of 28.03.1905 (GA 92). Typescript NSL 175-8 available from Library, Rudolf Steiner House, London. 'White Brotherhood' is not a racial term, but refers to the Lodge of exalted initiates said to guide humanity.
15. Rudolf Steiner, *Materialism and the Task of Anthroposophy* (Anthroposophic Press, Hudson 1987) (GA 204). Lecture of 16.04.1921.
16. Translated by P.M. Matarasso, Penguin Books, 1975.
17. *The Sovereign Adventure: The Grail of Mankind* (James Clarke & Co. Ltd., 1971).
18. Ibid.
19. Rudolf Steiner, *The Knights Templar*, ed. M. Jonas, op. cit. Lecture of 25.09.1916.

The Temple of Solomon and the Knights Templar

Rolf Speckner

The riddle of the name of the Order—the Poor Knights of Christ of the Temple of Solomon

An important question concerning the Knights Templar is why the Christian monastic/knightly order took the name of the main Hebrew temple in Jerusalem and a simple answer is that they took the name from the place where they were living at the time. We can ask: why question it as it seems so simple? But an Islamic legend tells us that the Byzantine Empress Helena found the true cross and built a great church over the tomb and place of Golgotha and at the same time disregarded the area of the Temple. Arab Muhallabi wrote: 'She turned "the Rock" into the rubbish dump of the area, and it passed into oblivion.' It was Caliph Umar, in 638, who gave the order to clean it.[1] It seems, therefore, that the Christians did not appreciate the site. The destruction of the Temple and its role in the condemnation of Christ had overshadowed the memory of Solomon's glory. However, the Templars gladly claimed the site and also its name which was the name of a Temple that had been destroyed hundreds of years earlier.

The Knights Templar within the development of monasticism

Many other monastic orders that had been similarly established on old heathen sanctuary sites did not take their name from the place. The first monastery of the Order of St Benedict was established on an Italian hill (*c.* 529) that was the site of the Roman military *castellum* (or stronghold) of Monte Cassino but originally had been an ancient heathen sanctuary dedicated to the Greek god Apollo. Benedict erected the altar of John the Baptist directly upon the altar of Apollo and placed an altar of St Martin nearby. Benedict did not take the name for his Order but the place he chose had a strong influence on his monastery, the Order and even on the whole Christian Church. It is symbolic that the walls of his monastery resembled a Roman *castellum* more than a Christian church and one might say that he built a strong fortress of Christianity.

How did Benedict form his order? Pope Gregory I has given us details of Benedict's life. The oldest form of Christian life outside Christian communities were the hermits living in Thebes, Egypt. St Anthony (*c.* 250–356) had led a devout life as a hermit, influencing others to imitate him. St Pachomius (*c.* 287–346) observed that the life of a hermit did not help develop the full spectrum of human virtues; in particular, social development could not take place in isolation. So he advised the hermits to live together, three in one cell. Such cells formed a hut and these huts formed a small village which was surrounded by a wall. Pachomius advised the hermits to wear similar clothes and to eat together. This was the transition from the hermit's life to that of monasticism.

Besides prayer, their central tasks were worldly. Ploughing, sowing, stockbreeding, gardening, weaving, craftwork, baking and cooking filled their days and the produce was sold in markets on behalf of the community. The needs of the community were met in this way. None of the monks were priests and so a priest had to be invited to take Mass. Pachomius wanted a deepening and Christianizing of the social sphere; we might say he wished for a 'common wealth'. He did not want a monasticism that was separate from the world. The monastery was part of the priest's parish, though a part that influenced him deeply, and so he too tried to lead a perfect life. The monks were the yeast in the dough of the human community.

The monks in Pachomius' community received no theological education and most of them only knew a little of the Gospels and perhaps some fragments from the Old Testament. Any education they had received had been gained previously, and further development was reliant on individual initiative as there were no schools within the communities. The influence from the community was purely moral and not intellectual—their hearts blossomed but not their intellectual life. Thus the monks had a deep influence on the souls of the people in their surroundings but little or no influence on intellectual debate.

Monks were not committed to Pachomius' communities for life and they could leave when they wanted. Some left the community, travelling alone and trying to lead a holy life; some of them succeeded, some didn't.

Born about 480 into a noble family, St Benedict first 'studied' jurisprudence in Rome. He soon left the city and began to lead a hermit's life in the mountains. Pope Gregory tells us that a monk with the telling name Romanus gave him the necessary clothing and brought meals to his cave. This 'friend' seems to have been his spiritual guide. After some years monks from a nearby monastery asked him to become their abbot. Benedict followed the call and failed! The older monks could not endure the strictness and earnestness of the regime and even wanted to kill him, so Benedict had to leave the community and return to the mountains near the River Anio where he founded another community in the style of that of St Pachomius. Again there was difficulty with some in this new community, which made it impossible for Benedict to remain.

When Benedict was 49 years old, in 529, he founded the monastery at Castrum Casinum, mentioned above. In the same year Justinian closed the philosophical schools of Athens and many of the Greek philosophers fled to Gondishapur in present-day Iraq.

Benedict destroyed the surviving remnants of paganism with this new foundation and he gave his monks a new 'rule'. When they entered the Order he now expected them to make a commitment for life. He expected strict observance of the *stabilitas loci*, which means they were to stay in the same monastery for life. This was not meant to be tyrannical but was a means to awaken the heart forces of the monks. Like Pachomius' hermits, Benedict's monks had to wear identical clothes. The rule also demanded a special haircut. They had to remove all the hair from the top part of the head, the place where the spirit connects to the human body, making the place open and visible. This meant that every Benedictine monk was recognized as such and thus was treated like a monk and always reminded of his vows.

Benedict's moderate demands concerning daily prayers and rites opened the possibility for the monks to receive a theological education. Benedictine monks had the task to read and listen to readings; Monte Cassino was one of the first monasteries to have a library. Through Benedict, monasticism became a lifelong learning and after a while the monasteries became centres of higher study, predating the later universities.

Because of Benedict's 'rule' and insistence on commitment, the Benedictine monks became important factors in intellectual life, their word having weight in the intellectual world of the time. This way Christianity not only reached the feelings of the heart but also the questioning mind.

Benedict, who has been called 'the last Roman', thought of his institution in terms of Roman military life. When monks took the vows they became *milites Christi*, 'the soldiers of Christ'. One can say that this meant an inner fight against the devil and the fight to find the living Christ. But the whole Church also became an *ecclesia militans*, a 'fighting church', and it was the task of every monk or clergyman to fight for the eternal salvation of all human beings.

The monks made an oath that Benedict called the *sacramentum,* using the same word that Roman soldiers gave to the oath to their flag. In the Prologue of the 'Rule' Benedict defines the purpose of the Order: *Constituenda est ergo nobis dominici schola servitii.* The word *schola* originally meant a group of guardians in the palace of the Roman Emperor. The declaration in St Benedict's rule reads: 'We have to be an army of guardians, for the service of God.' The Benedictine Order needed rules like all military troops. Benedict called the rule a *lex, sub qua militare vis* or 'the law, under which you wish to serve'. *Militare* means 'serve', a kind of military service, and by this law the monks were strictly separated from the rest of mankind.

His military concept of monasticism penetrated every aspect of the life of the monks. Even the library was called the *armatorium* which means the room containing the arms or weapons for the fight. The mental side of the fight becomes clearly visible.

In the third century Roman theologians had begun to introduce their thinking, in terms of juridical laws, into the Church. For the Greek Patriarchs, Christ was the redeemer or saviour. With his sacrifice everything was completed. It was wonderful news they brought to the people, an *euangelion.* Death had lost its sting. In Rome, however, Christ became the highest judge. One had to fulfil certain terms or conditions to gain redemption. The *eu-angelion* here became a testament whose writer was dead, and the heirs (*eu-angelists*) had to fulfil certain terms to achieve the inheritance. The Romans thought that redemption was not unconditional salvation but that people had to do something to achieve the inheritance. The conditions were moral ones, but Cyprian of Carthage found that there were also other ones: *Extra ecclesiam salus non est,* 'There is no salvation outside the Church'.[2]

In the sixth century the Romanization of the Church took another step. The forces of Mars penetrated the independence of the Church and the *worldly* imperial will of Rome and its Emperors went through a metamorphosis and became a will to *spiritually* conquer the world. This influence from the past, this incorporation of the Roman 'folk spirit', or 'Spirit of the Roman people', is what we observe in the life of Benedict of Nursia and his contemporary Cassiodorus (*c.* 490–583).

Rudolf Steiner tells us that the spiritual background of such outer manifestations lies in the sacrifice of the spirit who once was the Spirit of the Roman People.[3] The archangel relinquished his task for the Roman people and became the leading spirit of exoteric Christianity. The name Roman Catholic Church says it all. *Catholicos* is a Greek word meaning 'for everyone', but being 'Roman' and being 'for everyone' seems rather contradictory. The Spirit of the Roman People behaved as if he were a 'Spirit of Time', as if he were 'for everyone'. This Spirit was an archangel who worked like a 'Time Spirit'. This is reflected in the fact that Benedict chose a former military colony of the Roman army as the right place to found his order. This depicts the real evolution in the spiritual world that lies behind the outer facts.

Ferdinand Gregorovius, the writer of *History of the City of Rome in the Middle Ages*, described Benedict's work with the following words:

> [The Benedictine monasteries] became for the Roman Church what the military colonies had been for ancient Rome. Scarcely had the Empire been destroyed when Roman monks penetrated barefoot—the cord around their loins—without any fear into the outermost Thule and invaded into those wildernesses of the Occident, which the ancient Roman consuls and their legions had not been able to fully conquer.[4]

(By Thule he means the whole of Northern Europe outside the former Roman Empire, i.e. Scotland, Ireland, Scandinavia, etc.)

Our short voyage through Church history has shown us that in the eleventh century the idea that an order had a military task was not new to Christendom; it was normal. But through time the Church Fathers changed the physical fight into an inner or mental one.

What was new was that the Knights Templar combined spiritual combat with worldly combat. Was this some sort of backlash? No it was not. The Templar Knights were not allowed to attack the enemy first. Passions had to be controlled. If not in a declared war, they had to wait until an aggressor had attacked them three times before accepting the challenge. The combination of inner and outer challenge developed the physical body into a spiritualized physical body.

There are many witnesses who show that the metamorphosis of the Roman Spirit, who was taken for a real spirit, was known in the Middle Ages. On a Carolingian ivory plaque we find a scene that is not found in the Gospels but was living vividly in the minds of the Carolingian artists and their noble or ecclesiastical patrons with the result that it was carved many times.

We see on the right of the cross of Golgotha a woman sitting in front of a house or temple. She is sometimes depicted with an aura in the form of city walls and sometimes crowned, characterizing her as the city of Rome which means the Spirit of Rome. She has a round disc in her hand, showing her as ruler *urbi et orbi*, i.e. of the city and of the whole Earth.

Fig. 1 Ecclesia *and* Roma *under the cross. Ivory bookcover, about 870. (München. Staatsbibliothek; Clm. 4452)*

Another woman comes from the direction of the cross carrying a flag, as we know *Ecclesia* does, and takes the disc from the sitting Roma.[5] This shows that the task of the Spirit of Rome has passed to the *Ecclesia*, the Spirit of the Exoteric Church.

The Victoria and Albert Museum in London possesses a small ivory from the eleventh century. It shows St Peter dictating the Gospel to St Mark. An Angel is standing between them, seemingly inspiring Peter. Over the head of the angel are the Greek letters ΠΟΛΙC PϖMHI. The

Fig. 2   St Peter dictates the Evangile to St Mark. Ivory. Late eleventh century (Williamson) Victoria & Albert Museum, London. 270–1867 Nr. 3

words read *Polis Romei* and could be translated as 'City of Rome'. But there is no city to be seen. Therefore, the scholar Paul Williamson,[6] who seemingly does not believe in archangels, feels obliged to explain that there must have been an image of the city on a plate above the extant part. But *Polis* also means 'that which gives the order for all'. It was not meant as an abstract political unit but as a living being, so we might translate it better as 'The Common (Spirit) of Rome'. This indicates that people in the early Middle Ages were aware of Spirits of Nations and Spirits of Time, especially the leading and more developed citizens.

The Spirit of the place

We have already seen that the place on which Benedict founded his order was well chosen. Because of this he influenced the new 'Roman' Spirit of the Order. The remains of the ancient civilization, on which he built, gave the picture of the spirit on which he founded his new spirituality. Apollo has been described by Rudolf Steiner as the Greek form of the descending but-not-yet incarnated Christ.[7] Benedict consecrated Apollo's altar anew to John the Baptist, 'who prepared the way ... for the powers of Christ (to) permeate the existence of humanity'.[8]

The sites where churches and monasteries were founded were carefully chosen and the earlier history taken into account. Even the form of the place had a special importance. The founding of the monastery of Corvey at the Weser in Germany in the year 821, for example, was on a site that had the form of a triangle. The river Weser flowed along two sides of the triangle while along the third side a range of hills covered the land. This was taken as a sign that the threefold unity of the deity was living there. Paschasius Radbertus (785–860), who took part in the founding of Corvey, wrote of the form of the site and its meaning for its inhabitants: 'And if the triangle will be erected, as has been shown, this will be a sign, that those who live there shall ignite the fire of love.'[9]

As Rudolf Steiner often explained the symbolism of the figure of the triangle we can understand what Paschasius, the Carolingian theologian, meant. The symbol resembles a house. The living quarters have a form shaped like a square, whose corners represent fourfold man—the physical body, the etheric body, the astral body, and the 'I' or self. The roof forms a triangle over the square, representing the three parts of the human spirit, 'I' or ego, i.e. harmonized thinking, feeling and willing.[10]

If the three essential parts or members of our spirit shall rule over our fourfold physical or, better said, incarnated being, then this will happen by igniting the fire of love. The Spirit Self is developed through identifying oneself with an idea. This idea—which we love—becomes our Self. Through this the universal spirit becomes individual. Our beloved idea (moral intuition) is universal: *everyone* can think it and can have insight into it. On the other hand, the same idea is individual because *we* love it. We don't ask whether someone else loves it: we love it because we love it. Our love has its basis from the depth of ourselves, and through the love of the universal idea we start to know not only the universal being of the idea but also the individual being in our inner depths. *We will be in the future what we love now.*

All this indicates that there must have been clear reasons for the Templars' choice of site in Jerusalem and not just chance. The site of the Temple, the Spirit of the place, must have had an important influence on the founders of the Order. While the Spirit of Rome by a transition had become the Spirit of the Roman Church, the Knights Templar did not exclude military fighting from their spiritual development. It was kind of a counter-movement.

The wisdom of Solomon

Why did the Knights Templar choose the place of Solomon's Temple? When the knights entered Jerusalem the Temple was long destroyed. They knew about the Temple from the Bible and they also knew of the 'wisdom of Solomon'. Today the highest wisdom is still identified with the name of Solomon.

But what do we know of Solomon's wisdom? His Book of Proverbs was printed in hundreds of editions in former centuries. Nowadays we say it is part of the so-called wisdom-literature that flourished in the ancient world, similar to that of the Egyptian *Book of the Dead*,[11] written in the form of a father's speech to his son. But these are only formal comparisons that are made without real understanding.

Many modern academics do not believe in the authorship of Solomon, but at the time of the Knights Templar there were many books attributed to him. Albertus Magnus (1200–80) attributed a book *In speculum Astrologiae* to Solomon. Trithemius of Sponheim (1462–1516) believed in Solomon's authorship of the 'superstitious' and magic books *Clavicula Salomonis, Liber Lamene* and the *Liber Pentaculorum*. The Middle Ages thought of Solomon not only as a pious author but as an occult author, an author of Mystery wisdom.

At the beginning of the ninth chapter of Solomon's Book of Proverbs we read the following: *Sapientia aedificavit sibi domum, excidit columnas septem*. This strange sentence, which was central for some older occultists, can become a key for an understanding of Solomon's wisdom. The King James version of the Bible reads: 'Wisdom hath builded her house, she hath hewn out her seven pillars' (Proverbs, 9:1). Solomon speaks of the building of a house and a house is for someone to live in, so who will live in this house? Solomon says: 'Wisdom has built her house.' The house is built for wisdom. Wisdom is both the builder and the inhabitant. The second part of the sentence says: 'she (wisdom) has erected seven pillars' when building her house. If we look once more, we may notice the seven pillars are not only erected but also hewn out, which I understand as 'carved'. During the erection of the house each pillar gets hewn out or carved. It may be that each of them is carved in a different way.

The English translators of the seventeenth century have added a word to the Latin version that they used. In the Latin version 'wisdom hews out seven pillars', but in the English Authorized Version 'wisdom hews out *her* seven pillars'. This is a very interesting addition. Without it one could understand Solomon's proverb to mean that wisdom has built herself a house and that the edifice is erected in a beautiful way; it has seven pillars. The word *her* makes clear that the pillars have something to do with Solomon's wisdom; they either belong to it or are a part of it. We will see that Rudolf Steiner understands Solomon's words in the same way that James I, the 'English Solomon', understood them.

The wise translator, James I, speaks of wisdom as a female entity. In both versions Solomon first speaks of something that has no house or home, then she builds herself a house. The third phase, which he does not mention, would be that she is living in her house. Why doesn't Solomon mention it? Is she standing before her house and not entering? Is she unwilling to go inside? Is there a certain moment to wait before going in? He does not tell us. And why did wisdom build herself a house if she does not go in? Why does wisdom need a house at all? In looking repeatedly at this question one remembers that human thinking comes to consciousness by using the house of the body as a mirror. The human mind reflects on itself on the ground of its brain, which the mind has built for itself, and thereby comes to knowledge of itself. This wisdom needs her house not only as a dwelling place but to know herself. Can wisdom stay wisdom if she does not know herself?

If we remember that wisdom is a spiritual being then we notice that this resembles a process of incarnation. 'Wisdom' incarnates in seven phases by erecting seven kinds of support or props. We can say the first one is the physical body, it is hewn out in the first seven years of our life. However, the physical body alone would not be enough to attain sensory perceptions. It is necessary to structure the physical body so that it has its own etheric body, which is the second pillar that wisdom has to build or hew out in order to know her own essence. And so this process continues.

Where can we find the famous 'seven pillars of wisdom'? Rudolf Steiner gave a description of this some weeks before the outbreak of the First World War. He was speaking in Dornach about the erection of a 'House of the Word'. This house had a main hall with seven pillars on each side. Rudolf Steiner said:

The human being, as he enters the world, is really a highly complicated being. When he enters the world he cannot at first stand upright; he crawls, and at the very beginning of his existence he does not even crawl. Gradually he learns to control the forces which enable him to stand upright. Let me try to make a diagrammatic sketch of this process [Fig. 3].

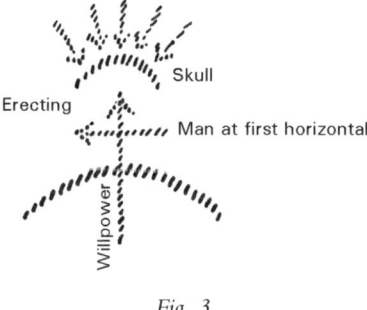

Fig. 3

Underneath we have the Earth. The human being is at first a horizontal being; then he stands upright—in the vertical position. It is an achievement of man's nature itself to attain the vertical position but he has the help of all the hierarchies as he passes through the course of his life. What is it that comes to his aid when he stands upright and walks? The forces that work from the Earth out into the expanses of cosmic space. These are the earthly forces. Today physicists only speak of purely physical forces of the Earth— forces of attraction, of gravity and the like.

The Earth, however, is not merely physical body but a being of spirit and soul and when, as little children, we raise ourselves to the upright position and walk, we are uniting ourselves with the forces of Will rising out of the Earth. The Earth-Will permeates our being; we allow the Earth-Will to flow into us and place ourselves in the upright position—the direction of the Earth-Will. This process is a union with the Earth-Will. But in opposition to the Earth-Will there is a will that works in from all sides of the cosmos. We have no knowledge of it, but yet it is the case that as we raise ourselves to the upright position, forces (from the cosmos) are working in from all sides and we come up against these forces that pour in from outside.

This has no particular significance today on the Earth but during the Ancient Moon period it had a tremendous significance. On the Ancient Moon, conditions were such that from his earliest childhood man had a different orientation, in that he had to place himself in line with the direction of the Moon-Will. As the result of this he acquired the first germs of the skull formation. Today we have inherited them, but on the Moon it was a question of acquiring them. In those times man worked in himself against the outer will-forces somewhat in the way a locomotive works when it has to push away snow. He pressed back the will-forces of the cosmos and his soft skull formation compressed itself into the hard skull covering. Today this process is no longer necessary. The skull formation is inherited. It is no longer necessary to build up the skull bones.

In the etheric body, however, we still build them, for as we rise to the upright position there is a densification in the head, representing the result of the fight between the forces streaming in from all sides of the cosmos. Thus, when we observe the etheric body, we may say that in his two legs, man builds up two lines of force and works against the forces that proceed from without. The etheric body is densified and this form arises [fig 4]. We raise ourselves upright. The physical legs have their junction above, but the etheric legs rise still higher.

As a result of this the etheric head is densified and as a result of the formation of the brain there arises in the etheric body, in our age as well, the densified etheric body. This does not only take place in childhood but as man passes through seven life periods (from the first to the seventh year, from the seventh to the fourteenth year and so on) new lines are formed, lines of different forces which pass upwards. So that when we have reached the age of full and complete adulthood—when we have passed the fiftieth year of life—we have added new pairs of pillars to that first strong pair formed during

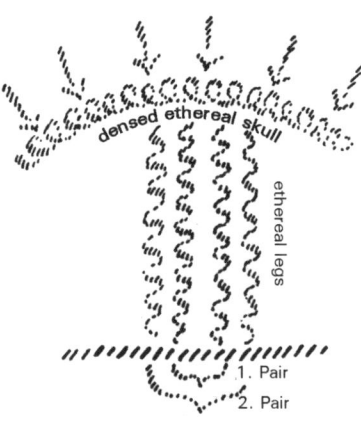

Fig. 4

the first seven years of life. They appear in the etheric body in different colours. We strengthen our etheric sheath every time we develop these 'life pillars' for so indeed they may be called. After the first period of seven years the first pair of life pillars is completed, at the fourteenth year the second pair, at the twenty-first year the third pair, and finally, with the forty-ninth year, the seventh pair. Each pair of life pillars makes our etheric skull covering more secure.[12]

Now we can have an inkling of the depth of Solomon's wisdom. He has a knowledge of the etheric world and especial knowledge of the seven pillars of life or processes of the human etheric body. These correspond to the seven planetary deities and so the 'seven pillars of the house of wisdom' can become seven doors of perception to the supersensible world. The human etheric body can become the means of re-membering the supersensible etheric world, the world of the plants and planets. The art of re-membering the spiritual world through the sevenfold etheric body was one of the esoteric arts of the Renaissance and the Middle Ages.[13]

Solomon knew how the house of wisdom, the human etheric body, had been built. Wisdom was able to get to know itself in this house. This wisdom that has found itself in the house of wisdom can be called Spirit Self. (The Spirit Self is the sum of the human free moral intuitions. But these moral intuitions are the air the spirit breathes, the water that refreshes it and the fire that inspires it. They are the life of the Spirit Self. Through our free deeds we impregnate the etheric body with our spirit and transform our daily self into the Spirit Self or transformed astral body.)

And this was the aim of a Templar Knight: to make his body a house of free and loving wisdom itself. His blood belonged to the 'I am the I am'.[14]

Solomon knew what was necessary to develop the human body in such a way that it could become the place where the human spirit enters the material world, rests, develops its hidden powers and, through this labour, gets to know itself. Christiane Schwarzweller has demonstrated that the impact of the Solomonic Temple in Jerusalem was based on its influence on the human etheric body, especially from the mighty pillars of Jachin and Boaz.[15] When visitors entered the Temple they had to pass between two pillars. They saw Jachin on their left with a cold red tone and Boaz on their right with a warm blue tone. The etheric movements, through which the visitor received the perception of the two pillars, intermingled with the etheric effect of the pillars. While the red pillar made the visitor shrink back, they were attracted by the blue colour. Because of this the human etheric body came into a spiral movement that led to a crossing of the etheric movements in the heart region. The heart was the centre of human consciousness in the times of Solomon and long afterwards. The influence of the Solomonic Temple on visiting mankind was to strengthen this etheric stream which crossed its own movement.

This way Solomon discovered and then made the plan of the Temple. But he could not bring it into a physical form. The wisdom and knowledge of Hiram of Tyre was necessary to build the Temple in the physical world.

The Solomonic Temple and the aims of the Order

The idea of the Solomonic Temple was to build an edifice to house the name of God. The Temple was not for God but for his name. It was forbidden to speak this name. Is there any name which one is not allowed to speak? This seems impossible as a name is by definition the word by which we address one another. But there is one exception. No one can speak to another individual and call him/her 'I'.

The riddle of the name 'I' deepens if we ask how each of us can call ourselves 'I'? Who is calling whom in that case? If 'I' ask 'myself' something, who is putting the question? Who is hearing the question and who is giving the answer? How can I give the answer if I ask the question? If I ask I don't know the answer—but I do know if I answer.

We can explore further. What does it mean when I ask a question? The spoken question is a sign that my inner self is wondering about something. I have noticed that I do not understand something. I have noticed that I long for some idea, something in the world that is missing. If I say 'I don't know', I presume there is something to know. But how do I know there is something to know if I do not know what it is? The fact that we have questions shows that we have some kind of glimpse of the answer. The question is the dawn of the answer. The following intuition is the sunrise. The question is a part of the answer, its first semblance.

In terms of Rudolf Steiner's *Theosophy*[16] the whole process can be described as follows. The consciousness soul[17] is asking the question. When the answer dawns the Spirit Self touches the consciousness soul. When intuition enters like a flash of lightning the Spirit Self enters the consciousness soul and I come to my self. We are asking the question and we are giving the answer. Every time we ask ourselves something and give ourselves the answer it is some kind of awakening of the soul: a self-awakening.

The human being's physical, etheric and astral bodies have been built in order to make this possible. The human body was and is meant to become a 'House for the (unspoken) name of God'.

We know the great myth of Paradise with Adam and Eve and the snake which describes how man lost his way. This story comes at the beginning of the Old Testament. At the end of the Old Testament there stands the figure of the predicted Messiah whom we, in so far as we are Christian readers, identify with the Christ. The whole story between the two events is the journey of the building of a house for the name of God. This is the reason why the Messiah was expected to incarnate in the Jewish race. The Jewish people were building the house of the 'I', the house of the name of God. The Temple of Solomon—planned by the king and erected by Hiram of Tyre—had a direct impact on the body of the visitor: through its form, its colours, its measures. The Solomonic Temple was a means of education for mankind.

The Knights Templar were striving for the same goal. When they said their body belonged to Christ, this meant that they wanted to take each step with the conscious power of the 'I' or self. Their body should become a house or a temple of the name of God. Therefore they chose to live at the place where the Solomonic Temple had been.

Rolf Speckner is a freelance writer born in Hamburg in 1949. He gives introductory courses at Rudolf Steiner House in Hamburg and lectures at the anthroposophic art school 'Kunstakademie Hamburg'. He is married with one son and is the second son in a merchant's family having a Protestant mother and a liberal minded Roman Catholic father.

He met anthroposophy at 17 through becoming a pupil of the anthroposophist and scholar Dr Hans Börnsen. Börnsen was an expert in Nordic mythology and medieval culture, and Rolf's interest was awakened to the ethical and spiritual background of the Knights Templar. Rolf then studied physics, mathematics and philosophy at the University of Hamburg.

After Börnsen's death in 1982 Rolf edited three books written by his anthroposophical 'father'. The second anthroposophical teacher he found was Professor Walther Matthes with whom he wrote a book on the medieval relief of the 'deposition of the cross' in the sanctuary of the rocks at the Externsteine near Paderborn in Germany, a place where Celtic and Germanic mysteries took place. During this time he worked for some years as a bookkeeper and trader. In 2002 he published a book, with a professional photographer, on the Externsteine (Rolf Speckner and Christian Stamm: Das Geheimnis der Externsteine. Bilder einer Mysterienstätte. 2002).

Rolf Speckner is a Council member of the Anthroposophical Society in Hamburg and has been responsible for some well-attended and important conferences in Ham-

burg, most notably an Anglo-German conference on the Knights Templar in October 2007, exactly 700 years to the day on which the first Templar arrests were made. In preparation for the Hamburg conference he published an article, 'Die Ursprungsimpulse der Templer nach Rudolf Steiner' in the Swiss magazine Gegenwart *in 2007.*

Notes

1. Priscilla Soucek, 'The Temple of Solomon in Islamic Legend and Art', included in Joseph Gutmann (ed.), *The Temple of Solomon*, Archaeological Fact and Medieval Tradition in Christian, Islamic and Jewish Art (Ann Arbor, Michigan, 1976).
2. *Letters of Cyprian.*
3. Rudolf Steiner, *The Mission of the Individual Folk Souls*, tr. A.H. Parker (Rudolf Steiner Press, London 1970) (GA 121). Lecture of 12.06.1910.
4. Ferdinand Gregorovius, *History of the City of Rome in the Middle Ages*, tr. Annie Hamilton (Cornell University Library, 2009).
5. Wolfgang Seiferth, *Synagoge und Kirche im Mittelalter* (München 1964). Abb. 5 und 6, München, Staatsbibliothek, Clm. 4452, coverplate (*c.* 870), and Paris, Bibliothèque Nationale, Cl. 9383, coverplate (*c.* 900).
6. Paul Williamson, *Medieval Ivory Carvings: Early Christian to Romanesque* (V&A Publishing, 2010).
7. Rudolf Steiner, *Approaching the Mystery of Golgotha*, lecture of 5.03.1914 (SteinerBooks 2006) (GA 152).
8. Karl König, 'St John the Baptist', in *The Mystery of John* (Camphill Books, 2000).
9. Paschasius Radbertus, 'Vita Adalhardi abbatis Corbeiensis', in Walther Matthes, *Corvey und die Externsteine. Schicksal eines vorchristlichen Heiligtums in karolingischer Zeit*, Chapter 66 (Stuttgart 1982). Allen Cabaniss translates the phrase thus: 'If it should be elevated upward, it is obligated to inflame those dwelling therein with the fire of charity.' In: Allen Cabaniss, *Charlemagne's Cousins. Contemporary lives of Adalard and Wala* (Syracuse University Press, New York 1967).
10. Rudolf Steiner, *The Mission of the Individual Folk Souls*, tr. A.H. Parker (Rudolf Steiner Press, London 1970) (GA 121). Lecture of 11.6.1910.
11. T. Eric Peet, *A Comparative Study of the Literatures of Egypt, Palestine and Mesopotamia* (Wipf & Stock Publishers, 2007).
12. Rudolf Steiner, *Architecture as a Synthesis of the Arts* (Rudolf Steiner Press, London 1999) (GA 286). Lecture of 28.6.1914.
13. See Frances A. Yates, *The Art of Memory* (Pimlico 1992). Sheila Mackay transports the Art of Memory to the Garden of Edzell, Scotland. See Sheila Mackay, *Early Scottish Gardens* (Polygon at Edinburgh, 2001).
14. Rolf Speckner, 'Die Ursprungsimpulse der Templer nach Rudolf Steiner', in *Gegenwart*, Nr. 2 (2007) pp. 10–14.
15. Christiane Schwarzweller, *Der Salomonische Tempel als Einweihungsweg*, Hamburg 2008.
16. Rudolf Steiner, *Theosophy*, tr. C.E. Creeger (Anthroposophic Press, Hudson 1994) (GA 9).

17. The consciousness soul is an anthroposophic term denoting a view of the human soul. It was introduced by the German philosopher Immanuel Hermann Fichte who was the son of the famous Johann Gottlieb Fichte. In Immanuel Fichte's and Steiner's view there are three main configurations of the human soul: sentient soul, mind and feeling soul and consciousness soul. The first part enables us to perceive things and beings; the second part enables us to store the perceptions in our mind and to live with these by reliving the moment from the past. This enables us, as well, to compare things and to connect them with the help of ideas. The third part, the consciousness soul, is that part of our soul which is able to reflect upon itself. This ability enables us to practise objectivity, for example, in scientific research. Scientists can describe their methods and work. They can differentiate what they have heard from what they have seen, what they have felt from what they have thought, and what they can imagine from their insight. This way people are able to construct and to state the strength of proof. The three configurations of our soul can be understood as belonging to every part of gaining knowledge.

The Knights Templar, Shipley and the Mission of Albion

Sylvia Francke

The tiny hamlet of Shipley in West Sussex was chosen by the Knights Templar as their southern headquarters in Britain. A visitor to Shipley once perceived it as having been the gateway to the Mysteries of this Island, referred to by William Blake as Albion which 'originally may have been the Celtic name of all Britain'.[1] Today Shipley still radiates a quiet peace which can give those who visit it an insight into the meditative work of the Templars.

I will attempt to trace a possible connection between the activities of the Knights Templar in Shipley with the development of the individual human being, an impulse which Rudolf Steiner described as having been prepared in the Hibernian Mysteries, the most ancient of the Mystery Centres of antiquity, which still waits its fulfilment in these islands.

Rudolf Steiner often spoke of a unique contribution that Britain has to give to the spiritual development of mankind, the fostering of which he described as 'the consciousness soul'. This impulse, which began in 1413 and through which we are still passing today, will continue for several centuries to come.[2] It is concerned with the development of the 'ego', the eternal human spirit, a centre from which the human being can begin to transform the bodily sheaths—the etheric, astral and physical bodies—in free cooperation with Christ.

There are powers that are seeking to thwart this impulse. Rudolf Steiner talks of Sorat the Anti-Sun Demon, the two-horned beast described in the Book of Revelation, who attacks the progressive course of evolution approximately every 666 years. He speaks of the first attack by Sorat being connected to the establishment of the Academy at Jundí Sábúr (Gondishapur), close to present-day Baghdad, where activities reached their height around the year 666.[3] Two years earlier, 664, marked the height of the Council of Whitby when the Church of Rome superseded Celtic Christianity in Britain. Rudolf Steiner describes how the arrest of the Knights Templar in 1307 took place in the preceding shadow of the second attack by Sorat in 1332. Moreover, he foretold that the third attack would occur around 1998.[4] We can perhaps identify for ourselves the various symptoms of such an onslaught.

Through that great change in the relationship of humanity to the spiritual worlds, known in biblical tradition as 'the Fall', man lost his connection with the source of creation but gained individual freedom. This freedom gradually begins to assert itself as the human soul develops in the widening gap between the worlds of spirit and matter. The establishment of this possibility is being developed during the time described by Rudolf Steiner as 'the age of the consciousness soul' which began in 1413. The Being who is to lead mankind through to this stage of spiritual development, especially during the period which began with the twentieth century, is the Archangel Michael who is closely connected with Britain's patron saint, St George.

In connecting Michael with Britain's task of developing the age of the consciousness soul, it is interesting to note that this country is traversed from west to east by a line of churches and sites dedicated to or connected with St Michael.[5] Most of the sites on this line have connections to the Knights Templar.

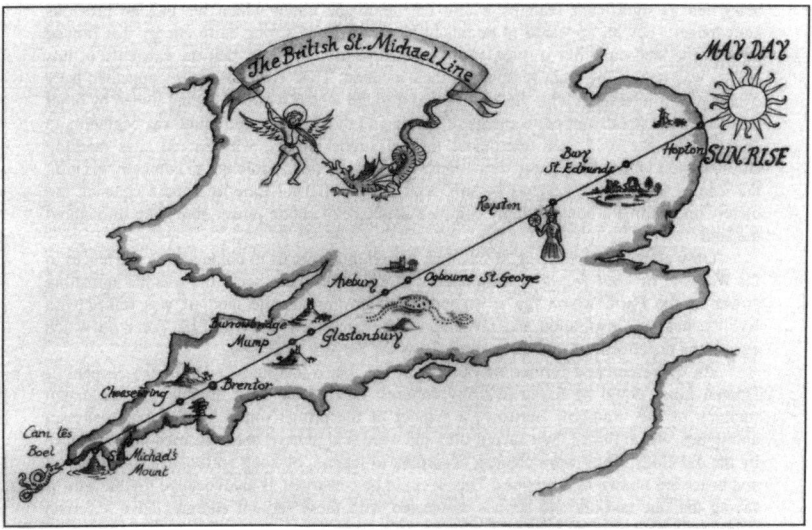

The late John Michell first discovered the Michael Line, as a line of Earth-energy, running between Glastonbury and Avebury. Paul Broadhurst and the late Hamish Miller then elaborated upon his initial findings in their book *The Sun and the Serpent*. Miller, a proficient dowser, found that these ancient sites manifest an intensification of the Earth's etheric energy. 'Dowsing these unseen energies,' say Miller and Broadhurst, 'leads into the world of multi-dimensional forces that lie behind the physical reality we observe with our ordinary senses.'[6]

I have interpreted this statement to be in accord with Rudolf Steiner's more detailed descriptions of the life force, the etheric realm, which works into all nature in higher octaves of four elements (or four *ethers*). The warmth ether relates to heat, the light ether to gas and air, the chemical ether to the fluid state, and the life ether to solid matter.

The life ether is the highest etheric state connected with the most sublime regions of the spiritual world although now reaching down deeply into matter bringing life into the solid state. It has been described as energy before matter, as 'the coming into being of matter' or the 'coming into matter of being'. The chemical, sound, number or tone ether is connected with the fluid state. It brings into matter 'information' which will qualify and differentiate emerging life forms.

During the time of 'Paradise'—a purely spiritual state of the Earth prior to the Fall—the full power of the life force manifested the Creative Word. Christ was within the undivided ethers that permeated the kingdoms of nature in perfect harmony:

> It is really not easy to portray the splendour of the Earth at that time. We must perceive it as a light-filled globe, shone round by light-bearing clouds and generating wonderful phenomena of light and colour ... Within them ... were all of the human beings of today, woven through by all the spiritual beings, who rayed forth light in manifold grandeur and beauty; outside was the Earth cosmos in its great variety, inside was man in close connection with the divine spiritual beings raying streams of light into the outer light sphere ... From the beginning the Earth was not only glowing and shining but was also resounding ...[7]

In the early period of world history known as the Lemurian epoch the original harmonious state of creation was interrupted by Lucifer's invasion of the early human astral body, which affected the etheric body as far as the light and warmth ethers. This meant that humanity gained control over these two ethers which gave us the faculty of independent thinking.

Steiner describes how independent thinking is caused by the activity of the warmth and light ethers. This is referred to in the Book of Genesis as the story of Adam and Eve eating from the Tree of Knowledge. The story continues with a description of the removal of the Tree of Life to the east of the Garden of Eden. Steiner says that man has gained control over the warmth and light ethers but to gain control over the two higher ethers, the chemical and life ethers, would have led to disaster for early humanity as these two ethers hold the mystery of life itself. In his collection of lectures *The Temple Legend*, Rudolf Steiner describes these two higher ethers as the Holy Grail.

> What then is the Holy Grail? For those who understand this legend correctly, it signifies—as can be proved by literary means—the following. Until now, man has only mastered the inanimate in nature. The transformation of the living forces—the transformation of what grows in the plants and of what manifests itself in animal and human reproduction—that is beyond his power. Man has to leave these mysterious powers of nature untouched. There he cannot encroach. What results from these forces cannot be fully comprehended by him.[8]

Steiner and Günther Wachsmuth have further interpreted the story of the Tree of Knowledge and the Tree of Life from the Book of Genesis. Wachsmuth investigated the ethers under Steiner's supervision for many years. It has been explained in various places by both of them how, as a result of Lucifer's intervention, the highest region of the ethers, the life ether—the 'Grail' as mentioned above—was separated from the Earth to form a new 'Sun-sphere' by six of the angelic hierarchy of Elohim or Exusai. The chemical ether was removed some time later to be incorporated into a 'Moon-sphere' by the seventh of the Elohim, Yahweh. These higher ethers manifested Christ, the Logos, who had sounded through Paradise before the Fall.

Wachsmuth continues

> Whence came the Christ? He came from those very regions which have been closed to man by the temptation of Lucifer, from the region of the Music of the Spheres, from the region of the cosmic life. With his soul, man really belongs to the region of the living cosmic ether. But he was driven out from it.[9]

Humanity lost Paradise but attained a new, independent faculty of thinking. We see the branches of the Tree of Knowledge fanning out and diversifying in medical diagrams of the central nervous system! Human freedom was gained through the estrangement of human thoughts from the creative thoughts of the angelic hierarchies. Following the individualization of humanity on Earth, the 'kindling of the I' came as a gift from the Sun Elohim who donated a spark of their own fire to form the future human ego. Before this human beings had been 'soul beings' but were now given the potential to become individual eternal 'spirits'. From that time onwards, as the gap widened between the original Paradise state and an increasingly solid material world, the human soul gradually began its long development as the link between spirit and matter.

The ancient Atlantean Sun Mysteries continued to foster the activity of the six Sun Elohim who had begun to work upon human individuality after the Fall. These Mysteries were located in what is now the northern Atlantic near the Arctic Circle and moved, first, to a region north-west of Ireland, where they became the Hibernian Mysteries, and then to the Irish mainland at the end of the Atlantean period. They were places where the most advanced men were initiated into cosmic secrets. At the same time they were taught how to master earthly tasks.

> The Mysteries of the Sun, including all the various types, combined them into a higher unity.[10]

This was how the first foundations were laid for future esoteric Christianity whose development throughout the world would be the particular responsibility of Europe when it came into being.

Britain marks part of the area permeated by the influence of this most ancient and far reaching of all the ancient Mystery Centres. In these Mysteries initiates were trained to combine direct spiritual revelation with human concepts. Steiner describes how 'these Mysteries can be discovered only by the exercise of a human being's own conscious inner activity, by the rekindling of one's own inwardly acquired knowledge'.[11] This training can be seen as potential for Britain's mission of directing emerging human individuality worldwide at the birth of the consciousness soul in 1413.[12] Steiner speaks of how the Hibernian Mysteries were central to the spiritual evolution of Europe for many centuries and of how ego consciousness first manifested in the region of modern Ireland towards the end of the Atlantean period when the forerunner of clear and logical thinking first began to emerge.

With this activity comes the awakening of human conscience, which was also connected with ancient Ireland. Sergei Prokofieff says, for instance:

> Conscience has been described as the calling forth from within man of a kind of dim memory of his condition before the Fall, and at the same time enables him to be inwardly aware of the voice of that part of his soul—a kind of 'inner Ireland' where divine forces, untouched by anything earthly are still preserved.[13]

As the time approached for human individuality to evolve, the Hibernian Mysteries ceased to exist in the outer world. Now, the Sun

Archangel, Michael, has particularly bestowed his special characteristic—the activation of human initiative—during the twentieth and twenty-first centuries. Michael is the being who waits for human beings to act out of themselves in furthering their individual spiritual progress and the progress of world-evolution.[14]

We can consider how closely these characteristics of the Archangel Michael are connected to the development of the human ego through the activity of the six Sun Elohim manifesting Christ. We can see that this was also the aim of the High Sun Mysteries and the Hibernian Mysteries which prepared for the maturing of these ego forces in the consciousness soul age which would begin to take place in Britain. We can then look at the line stretching through Britain where the Archangel Michael is repeatedly represented overcoming the Dragon, reminding us that each individual human being affected by the impulse of the consciousness soul age can begin to take up this task of individual transformation.

We can, furthermore, look at this connection between the mission of Albion, the development of individuality and Michael's fight with the Dragon in more detail. In his lectures on the Book of Genesis, Steiner describes how, at the Fall, the physical body, which was formerly composed of warmth and air, contracted and condensed and formed a body that was all fluid and only later solid. The etheric body of the Earth (with its four ethers) also became subject to the dynamic of the Fall and formed a 'sub-material realm' indwelt by three ranks of fallen beings.

The result of this dynamic within the layers of the Earth caused the fallen light ether to descend to a sub-material realm where it became electricity, indwelt by luciferic beings. The fallen chemical ether likewise became magnetism, indwelt by satanic beings often referred to as ahrimanic (after Ahriman, the dark brother of the Sun-god Ahura Mazda in the Zoroastrian religion). The fallen life ether, which Rudolf Steiner has described as 'the third force', manifests a realm connected with the Asuras, a hierarchy of fallen beings of whom Steiner seldom spoke.

Where there are geological faults or where geological strata meet, fallen etheric energy (electromagnetic energy) is funnelled to the surface and can be experienced as powerful earth-energy. It is possible for human beings to transform this to its original etheric state by working on the corresponding etheric structure within themselves. This will be referred to in more detail when we describe the meditative work of the Knights Templar in connection with their relationship to the powerful energy spots over which they chose to settle. Many such powerful areas also manifest the Threefold Goddess together with the centric forces, the

Earthbound ethers with their respective fallen beings. One can see that many Cathedrals not only have many representations of a figure often connected with earth-energy, the Green Man, but also the Black Virgin. There was a Templar presence in Chartres Cathedral, in France, and the Black Virgin was venerated at Chartres thousands of years before the birth of Christianity.

In his lectures on 'The Problem of Faust', Steiner described the Triple Goddess, the Mothers, as personifications of the evolutionary development of the forces of life working into the human cell, the same forces that were trapped within the Earth by the dynamic of the Fall. Walter Johannes Stein developed this description further,

> ... these layers are the Earth's past, the relic of its past evolution still buried within it ... Mephistopheles spoke of the Mothers with the greatest awe as goddesses unknown to men, and told Faust that he 'must burrow to the uttermost profound' if he would find them in the 'ever-empty far'.[15]

Box Hill in Surrey manifests powerful electromagnetic energy. This is a location where the chalk deposits end and London clay begins. The village of Mickleham, or Michaelham, in the valley below is not only named after St Michael but some of the roofs of the village houses are adorned with terracotta dragons. Where there is powerful Dragon energy there is the possibility of overcoming it or transforming it. Random observations gathered from people living on the hill bear witness to the fact that it is an emotionally turbulent place in which to live.

Rudolf Steiner sometimes referred to the 'fallen' etheric energy as it manifests in the human being as an ahrimanic 'double' or *Doppelgänger* living within the electromagnetic impulses of the nervous system (within the Tree of Knowledge). He described how the double seeks out locations on the Earth from which these same electromagnetic forces radiate so that it can connect with them and increase its domination over the human host on which it thrives.[16] In these powerful places the challenge to overcome the forces working below the level of human consciousness is far greater, presenting the individual with an opportunity to emulate St Michael's fight with the Dragon.

Let us draw these threads of conjecture together in relation to the mission of Britain and the Knights Templars' role as guardians of the Grail in the tiny hamlet of Shipley in West Sussex. The discovery of the Michael line in modern times began when John Michell, standing on Glastonbury Tor in Somerset, 'observed' that its axis seemed to point directly towards the projecting mound of Burrowbridge Mump, located between St Michael's Church at Trull and St Michael's Church at Othery.

> An image began to form. It was of a great line stretching across country, from the Mump a few miles away in the south-west over the low-lying landscape of the area to pass through the remains of the great megalithic temple complex at . . . Avebury.[17]

There is possibly another significant line that runs eastwards from Glastonbury. Nicholas Mann, a Glastonbury author speaks of 'Classic ley stories, such as the arrow being fired from Old Sarum to mark the location of Salisbury Cathedral and happening to coincide with an alignment to Stonehenge to appear in the Glastonbury corpus.'[18]

One favourite story is that of St Cuthbert who carried his 'mother' in a wheelbarrow from Glastonbury until the straps broke in Shipley in Sussex. At that place he founded his church. Unremarkable you may think, but it happens that Shipley was the major seat of the Knights Templar in southern Britain. The Templars were a mystical order accused of practising earth magic or geomancy. If a line is drawn from Shipley to Glastonbury it passes through the ecclesiastical centres of Shaftesbury and Salisbury. It makes one wonder what St Cuthbert was wheeling from the 'Mother Church' of Glastonbury. Is the story an allegory of far deeper wisdom?

Shipley, although not on the Michael Line, demonstrates its close connection with St Michael and St George through the ancient name of the neighbouring tiny hamlet, Dragon's Green. A carved stone serpent or dragon arching over the first step up to the altar indicates the location of a very intense source of etheric energy inside Shipley Church.

When I, and a group of friends, visited Shipley many years ago we came upon the then-new vicar outside the church and asked him about the Knights Templar. He obviously didn't know much but

referred to them vaguely as 'a bunch of vagabonds'. Ten years later I had
to call in at the vicarage to ask the same vicar if he could open the church
so that a friend of mine might see it. As we entered my friend com-
mented: 'What a holy place.' The Vicar turned to her and said, 'Yes, the
Templars prayed this into these walls.' His change of attitude would seem
to corroborate my feeling that the Templars' mission was to return
original Paradise forces, the Grail energy, to the Earth by applying their
deeply meditative work to locations like Shipley.

If we repeat the earlier quotation from Günther Wachsmuth we can
make a link with the aims of the work of the Templars 700 years ago.

> Whence came the Christ? He came from those very regions which
> have been closed to man by the temptation of Lucifer, from the region
> of the Music of the Spheres, from the region of the cosmic life. With
> his soul man really belongs to the region of the living cosmic ether. But
> he was driven out from it. And so it is given to him again, so that by
> degrees he may once more be able to imbue himself with that which he
> had forfeited.[19]

In what way might the Templars have been working with the
Earth's energy? Rudolf Steiner has described how, at the moment that

Christ's blood fell from the cross on Golgotha a change took place in the Earth.

> If someone had observed clairvoyantly the astral body of the Earth during the course of the Earth's evolution, during the course of long periods of time, he would have seen ... the Earth surrounded by an aura of light, for he would have been perceiving the Earth's etheric and astral bodies. If this clairvoyant person ... observed the pre-Christian periods of the Earth pass by and the Event of Golgotha approaching, the following spectacle would have presented itself to him. Before the Event of Golgotha the aura of the Earth, the astral and etheric bodies, offered a certain aspect of colour and form, but following a definite moment of time he would have seen the colour of the entire aura changing. What was this particular moment of time? It was the very moment when the blood flowed from the wounds of Christ Jesus upon Golgotha. All spiritual earthly relationships changed from this moment.[20]

However, although this change has taken place, Rudolf Steiner has constantly indicated that humanity has the task of continuing this process. The transformation of the sheaths of the Earth cannot be complete until we transform our own individual bodily sheaths (astral, etheric and, finally, physical bodies). As we have begun to see, the transformation of matter will be involved in the redemption of the fallen beings which were involved in its formation from an original purely spiritual state.

In a different connection Rudolf Steiner has described how

> We find that the Order of the Knights Templar, inwardly considered, expresses a specially deep approach to the Mystery of Golgotha on the part of modern humanity ... The blood of the Templars belonged to Christ Jesus ... Every moment of their life was to be filled with the perpetual consciousness of how in their soul there dwelt 'Not I, but Christ in Me'.[21]

Elsewhere he has described how the free application of meditative work, an intense contemplative preoccupation with the life of Christ, can cause the electrical impulses of the nerves to be withdrawn from the blood, allowing pure etheric energy to replace them.[22]

Günther Wachsmuth has linked this possibility with the etheric body of the Earth:

> Certain forces mould the body of the Earth and of man in accordance with uniform, harmonious laws ... The destiny of man is bound up

with the Earth ... the face of the Earth becomes part of the destiny of man ... the configuration of the etheric body of the Earth ... is a reflection of our own inner being ... the etheric forces moulding the body of the Earth are the same as those in our blood corpuscles ... If new etheric forces arise within the Earth in the course of cosmic 'becoming', this reflects itself right into the corpuscles of human blood. On the other hand, when a change takes place in the etheric structure of human blood, this will be reflected into the etheric sphere of the Earth, because, in effect, the Earth and the blood corpuscles are formed according to the same laws ... We are thus led into a quite different relationship with the Earth, a truly Christian knowledge of the spirituality of the Earth, to a Gaia-Sophia.[23]

This began a process that can be continued today. It was once observed that long ago Shipley was 'the gateway to the Sacred Isle of Britain, and that people came here from very far afield because there are and were special aspects of the Mysteries which could only be learned here'.[24]

This would seem to point to the possibility that where the etheric landscape of Britain is intensified and returned to the 'Paradise state', the original aim of the Hibernian Mysteries can be released as a strength that carries us towards the future destiny of Britain.

Sylvia Francke's first reaction to the initial publication of The Holy Blood and the Holy Grail *by Michael Baigent, Richard Leigh and Henry Lincoln in 1982 was one of anxiety at what appeared to be a calculated attack on Christianity. Having separated the sensational style from what appeared to be a genuine desire on the part of the authors to solve many unanswered questions posed by exoteric Christianity, she felt a strong compulsion to attempt to tackle those questions from another direction: from the ancient traditions of esoteric Christianity which have re-surfaced in Rudolf Steiner's anthroposophy (or spiritual science). Here the many strands of hidden Christian initiation have emerged again in a form in keeping with the twentieth and twenty-first centuries. She then attempted an answer to the three authors' questions in her book* The Tree of Life and the Holy Grail.* In 2009 the Templar Conference at Emerson College gave her an opportunity to link the Knights Templar's Christian esotericism to another subject about which she feels passionately, the mission of Britain in fostering the future development of esoteric Christianity on a wider scale. In connection with this, her suspicions of a calculated attack on Christianity have been revived by the many recent attempts to discredit Britain and to deny the possibility of its role, which entails developing the sovereignty and dignity of the individual human being.*

---

*Sylvia Francke, *The Tree of Life and the Holy Grail* (Temple Lodge, 2007).

Notes

1. Adrian Room, ed., *A Dictionary of Phrase and Fable*, Millenium Edition (Cassell, 1999).

2. Humanity began as a purely spiritual being, having no independent existence. As a result of the Fall we gained freedom, a newly formed separate human spirit or 'ego', while losing direct connection with the spiritual world and gradually developing a body composed of matter. The human 'soul' is that part of our being which, developing through time-periods, forms a continuous link between our spiritual origin and the constantly changing bodily consciousness. Rudolf Steiner described this developing relationship as follows: sentient soul began *c.* 1900 BC; intellectual soul began *c.* 747 BC; consciousness soul began *c.* AD 1413 and is still continuing.

   And Rudolf Steiner has described how the Knights Templar belong to the same stream of Mystery knowledge as the Rosicrucians. The Rosicrucians' mission in the fifteenth and sixteenth centuries was to prepare human soul-development in a way that was crucial to the transformation of the human being in reversing the effects of the Fall. Steiner describes the human 'soul' as the mediator between the physical body and the eternal spirit, the ego, which was liberated by the Fall of Lucifer. He describes how the soul's relationship to physical experience of the outer world on one side and the emerging independence of the ego on the other gradually brought about humanity's awakening consciousness. The latest stage through which it has passed is the stage of the consciousness soul, which still continues.

3. Rudolf Steiner, *Three Streams in the Evolution of Mankind*, tr. C. Davy (Rudolf Steiner Press, 2nd impr. 1985) (GA 184). Lecture of 12.10.1918.

4. Rudolf Steiner, *The Book of Revelation and the Work of the Priest* (Rudolf Steiner Press, 1998) (GA 346). Lecture of 12.09.1919.

5. Main sites on the Michael Line: Carn Lës Boel; St Michael's Mount; Cheesewring; St Michael's Church, Brentnor; St Michael's Church, Trull; Burrowbridge Mump; St Michael's Church, Othery; Glastonbury; Stoke; St Michael's Church, Avebury; Ogbourne St George; St Michael's Church, Clifton Hampden; Royston; Bury St Edmunds; St Margaret's Church, Hopton.

6. Paul Broadhurst and Hamish Miller, *The Sun and the Serpent* (Pendragon Press, 1982).

7. Rudolf Steiner, *Egyptian Myths and Mysteries* (Anthroposophic Press, New York 1971) (GA 106). Lecture of 07.09.1908.

8. Rudolf Steiner, *The Temple Legend*, tr. J. Wood (Rudolf Steiner Press, London 1997) (GA 93). Lecture of 02.01.1906.

9. Günther Wachsmuth, *Etheric Formative Forces in Science, Art and Religion*, Book 2, Chap. 12, Typescript, Rudolf Steiner House Library, London.

10. Rudolf Steiner, *Mystery Knowledge and Mystery Centres*, ed. A. Welburn (Rudolf Steiner Press, 1997) (GA 232). Lecture of 09.12.1923.

11. Rudolf Steiner, *Esoteric Cosmology* (St George Publications, Spring Valley, USA, 1978) (GA 94).

12. See note 3.

13. Sergei Prokofieff, *The Spiritual Origins of Eastern Europe and the Future Mysteries of the Holy Grail* (Temple Lodge, 1993).

14. Rudolf Steiner has described how, in the evolution of the Earth, each of the archangels, in turn, rules over a period of 260 years. Michael's last period of rulership was before the birth of Christ. He rules again now in a period which began in the year 1879.

15. Walter Johannes Stein, 'The Interrelation of Man and Cosmos', 01.02.1947. Quoted by M. Cotterel in 'The Undiscovered Third Force' in Anthroposophical Quarterly, Autumn (1961).

16. Rudolf Steiner, *Geographic Medicine. The Secret of the Double* (Mercury Press, Spring Valley, New York 1986) (GA 178).

17. Paul Broadhurst and Hamish Miller. op. cit.

18. Nicholas Mann, *The Isle of Avalon* (Llewellyn Worldwide Ltd., 1996).

19. Günther Wachsmuth, *Etheric Formative Forces in Science, Art and Religion*, op. cit.

20. Rudolf Steiner, *The Gospel of St John*, tr. Monges (Anthroposophic Press, New York 1984) (GA 103). Lecture of 26.05.1908.

21. Rudolf Steiner, lecture of 02.10.1916 in *The Knights Templar*, ed. M. Jonas (Rudolf Steiner Press, 2007).

22. Rudolf Steiner, *An Occult Physiology* (Rudolf Steiner Press, 1983) (GA 128). Lecture of 21.03.1911.

23. Günther Wachsmuth, 'The Face of the Earth and the Destiny of Mankind', a lecture given in Dornach, 27.12.1923, published in *Gäia-Sophia*, the first yearbook issued by the Section for Natural Science at the Goetheanum.

24. Jehanne Mehta, written account of a Gatekeeper Trust outing to Shipley, 08.02.1981.

Bound with Gold

Jacques de Molay and King Philip the Fair

Scene 1

Antechamber in the Paris Temple. King Philip IV paces anxiously. A veiled figure (ahrimanic spirit) looms in a corner.

PHILIP [*to audience*]   I escape from the claws of a mob and he makes me wait—when the whole country shrieks for my head over our noble mint. [*A beat*] But never one to squander an opportunity, I'll strike while the iron is hot—for all their gold, these Poor Knights of the Temple reveal a baser metal!

[*PHILIP bangs a table.*]

PHILIP [*in mock weakness*]   Your King awaits!

[*Enter JACQUES DE MOLAY*]

DE MOLAY   Forgive the delay, a snake loose in the halls. A party of knights hunt it—but it proves more elusive than Saladin!

PHILIP   An ill omen.

DE MOLAY   Perhaps ... but welcome to the Temple, my liege. Stay at your leisure, that rabble looked murderous.

PHILIP [*feigning weakness*]   My heart's taken flight, but my royal head sends its thanks.

DE MOLAY   Please sit.

DE MOLAY   We received the invitation to your sister's funeral; it will be an honour to bear her body.

PHILIP   Good. You'll be informed of the date.

[*PHILIP studies Jacques' Templar dress.*]

PHILIP   You look magnificent—a more noble vision is hard to imagine. Did you not think me worthy of this honour?

DE MOLAY   These are council verdicts. I submit to a higher will.

PHILIP [*mock sad*]   But am I not as entitled as Coeur-de-Lion? I could have been your brother.

DE MOLAY   This is hard to take, I understand—

PHILIP [*suddenly sharp*]   Do you?

DE MOLAY   What's done is done—

PHILIP [*petulant*]   Now Edward's no more you stand in need of royal protection.

DE MOLAY   Disappointment teaches peasants and kings alike.

PHILIP [*sharp*]   You philosophize like a true soldier, but I can muster no argument ... [*he sits with mock sadness*] ... A week from hell, yet I survive.

[*The ahrimanic shadow moves to the centre of the room. Philip is suspicious. Does De Molay see it? It remains ambiguous.*]

PHILIP   It's said that you *initiated knights* have the sight. I believe it true.

DE MOLAY   True like: blasphemy, sodomy, witchcraft? It's unwise to trust wagging tongues.

PHILIP   A fair point; I trust only what weighs my purse, but the spirit realms interest me. My childhood visions often scared my little playmates.

DE MOLAY   As a boy, a grey knight hunted me for a season. One day I made a wooden cross and chased it through a field of sunflowers until it shrank into the earth. It never returned.

PHILIP   Pity, I accept all bounties seen or unseen—but keep that to yourself. [*A beat*] I'll cut to the bone—you saw it with your own eyes—the crown of France needs your help.

DE MOLAY   More gold—

PHILIP   For the security of the realm.

DE MOLAY   What did you expect, debasing the coinage. The Denier is nothing but tin!

PHILIP   I know what you think, but it was a necessary measure. [*with pathos*] My fair head is on the block ... but it was unavoidable. Crown finance languishes in dark waters.

DE MOLAY   Well, we too are deeply vexed by the ideas of that mystic Spaniard!

PHILIP   An idea whose time has come. Ramon Lull was renowned for his wisdom. We have to embrace change, Jacques—unification with the Hospitallers could be good for everyone—

DE MOLAY   Except us! Would you dilute pure spirit with harsh wine? Besides, Foulques is an overbearing ass who will lead us all to ruin.

PHILIP   150 thousand in gold?

DE MOLAY   A bribe?

PHILIP   How so? You are free to seek or reject my influence in this matter, but a king doesn't come cheap.

DE MOLAY   That's 300 thousand in a year. [*A beat*] This will need careful consideration.

PHILIP   Then think on it—while the rabble removes my limbs.

DE MOLAY   What of your current debt?

PHILIP   Neither of us will live to see it absolved completely. [*aside to audience*] Even Methuselah didn't live that long. My father taught me: muddy the waters and you can't see the bottom. [*to Jacques*] It's the way it's always been!

DE MOLAY   Without us the bones of your saintly grandfather would line a heathen pit. He would counsel prudence and virtue?

PHILIP [*bored*]   My ears seem to suffer with age, they no longer pick up such *high* tones. [*serious*] Help me, Jacques. The wine you crush today will intoxicate the whole of Christendom for centuries—we serve the same master. [*tempting*] I can raise a new Crusade—your last chance to drive the heathen from the scene.

[*The shadow draws near to De Molay.*]

DE MOLAY   It remains my only dream. [*A beat*] But I feel a tide has turned.

PHILIP   I understand your weariness . . . but there's always gold!

DE MOLAY   The gold of heaven?

PHILIP   It's heaven in my hands!

DE MOLAY   Our coffers are full enough.

PHILIP   Really! Do you keep it *all* here? I would like to see the treasury.

[*De Molay is silent.*]

PHILIP [*cold*]   I demand it!

DE MOLAY   Bury talk of this merger and I'll see what more can be done. I'll take it to the council—You'll have my weight behind you.

PHILIP   Good, let's work together on this. [*A beat*] Your presence at the funeral will be a statement to all. You'll make a magnificent bearer.

DE MOLAY   I pray dignity for us all.

PHILIP   She was a drunk, just like my mother.

DE MOLAY   The soul purges itself eventually. She will find rest.

PHILIP   You didn't know her.

DE MOLAY   You have your son.

PHILIP   Ah yes, the little thing may yet prove a useful heir. Have you no kin?

DE MOLAY   The Temple is our blood; a pure ether fire that binds as one.

PHILIP [*getting a sudden idea*]   Jacques, you may be a father yet—honour me, bless the little cur with your holy blood, be his father in God!

DE MOLAY   This is . . . unexpected. I'll need to ponder—

PHILIP [*laughing*]   You cannot refuse your King.

DE MOLAY [*warmly*]   Of course . . . my head is filled with chaos and snakes this morning. I'd be . . . honoured.

PHILIP [*warmish*]   Good. [*sighs*] I'll retire now. That rabble and my *grief* have left me drained. On the morrow I'll visit the treasury.

DE MOLAY   I'll arrange it.

PHILIP [*suddenly cold*]   Oh, my accountants have already drawn up a *fair* repayment plan. We don't want usury added to the rumours?

Exit Philip with the shadow following

[*BLACKOUT*]

Scene 2

Jacques alone.

DE MOLAY   I long for a straight road. I godfather to his son and the Order bound to his yoke. His face draws out the devil in me. Yet present a civil mask to Satan himself. I can take no more of this viper. [*pause*] But this merger with the Hospitallers is beyond idle talk—a new order to conquer the world led by a war king with the face of a fallen angel—not this! [*A beat*] I'll give him what he wants—after all, the well-being of France is no little matter to us. But I want security in the provinces.

[*DE MOLAY wanders sighing, heavy of heart.*]

DE MOLAY   I sense a story sprung from ancient darkness. Why always this Judas signature? [*resolute*] My instincts say fight, counter every move. I'll pray for the strength to confront our enemies.

[*DE MOLAY gets down on one knee and bows before his sword.*]

[*BLACKOUT*]

Scene 3

The SHADOW is slipping into the room.

Enter DE MOLAY, supporting Philip who can barely hold himself upright.

PHILIP   I can find no words.

DE MOLAY [*ironic*]   It stirs fierce emotion, Sire—calm yourself.

PHILIP [*spits*]   Calm! I've never seen so much gold and in my own kingdom! Did I dream this past hour?

DE MOLAY   No man can witness such a sight and not be affected. The power of gold reaches into realms that can annihilate the little 'I' of man.

PHILIP   This is not about *man*, this echoes something greater. That strange idol, where did it come from?

DE MOLAY   Our ships trade with a great western land. It was bartered there by painted natives who brought it from a dark forest.

PHILIP   Its eyes flash blood and horror, a torrent of screams yet—

DE MOLAY   It's some dread animal god, dark and ugly.

PHILIP   Oh, on the contrary. It has a savage beauty; it radiates a cold intelligence.

DE MOLAY   Take it with you. It will not be missed. I'll arrange transportation.

Exit DE MOLAY

[*Philip is entranced. The shadow moves towards him.*]

PHILIP [*to shadow*]   What you insinuate tingles my blood . . . but it is too bold, surely impossible. [*A beat*] Yet as inevitable as a winter frost.

[*DE MOLAY returns. Philip wrenches himself from the trance and confronts him.*]

PHILIP   We have a deep concern! It's emerged that the ringleaders of that street rabble were former Knights of the Temple?

DE MOLAY [*uncomfortable*]   Sadly, yes. Spurned insiders often make the greatest enemies.

PHILIP [*to audience*]   Then I'll take their names and abodes. [*A beat*] So, it's agreed then?

DE MOLAY   The council has agreed to your request.

PHILIP   Good! Some wine?

DE MOLAY [*reluctant*]   My lord [*leaves to fetch some wine*].

PHILIP [*to audience*]   I always get what I want, but it never feels enough to quell this sense of doom . . . [*PHILIP contemplates the golden statuette and seems aroused by it and all the gold before him*] But I'm sure it's just a question of amount! [*Surveys the staggering treasure and stabs at the heart of the idol.*]

[*DE MOLAY returns. PHILIP attempts to hide his mood.*]

DE MOLAY   The council has agreed to your request, but the gold is dependent on Benedict—

PHILIP [*to audience*]   Serving God rather than himself!

DE MOLAY   Benedict must rescind your excommunication. [*PHILIP laughs*]

PHILIP   I expected that. It's already done, dear Jacques.

DE MOLAY [*shocked*]   This is true?

PHILIP   From the Pope of vice himself—but now he is after de Nogaret! This extreme folly will prove his undoing.

DE MOLAY   I've never understood your need for these knights that bear not arms.

PHILIP   My legists prove their worth. De Nogaret's smile is just as deadly as your sword.

DE MOLAY   Of that I've no doubt.

PHILIP   Benedict is finished. Rome must learn: In temporals I am subject to no one!

DE MOLAY   But surely all this chaos in Rome breeds only food for the dark one—[*PHILIP laughs*]

PHILIP   Rome's long been full of overstuffed devils! Allay your fears, Jacques—we'll soon manage a firmer orthodoxy, and on French soil.

[*BLACKOUT*]

Scene 4

PHILIP holds the golden idol and confronts the SHADOW.

PHILIP [*to shadow*]   You appear to me like an old friend—reveal your secret.

SHADOW   Its secret lies in me, your companion through the ages!

PHILIP   Yes . . . in the eyes, it's you encased in gold.

SHADOW   The heart of your power.

PHILIP   What are you?

SHADOW   Your greater self! [*PHILIP holds his head in fear*]

PHILIP [*despairingly*]   I feel the breath of the pit—I am less than nothing!

SHADOW   Yet more than all! Your fear will grow into the power to compel the Dark Temple from existence!

[*BLACKOUT*]

Scene 5

DE MOLAY is alone in his chamber.

DE MOLAY   My vision reveals the gathering storm. Many would stand and fight, but the true Temple Gold must withdraw to higher realms for future times. But to turn the other cheek at this crucial moment feels like weakness!

[*DE MOLAY kneels.*]

DE MOLAY   I must seek a higher will.

A FIGURE OF LIGHT, appears behind DE MOLAY.

FIGURE OF LIGHT   Seek in powerlessness the one true power. Love to conquer all thyself.

DE MOLAY   What riddle is this? Look for power where there is none? [*pause*] Thy will be done.

[*BLACKOUT*]

Scene 6

PHILIP *enters with the* SHADOW *at his side.*

PHILIP   My heart returns and we thank you.

DE MOLAY   You seem freshly resolved, a man new born.

PHILIP   A king too must be the instrument of a greater will.

DE MOLAY   Like two sides of a coin our destinies are bound—I through others entrusted, you through blood, seal—

PHILIP   And countenance fair! [*snatches the gold coin from Jacques' fingers*] But poetry or a prophetic riddle, it's all the same. [*PHILIP flicks the coin in the air. It rattles on the floor.*]

PHILIP [*with childish delight*]   I win! A good omen!

DE MOLAY   The broad stroke is resolved but the details remain to love.

PHILIP   Romance! Well ... our business this day is finance.

DE MOLAY   Our story rattles to its bony grave.

PHILIP   What black mood is this? We've yet to sign your generous terms.

DE MOLAY   *Your* terms are generous indeed! But someone will have to pay.

[*PHILIP signs the document before them.*]

PHILIP [*archly*]   Oh, have no doubt, someone will pay. [*He passes the quill to* DE MOLAY, *who signs*]

Exit PHILIP

[*THE SHADOW comes to rest at* DE MOLAY's *side. It's clear that DE MOLAY does see it.*]

DE MOLAY   I see my trial of fear approaches.

[*DE MOLAY kneels.*]

DE MOLAY   One last step through the dread valley—a brief scene before the final act.

[*BLACKOUT*]

Scene 7

Philip on his throne. He picks up a proclamation and reads it to the audience. Unseen by PHILIP one sheet of paper drops to the floor out of sight.

PHILIP   News has reached our ears from many persons worthy of faith, striking us with astonishment and causing us to tremble with violent horror—the accused to be charged with ...

[*PHILIP stops, shuffles the papers, expecting something more, but finds nothing and so carries on reading.*]

PHILIP   '... all members of said order will be arrested, without

exception, imprisoned and reserved for the judgment of the Church.'
[*He gets up from his throne and wanders.*]

PHILIP [*panting*]   I tear out their heart, yet fear claws at my breath. I dread such boldness will bring disaster.

[*PHILIP turns and sees the missing sheet near his throne.*]

PHILIP   What have I done? [*He picks the sheet up, walks to the front of the stage, and slowly reads it aloud.*]

PHILIP [*perplexed*]   A bitter thing, a lamentable thing, a thing horrible to think of, too terrible to hear. [*Each line reinforces his feelings of disaster.*] A detestable, inhuman crime, foreign to all humanity.

[*PHILIP stares menacingly into the distance.*]

PHILIP   Then so be it.

Scene 7

Chinon Prison. DE MOLAY in a cell, alone and shattered.

DE MOLAY   That poor knight, forced to watch his entrails drawn before him. And that youth his feet roasted till the bones fell from the flesh. [*A beat*] Then so will my confession fall from me—to deny the Order again would be to shame the Lord himself. [*A beat*] And though my bones be twisted by the rack, within them burns one last cry, to wing its way above the smoke and flames and summon my enemies within one year to stand with me before the throne of Light.

Simon Cade-Williams is a London based screenwriter and lecturer. He was born in Wales and grew in the small Victorian seaside town of Penarth. His early interest in music brought him, in 1977, to join one of the original punk bands, and tour England. Further bands in New York led to a meeting with the beat poet Alan Ginsberg who introduced Simon to the discipline of Buddhist meditation.

But it was back in England in 1979 that Simon found his path and teacher, Rudolf Steiner. Simon's interest in the Templars arises from his intensive work with Rudolf Steiner's anthroposophy over a period of 30 years and his personal researches into karma.

The short play Bound with Gold *is an adaptation from Simon's original feature film script,* The Downfall of the Knights Templar. *The initial research and planning for this script was conducted at a resort on the island of Majorca, which lies below St Martin's mountain in Alcudia. A number of spiritual experiences at the resort, which lies at the foot of the mountain, led to the discovery that below the mountain was a cave used by the Knights Templar as an initiation centre. Simon has felt a spiritual connection to the Order of the Knights Templar ever since.*

Simon is currently working on a stage adaptation of Owen Barfield's novel Unancestral Voice.

THE PRESENT

Finding Inspiration in the Twenty-first Century through the Wisdom of the Knights Templar

Jaap van der Haar

First, I should like to describe my work. One can have beautiful ideas but it is in the doing that one expresses who one is. There are now four areas in which I am mainly active. I am treasurer of the Green Party in the Netherlands, so I am active in the field of politics. I believe that the impulse of the Knights Templar has an importance in political life to which I will refer later.

Secondly, I run an organization that currently owns about 300 hectares of land that is rented to farmers working out of biodynamic principles.[1] Land is rented at a reasonable price in order to make it possible to encourage work worthy of the Earth. It is essential to support efforts of organic farming and to show clearly the consequences of charging high prices for land and land rental which leads to misuse of the land. It is vital that this point is on political agendas. We give examples of how changes can be made, and why they have to be made, by showing small-scale, alternative ways within a non-profit-making organization.

The organization Non Nobis is the third venture in which I am involved. *Non nobis* means 'not for us'. This non-profit-making organization owns a substantial amount of real estate worth about £15 million and the market value of this land increases annually. Due to this inflated value we have been able to obtain loans from banks and purchase new real estate, which we rent to people with moral and sustainable initiatives. Our criteria for leasing land are based on initiatives that help create a better world, i.e. education, providing homes for child-soldiers from Africa, etc. We rent the real estate to people at reasonable prices so they can contribute to a better world.

The last of my activities is with a global organization that works in the field of development aid outside the European Union. We have about 60 projects in South Africa, Asia, India and Eastern Europe focusing on psychiatry, addiction, care for the mentally disabled, and so on. We try to initiate these projects and help others develop higher standards in similar fields.

I hope to make clear that all these activities have to do with Templar impulses. It is not enough to look into the past and say that important initiatives were happening 500 to 700 years ago; they are still happening now and there are still Knights Templar. The Templars of our time have other weapons than those of the past and have to use these weapons in a different way today.[2] But the inspiration that guided the Order of the Knights Templar is still present and can continue to let its influence be felt. The Templars were a small group of men but they had great influence. Their power and energy in tackling important tasks came from their esoteric knowledge.[3]

The first picture I want to give comes from the first appearance of the Order. The Order of the Knights Templar, also called the Order of the Poor Knights of Christ and the Temple of Solomon, was founded at the beginning of the twelfth century though the exact date is unknown. But what is commonly known is that it started with a group of men in Jerusalem. Where did they come from? Where did their impulse come from? Some say that it was an impulse that first expressed itself in a family or a group of families of ancient lineage who had lived a little over a thousand years on European soil. These families had a special vision of the meaning of Christianity.

The central idea was that they perceived that Christ's knowledge and wisdom was received by Him when He was baptized by John the Baptist. This baptism made it possible for Jesus to receive the Christ spirit. The message of Christ that lives in exoteric Christianity is: 'I have come as the Redeemer; all your sins will be forgiven.' The Templars, however, followed a subtly different teaching that derived from the esoteric source of their inspiration. It was, in essence, that Christ came to show us the path of individual self-initiation. This message, however, gradually faded from our perceptions of the Templars in the course of time.

In the mid-nineteenth century however, Pope Pius IX, made some observations about the Templars. He was one of the few popes who mentioned them and said they were heretical because they gave special meaning to John the Baptist and were the followers of the philosophy and ideas of John the Evangelist.

Here we find three elements: John the Baptist, John the Evangelist and the special relationship both had to Christ. I mention these things partly in connection with those families of the first Templars and their history, and partly to show that the Catholic Church, through the figure of Pius IX, more or less confirmed that the Templars had special knowledge.

How did this knowledge manifest itself among the Templars? There were different levels of initiation in the Order with more insight and knowledge gained at each level until the whole truth, as they conceived it, was revealed. A similar process is found in all Mystery streams. Rudolf Steiner said: 'There were many in the circle of the Knights Templar who could gain a deep insight into the Mystery of Golgotha and its meaning ...'[4] On another occasion, Steiner had this to say:

> And they said, 'everything we have experienced so far is a preparation for what the Redeemer has wished for. For Christianity has a future, a new task. And we have the task of preparing the various sects of the Middle Ages, and humanity generally, for a future in which Christianity will emerge into a new clarity, as the Redeemer actually intended that it should. We saw Christianity rise in the fourth cultural epoch; it will develop further in the fifth (the present time) but only in the sixth is it to celebrate the glory of its resurrection. We have to prepare for that. We must guide human souls in such a way that a genuine, true and pure Christianity may come to expression, in which the Name of the Most High may find its dwelling place.[5]

In several of his lectures, Rudolf Steiner spoke about the Essenes, who were one of the communities living at the time of Christ. They lived in the Negev desert from about 500 BC onwards. They left their families and groups to live a single life and took part in the teachings of a strict Mystery school. They practised new forces of human individuality and, in Steiner's words, their teachings 'were to prepare humanity to grasp the mighty event of the coming of Christ'.[6] They were convinced, according to Steiner, that through reincarnation the individual would reach a higher stage of being in the course of time by purging his soul of impurities through successive incarnations. They were also convinced that initiation would be a common process in future times. At that time this kind of knowledge was found only in a few individuals living in small isolated communities, but it would spread out over the world in due time.

> It was the mission of the Essenes to see that among a few at least there should be an understanding of what the Christ would be.[7]

The Essenes were convinced that as individuality was developed within mankind more and more, contact would be lost with the spiritual meaning of life. The connection to the spiritual world would lessen over the course of time. This process was necessary, however, in order for individual development to happen, otherwise further development would not be possible. This connection had to be lost. The 'coming down' to Earth from the spiritual world means forgetting the spiritual world—and then re-finding it. This is the process the individual has to step into. The Essenes said that in the future this loss of the spirit could be amended by education. Education was going to be most important to help mankind through this process and to achieve a more spiritual stage in the future.

One of the first books Rudolf Steiner wrote was *Christianity as Mystical Fact*.[8] In this book, he speaks of Christ attending a wedding and being told that Lazarus was ill and likely to die. Christ stayed at the wedding instead of leaving. It was only after two days that He went to Lazarus who had indeed died and was already in his tomb. He said to Lazarus, 'Arise,' and Lazarus arose from the dead. Later, on Palm Sunday, Christ went to Jerusalem riding on an ass, with people laying palm leaves on the street before Him to show that an initiate had come. He was arrested and, according to Luke's Gospel, brought before Herod with the charge that He had committed high treason and would be sentenced to death. But what did high treason mean in those times?

If the history of that time is researched it will be seen that this also happened to three philosophers. They were forced to kill themselves by drinking poisoned wine because they revealed forbidden knowledge. They had included aspects in their philosophy that were highly spiritual and so kept hidden as this was then secret knowledge. Making this knowledge available to everyone was regarded as high treason. This was one of the outer reasons why Christ could be tried before Pontius Pilate.

Christ initiated Lazarus, who had been 'dead' for three days, and after these three days He resurrected Lazarus. He carried out in public what the old initiates did in the Mystery centres, initiating people three days after their 'death'. This was the reason, given publicly, why Christ was sentenced to death. Christ died and was put in a grave and Resurrection took place after three days. He initiated Himself; no hierophant was present. No one was there to awaken Him from the dead, but the preparations that He had undergone, as a sublime Spiritual Being, allowed Him to be resurrected.[9]

After Christ's death on the cross at Golgotha, Christianity, as a religion distinct from Judaism, developed slowly. The first Christian communities developed in the regions of Georgia and Turkey, and Constantinople became an important centre. Christianity then moved in the direction of Europe. Through Emperor Constantine, the Romans made Christianity the state religion and the European Christian impulse became more dominant. Its religious concepts developed gradually within the churches of Constantinople and Rome. Christianity was structured, centralized, and indeed politicized in the way we are still familiar with today. The

Pope received a very special status representing God on Earth. Much later, notably during the sixteenth century, people started to think about different ways of practising Christianity, and the Roman Catholic Church split up into several different religious streams each with its own churches. That is how we entered the twentieth century. Before then almost everybody had some kind of relationship to some kind of church. This changed during the twentieth century. When I was born 80 per cent of Dutch people were members of a church, now only about 30 per cent are members of churches and this figure continues to decrease.

The Rosicrucians and those following the Templar impulses carried secrets of spiritual esoteric wisdom throughout this time. The Templars made it visible during a certain period, but this spiritual wisdom had come into the world before its rightful time. People were not ready for it and that is why it could not survive. But they carried this Christian esoteric impulse of which Steiner refers when he speaks about Christianity.

The beginning of the twentieth century saw many profound changes. Sigmund Freud began to talk about our inner world and Maria Montessori felt that a change was needed within the field of education. It was also a time when architects developed new ways of building. Different types of dancing began to be introduced. Christianity also began to move away from its traditional means of expression. Perhaps most profoundly of all Rudolf Steiner introduced anthroposophy.[10] After a long period of spiritual darkness, the so-called Kali Yuga, ended in 1899, new impulses began in the world.

The Templars held the conviction that Christianity would, in the end, mean that the individual would be able to follow the same process within himself that Christ did, which is to work towards one's own initiation. In his book *Knowledge of Higher Worlds* Steiner gives a path of self-initiation that is entirely within this stream of esoteric Christianity.[11]

When we look at the life of Rudolf Steiner we see that he started by writing his ideas. Then, in the second part of life, he concentrated on artistic impulses. And in the third period of his active life he gave impulses that could improve the world. He started the Waldorf School movement, for instance, and biodynamic farming. Imagine talking about biodynamics at a time when there were hardly any chemical fertilizers. This is an example of the kind of thinking that can look into the future and see what will be needed a hundred years later. His impulses inspired people to work towards better care for the Earth, better education, better health and improved care for handicapped people, suitable architecture with forms connected to the souls of people, and so on. All this asks to be carried on into the twenty-first century. In our time there are few individuals like Rudolf Steiner, but there are individuals on that path of initiation who can carry into today's world and into the future the knowledge that the Templars had.

How can this be managed? I will take the three main domains of life: religion, science and politics.

First let us consider the political process. In the distant past there were gods that led mankind, then there were demi-gods in the Egyptian period. Thereafter the royal, or ruling families, took over. Their role started to disappear in Greece with the first experiments with democracy. The old way finally came to a close with the French Revolution. Individuals took power using the democratic system.

In Europe we now have a world that is not led and regulated by gods or priests; we have democracy that says that the population can be trusted to access sufficient information to make right decisions. Therefore if 51 per cent of the population chooses something one can rely on its being a good decision. The question is heard more and more, however, whether or not 51 per cent is really enough to represent the wishes of the people.

But what is the next step? Is it that there should still be political parties each with their group philosophy or should democracy change? This discussion is already happening. What do we have to do with the other 49 per cent? If 51 per cent says that we need nuclear power and 49 per cent says we don't who, then, is right? We have to bring democracy a step forward and a lot of research is taking place on how democracy can develop in the future. One of the main questions is how individuals can become involved in the process of decision-making.

In today's political systems there is a huge need for people to partici-pate. Within a political system there is the possibility to contribute to the process of the emancipation of the individual. Nevertheless, at local level it is very difficult to find people who want to take part in the system, so given this lack of competition getting into politics is quite easy.

In a modern political system one takes on the role that the gods had 3000 years ago. In 2005 I became a member of the Dutch Green Party. In the congress of 2006 I was elected as National Treasurer and in November 2010 I hope to be re-elected for a second period of three years. It is so good to contribute to a system where individuals take responsibility for their own lives, especially if one does so bearing in mind the necessary development of Christianity as a process of self-initiation. I experience this as a modern Templar impulse.

I have been working for the Dutch Government for eight years, in a

Health Council commission, to develop drug policy. Leading scientists participate, and their brief is to make proposals so that the government can make the right decisions and develop appropriate policies on health issues. I experienced the members of the Health Council as highly intelligent people but I observed no intuition, no spirituality. They had an analytic research attitude, but it was cold and with no real love for the problems they were researching. In my experience the most significant aspect I observed in the scientific world was that the human heart was not involved in the science. And this heart, this love for the things that one is researching must return to science. This can start in education, in medical health, in psychology and in sociology: in the scientific areas where we research the human being.

In all the areas where modern individuality is developing we will gradually discover that the heart has to be involved again. Rudolf Steiner mentioned the fact that what will be discovered in the twentieth century is that the process of life is the same process as that of illness. Illness is usually experienced as something negative, as something bad. Even if we take homoeopathic medicine, deep within us we have the feeling that illness is not good. Steiner says that this will change, and that the more we understand karma the more we will feel that illness allows development. That is why illness exists, that is why problems are there. Suffering and crises foster the development of forces that lie dormant within the human being. To understand this fully, however, one has to love the developing individual.

This is a completely different way of looking at individual development and it is crucial that we now understand this. We can find it in those sciences that represent individual human development. There we start to understand that when we stimulate the development of the individual illness will lessen.

Development means healing and here we meet Essene wisdom again as a principle of Christianity. This knowledge also lived in the Templars, though not in the way we formulate it now. But they knew Christ as healer, showing the healing path of individual initiation. Many therapists work out of an inner knowledge that the best healing comes from the individual's own forces. The path of healing could be said to be the same as the path of self-knowledge. The process of healing illness is that of finding the spiritual in us, discovering the temple within.

The third aspect is that of religion or spiritual life. I have tried to show briefly how Christianity developed up until the beginning of the twentieth century and the subsequent dwindling in church membership.

Instead there is now a growing interest in spirituality, not for those streams that claim to have the only wisdom but for streams that are open and orientated to individual development. This individual spirituality might gradually takes over from traditional religion.

The Templars had a moral attitude towards money that was devoid of selfishness and greed and stemmed from their relationship to Christ. The generally accepted reason why the Templars were eliminated was their supposed wealth. Philip the Fair knew of the wealth that they held in trust for others. He debased the coinage and one could say he reached a stage where he was creating money out of nothing, just as the central banks are doing now. A crowd outside the Templars' main preceptory in Paris attacked Philip. He was rescued and taken into the Temple where he was confronted by the riches of which the Templars were the guardians; but he was also confronted by another way of dealing with money, one born out of moral impulses.

'Non Nobis'—the opening words of their famous motto—means 'not for us'. The Templars had developed an inner quality of being rich without having wealth. The order was rich but the individual possessed nothing. They had overcome certain inner forces that appear in a person when he has too much wealth. This egoistic element is there in every person but the Templar Knights had overcome this by developing qualities of selflessness and sacrifice. This confronted Philip but it was a step too far for him as he was blinded by greed for the gold the Templars held as the first bankers. He had to destroy the Order to obtain this wealth.

We can translate this scenario to the twenty-first century. What was and is the central problem of our financial crises? It comes from an immoral way of dealing with money. Bankers always used to have a moral quality in their profession which lasted up to 1955–1960. Then something changed and a political system developed whereby the leading principle could be characterized as 'survival of the fittest'. One could call it *Darwinism* or *neo-liberalism* or whatever, but the point is that one was not earning money for the well-being of the whole but for individual profit. And annual salaries ranging from $500.000 to $3000.000 or more started to be seen as a right in the banking world, but this is not right when looked at from other perspectives. However, there is no law yet that tells us a banker may not have such a salary. Here we see a similarity to the Templars and Philip IV. The problem is that of loss of morality and the need to find a new individual inner morality.

We will only be able to solve the problems we are now facing, and which will increase, when we develop new moral standards—not those handed down from the past, but those we have developed ourselves. This can only be done by a new, individualized Christianity. Only then are we able reach the modern moral standard that the Knights Templar developed and which gave them the power to be who they were. Working out of a new moral standard is the Templar impulse translated into the twenty-first century.

Is this simply all theory without any practical basis? Consider this: in the 1950s, Peter Smith, a native of Holland, took his family to start a new life in Brazil. They started farming, and 50 years later had built up a company with 15,000 hectares of land and 1500 employees. In the 1980s they met anthroposophy, and within that world-view met moral impulses that they found inspiring. Now, the profits of their company finance anthroposophical activities in Brazil.

They only grow flowers and use a lot of pesticides. But they have social security for their employees, medical care for the families and schools for the children. They know they are doing a lot wrong but they have started a social impulse that is born out of the profits of their enterprise.

This is what life is all about: you cannot be 100 per cent right all the time but changes can still be made to improve the situation for substantial numbers of people. If one, as a Christian (or a follower of any other religion), as a priest within one's own temple—the body—takes responsibility in such areas as politics, science or religion, then one is confronted with these kinds of questions and it sometimes becomes difficult to sleep. This is our life. It is our time. Being at the edge of what is good and not good, making decisions, making mistakes: that is the impulse of the Templars in the twenty-first century and one can find inspiration from this thought. I hope others can also find inspiration.

Jaap van der Haar was born in 1952 in the Hoogeveen, Holland. The main concerns in his life are economics, mental health care, global awareness and politics.

From 1976 to 2002 he was one of the founders and director of Arta, an organization that developed different programmes for people who struggle with addiction. He was also treasurer for GGZ-Nederland (the Dutch umbrella organization for mental health and addiction), where he was responsible for the addiction care organization Next, and was founder and chairman of the IVAES (an international umbrella-organization for addiction care based on humanistic and anthroposophical approaches).

Jaap was a member of the advisory committee for the Department of Health until 2004 and was co-responsible for the Dutch Government's approach to drugs and addiction. He is now active as an independent advisor and coach/manager in the field of addiction-care and mental health.

As treasurer and active member of GIP (Global Initiative on Psychiatry), he helps set up new mental health services in post-Soviet countries and Third World countries. He travels extensively—training teams, lecturing and facilitating reorganizations. Since 2007 he has been treasurer of the Green Party in the Netherlands.

Notes

1. Biodynamic agriculture sees the farm as a living organism, not as an industrial production unit. We are already seeing the material effects of farming with monocultures, artificial fertilizers, factory conditions for stock. This gives an impulse to create an agricultural system which adds a spiritual dimension to that of the organic farm.

2. There is a knighthood of the twentieth century whose riders do not ride through the darkness of physical forces, as of old, but through the forest of darkened minds. They are armed with a spiritual armour and an inner Sun makes them radiant. Out of them shines healing, healing that flows from the knowledge of the image of man as a spiritual being. They must create inner order, inner justice; peace and conviction in the darkness of our time.' Karl König.

3. Rudolf Steiner, *Inner Impulses of Evolution*, tr. Church, Kozlik, Easton (Anthroposophic Press, New York 1984) (GA 171). Lecture of 25.9.1916. Lecture also in Rudolf Steiner, *The Knights Templar*, ed. Margaret Jonas (Rudolf Steiner Press, 2007).

4. Ibid.

5. Rudolf Steiner, *The Temple Legend*, tr. J. Wood (Rudolf Steiner Press, London 1997) (GA 93).

6. Rudolf Steiner, *The Gospel of Matthew*, tr. D.S. Osmond and M. Kirkcaldy (Rudolf Steiner Press, London 1965) (GA 123).

7. Ibid.

8. Rudolf Steiner, *Christianity as Mystical Fact* (Anthroposophic Press Hudson 1997) (GA 8).

9. Ibid.

10. The grandfather of my wife was connected to the movement in which Mondriaan was active, and they were communicating with and participating in the Anthroposophical Society, working and discussing what modern art, of that time, should be.

11. Rudolf Steiner, *Knowledge of the Higher Worlds*, 6th ed. tr. G. Metaxa, D.S. Osmond and C. Davy (Rudolf Steiner Press, Bristol 2004) (GA 10).

The Knights Templar and their Meaning for the Twenty-first Century

Rolf Speckner

The following contribution comes from the observation that very many people today show a strong interest in the Order of the Knights Templar. The article attempts to give an explanation of why the Order was destroyed in such a strange and particular way, and what this has to do with our century. The aim of the Templar Knight was to develop his body and soul into a Temple for the name and presence of God. The aim of the torturer was to destroy this temple that each of the Knights had built, more or less perfectly.

King Philip IV of France and his destruction of the Order of the Knights Templar

The way the destruction of the Order of the Knights Templar was carried out and the intensity of the destruction is, in some ways, a reverse mirror that indicates the spiritual depth of their aims. We can see that King Philip IV of France (known as 'Philip the Fair') seems to have had an awareness of the importance of their spiritual goals. The king himself gave detailed instructions on the methods that were to be used to torture the knights. These methods of torture were specifically aimed to destroy their spiritual discipline. This, I believe, shows that he was an antichristian initiate.

So how did Philip destroy the order?

One of the first measures was the *destruction of their reputation*. Philip considered the lie to be a legitimate political tool and Guillaume de Nogaret, his chief henchman, began to smear the reputation of the Order in the eyes of the people through slander and libel. He declared them heretics and denounced their habits and customs as godless, impious and wicked. Nogaret reinforced this by using physical force at key moments.

Another means were the *cloak and dagger* activities. No one knew of Philip's preparations before the time of the first attack, except his closest henchmen. On 13 September 1307 Philip signed an order to arrest all Knights Templar in France. The order was to be carried out on 13 October. The Royal order was sent to hundreds of baillies, seneschals, prelates, barons, knights and officials of France. The details were enclosed in a letter which was not to be opened until shortly before the time of the arrests.

At dawn on 13 October 1307 about 220 Knights Templar from all over France were taken into custody at exactly the same time. They were still in their beds when their enemies arrived. In Paris Nogaret himself advanced against them with a strongly armed group of men.

In order to achieve his goals the king not only persecuted the Knights Templar but also other wealthy groups, especially the Jews. In 1306 Guillaume de Nogaret had organized a campaign to rob and expel Jews from the Languedoc. It seems that he and Philip had no racial prejudice but calculatedly used the racial and religious prejudices of the people to gain property and assets. The *persecution of the Jews* was followed by persecution of Northern Italian merchants and bankers who lived in France and so on.

King Philip liked to take *hostages*. As early as 1296, when Philip quarrelled with the Count of Flanders, he demanded an oath of loyalty and took the Count's daughter, Philippa, hostage even though he was her godfather. She was imprisoned in Paris until her death in 1307. Philip supported the Archbishop of Bordeaux' election as Pope Clement V and expected services in return. Pope Clement V had to place his brother and two of his nephews under the king's control as hostages.

Philip did not trust anyone and used *indirect threats* against his followers. For example, when Clement V hesitatingly disagreed with the king's aggressive actions Philip wrote him a seemingly friendly letter saying that as a true Christian king he would not hesitate to attack anyone who supported the heretics and would do with them what was necessary.

The French king seems to have been the first ruler at the end of the Middle Ages who tried to gain the consent of the people through *mass gatherings*. On the day of the Templars' arrest the citizens were called together in the royal gardens. Monks preached and lectured to them about the events—presumably these were the Dominicans whose task was to fight against heretics. This way the King involved thousands of people in his demonic ways.

Through *show trials* Philip the Fair obtained the consent of the university. The teachers and students were invited to the Temple in Paris and had to take part in the interrogation of Jacques de Molay and other Templar Knights. The confessions of the Templars made a deep impression on people even though it was known that they were extorted by torture. Many thought that torture brought the truth to light. This idea lasted until the seventeenth century. Even today, after the actions of the Third Reich, some officials of the US Government share and act on this idea. On 25 March 1308 the University of Paris agreed with Philip's actions.

Philip also reached his goals by *misrepresenting words* both in the gatherings of the masses and in the show trials held before leading intellectuals. There are many examples and one could say it was usual. For example, he called the criminal arrest of the Knights *besoigne*, which only means 'the affair' or 'the matter' (in German it would be *die Angelegenheit*). This way the heinous activities rarely appeared in spoken or written word because Philip had so skilfully concealed them.

Philip exercised *arbitrary lawlessness*. He called upon those Templars who were not in prison to defend their knightly brothers. They gained the impression that they were free and could travel safely. Hundreds of them believed Philip and were then taken into prison and tortured. The Knights were forbidden all legal representation and Philip also ordered that the imprisoned Knights were not allowed to take part in the Mass. This was illegal as long as they had not been sentenced.

The appalling torture used *dehumanized the servants* as well as the tortured Knights. The torturers used the noose to lift the Knights millimetre by millimetre from the ground. They used iron shoes that could be compressed. They burned their feet to the bone. They put small rods between their fingers and pressed their hands together until the bones broke. They pulled out their teeth. They hung weights on the genitals and other parts of the body until the last breath.[1]

Philip liked to watch these proceedings in the torture chamber. We do not know whether he took part in the tortures himself but he wanted to see the Knights being tortured. The burning of Jacques de Molay and his companion had to be carried out where Philip could see the pyre. The king wanted to see whether or how long they could withstand the pain, in other words how long their consciousness, their 'I' forces, could stay in their bodies. He tried to destroy their deepest spiritual aims through using torture.

The meaning of the Knights Templar for today

We have seen all these things repeated in the twentieth century within the Third Reich in Germany and Austria. The power that first entered European culture in 1307 returned in 1933.

It returned at the same time when many people would gain the ability to see Christ in the etheric world. There are reports of those that have seen Him. Victor Frankl, a Jewish psychiatrist, was sent to Auschwitz in

1942 and wrote of his experiences in 1945. In the concentration camp every circumstance conspired to make the prisoner lose his hold on self and life; all the familiar situations and goals in life were taken away. What alone remains 'is the last of human freedoms'—the ability to 'choose one's attitude in a given set of circumstances'.[2]

Frankl managed to rise above his fate and conquer hatred, for he realized that if he hated his oppressors he would become one of them. He would have opened himself to the same powers that controlled or directed the evil. This saved his life. One day Victor Frankl, talking to a dying girl lying on a wooden 'bed'—one cannot say bed, but what else—observed that she was cheerful. She pointed through the window of the hut and said, 'This tree here is the only friend I have in my loneliness.' She could see just one branch of a chestnut tree with two blossoms. 'I often talk to this tree and the tree replies saying, "I am here—I am here—I am life, eternal life." ' The girl did not survive.

During the last few weeks Frankl was given the task of helping prisoners with minor medical care although he was helping his fellow prisoners all through the war, as becoming ill meant death in the concentration camps. Victor Frankl survived. He went to Vienna and resumed his practice and developed an influential psychotherapy known as Logotherapy. He married an Austrian wife, remained in Vienna and did not hate the Germans.

Paul Antschel, who wrote under the pseudonym of Paul Celan, was born in Czernowitz, Romania, in 1920, into a German-speaking Jewish family. He studied medicine in Paris in 1938, and in 1939 returned to Czernowitz to study literature and languages. German troops occupied the country in 1941 and the Jews were sent to camps. His parents were deported and died in Nazi labour camps. Celan himself was interned in a camp for 18 months, then managed to escape to the Red Army. After the war he still used the German language, which his mother had loved so much, and emigrated from Romania to Vienna and from there to Paris, where he lived. He wrote his poems in German. And he seems to have thought that only in the German language can you write a poem on the horrors of the concentration camps. He committed suicide in 1970.

Death Fugue

Black milk of dawn we drink it at dusk
we drink it at noon and at morning we drink it at night
we drink it and drink it

we scoop out a grave in the sky where it's roomy to lie
A man lives in the house he plays with his vipers he writes
he writes when dusk falls to Germany your golden hair Margarete
he writes it and walks from the house the stars glitter he whistles his dogs
he whistles his Jews and orders a grave dug in the ground
he commands us to strike up for the dance

Black milk of dawn we drink you at night
we drink you at dawn and at noon we drink you at dusk
we drink and we drink
A man lives in the house he plays with his vipers he writes
he writes when dusk falls to Germany your golden hair Margarete
your ashen hair Shulamite we scoop out a grave in the sky where it's
roomy to lie
He shouts jab this earth deeper you lot there you others you sing and you
play
he grabs at the iron at his belt he swings it his eyes that are blue
jab deeper you lot with your spades you others play on for the dance

Black milk of dawn we drink you at night
we drink you at noon and at morning we drink you at dusk
we drink and we drink
a man lives in the house your golden hair Margarete
your ashen hair Shulamite he plays with his vipers

He calls play death's music sweeter Death is the Master from Deutschland
he calls stroke darker the strings and as smoke you shall rise to the skies
then scoop out a grave in the clouds where it's roomy to lie

Black milk of dawn we drink you at night
we drink you at noon Death is the Master from Deutschland
we drink you at dusk and at noon we drink and we drink you
Death is the Master from Deutschland with eyes that are blue
he shoots you with shot made of lead shoots you level and true
a man lives in the house your golden hair Margarete
he hunts us down with his dogs he gives us a grave in the air
he plays with his vipers and dreams Death is the Master from Deutschland

your golden hair Margarete
your ashen hair Shulamite

Paul Celan

Others also noticed signs of the Antichrist working. There was a Resistance in Germany which the historians in Germany tend to overlook. It was and is easier that way. They find it difficult to understand the central agents of the opposition because these young students, who were often soldiers too, spread leaflets in the University in Munich in July 1942, i.e. when the Third Reich was at the apex of its power.

On these leaflets they publicly declared:

> Every word that comes from Hitler's mouth is a lie. When he says peace he means war, and when he blasphemously uses the name of the Almighty he means the power of evil, the fallen angel, Satan. His mouth is the foul-smelling maw of hell, and his might is at bottom accursed. True, we must conduct a struggle against the National Socialist terrorist state with rational means; but whoever today still doubts the reality, the existence of demonic powers has failed by a wide margin to understand the metaphysical background of this war. Behind the concrete, behind what is perceptible through the senses, behind all the rational, logical reflections stands the Irrational, that is the fight against the demon, against the messenger of the Antichrist.[3]

How can a historian deal with this? It is either the end of the usual sort of writing of history and the reawakening of another kind of history, a history of salvation, or it is nonsense. The German historians are in a difficult position. If they take this seriously they have to change their whole attitude of mind. They do not want to do this. But they also do not want to say that these brave young people were mad.

As we have seen in the case of the Knights Templar, we can also see here again and can trust that, as the poet Friedrich Hölderlin says, 'but where the danger is, groweth the saviour too . . .'[4]

The virtues of the Knights Templar are today needed now as never before.

Today we face a new attack from the same antichristian powers. They showed themselves in the so-called Third Reich. This name was blasphemous as was everything that was said and done in the name of this force. The name Third Reich has been in use since medieval times. Joachim de Fiore used it as a pseudonym for the time when Christ would be present again. The falsely called Third Reich was the beginning of a renewed attack from those powers that extinguished the Knights Templar.

What began in France and returned again in Germany has spread all over the world. Newspapers are full of it. Behind the façade there is a mighty war between the Christian and the antichristian powers and this is fought in every human soul. Unfree persons can be drawn into a whirlwind of emotion and moral aberration. Nearly every thinkable seduction is aimed at them. And only the gaining of an inner strength, the development of a free will, can save them. We all need an inner Foundation Stone.

The free human being cannot be overthrown by the powers of evil so therefore we see another attack today, an attack against the daily necessities—education, food, medicine. It all gains a post-Christian or, better stated, antichristian stance.

The Knights Templar were Knights of the sword. Within the process of the law it was obvious that they were not the best defenders of themselves with their 'tongues'. Today a new knighthood would be a 'Knighthood of the Word'. The new Knights would never leave their posts—even when there were three enemies around them. They would not leave their posts when there were three enemies or animals within them. The new Knights would fight against their soul sleeping within and around themselves. They will do this not because they seek praise but because of love for their own ideals and because of their compassion and understanding towards others.

They will be able to do this because the power of the Sun has found a home in their hearts and begins to warm it and stream out in the form of love. This will be the force that changes the whole physical being of mankind and binds humanity to Christ who works for all, whatever their belief.

Therefore the new Knight will not speak with satirical sharpness. Good will flow from their tongues. The WORD will live in their words.

Such Knights will be necessary in the future in every newspaper and on every railway station. They will be men and women. They will work as teachers and doctors, as shopkeepers, refuse collectors, architects and farmers, etc. They will be able to confront the future.

Notes

1. John Charpentier, *Die Templer*, 2nd ed. (Stuttgart 1965).
2. Victor Frankl, *Man's Search for Meaning* (Beacon, 2006).
3. Fourth leaflet of the Group, *The White Rose* (Die Weiße Rose) (July 1942). See also Peter Tradowsky, *Und das Licht schein in die Finsternis . . .* (And the Light Shines in the Darkness) (Verlag, Dornach 2008).
4. 'wo aber Gefahr ist, wächst auch das Rettende'.

Knighthood's Contribution to Future Spirituality

A New Method of Historical Research and its Relationship to the History of the Knights Templar

Alfred Kon

Rudolf Steiner, in his *Twelve Cosmic Moods*, wrote for the sign of Capricorn:

> The future shall rest on what is past.
> The past feels forwards to the future
> for a vigorous present existence.
> Resilience in innermost life
> gives strength to the guarding of worlds.
> The blossoming might of life unfurls:
> the past must bear with the future.[1]

This meditation brings us to the very core of historiography. The theme of the flow of time and what might flow from beyond time into time can lead us towards a new method of historical research that accords with what Steiner refers to as 'historical symptomatology'.[2] Those who represent the forces of Capricorn, in the sense that Steiner intends, show us what historical investigation could be today. One could say that in critical moments they show trust in the heavens when dealing with life's unpredictability through the virtue of courage. In Steiner's phrase, this quality then becomes 'liberating or redemptive power'. The sign of Capricorn is connected, in old Hermetic wisdom, with the knees where the bodily sense organ of movement and equilibrium can be felt. Remember, for instance, how in the *Odyssey*, Homer refers to moments where life and death are at stake with the phrase 'his knees began to tremble'. Here we see the first awakening of what is to become an organ of knowledge of one's destiny.

Wolfram von Eschenbach's legendary epic *Parzival* could be said to be a work that prepares us for modern times. Parzival, the Grail-seeker, develops this organ of knowledge into a power of redemption, through his unbending courage, even in the worst situations of his young life and through his burgeoning interest in the sufferings of others. He learned to read the 'Book of Nature'—which is the book of our hidden karma—and we too can learn to read what comes to us personally: the message that we must, no matter how much our knees may tremble, develop redemptive forces.

Thus we can also begin to identify qualities in historical research as qualities of karmic research, of liberating or even redemptive karmic research. We leave behind the world of mechanistic searches for the causes, to enter an infinite continent of discovery and of individual development. We enter into the flow where what announces itself as history becomes alive in the present moment, where it becomes impulse for the future, where the future announces itself to us. We begin to understand one of the meditative lines from the *Foundation Stone Meditation*, given by Rudolf Steiner during the decisive Christmas Assembly of 1923: 'Practise spirit remembering'.[3]

It was Rudolf Steiner who invited the highly gifted Viennese mathematician and philosopher Walter Johannes Stein to be teacher of history in the senior classes of the first Waldorf School in Stuttgart in 1919. Steiner cooperated with W.J. Stein in creating a method of historical research during their work together on the *Parzival* main lesson, a period of study for the 16–17-year-old pupils, based on Wolfram von Eschenbach's thirteenth-century poem about the Grail quest, set in the ninth century. Stein had no formal training as a historian. However, his studies of maths, physics and philosophy had given him a firm grounding in scientific study. Mathematics had been the central pillar of the study of natural sciences from the very beginning. The question now began to take shape in Stein's mind: What is the 'mathematics' of historical research? What, indeed, can we really call 'historical research'?

The question arises because what we receive as history is often no more than a series of images or imaginative renderings based on whatever sources are available. We see movements of peoples: discussing, fighting, travelling from place to place; a manifold activity of tribes, nations, races, religions making their contribution to their epoch in fruitful or destructive ways. Can such chaos really be called 'history'? How are we to find an order within this akin to its true being?

Then there is the further question: What does it really mean to be a historian? Whose impulses can be recognized by whom as a *researcher*? To take it further still: What impact can the discussion of such questions have on historical research? Must we simply accept what so-called authorities have already written, bearing in mind that such authority often gives us no more than a *fable convenue* based on the preoccupations, prejudices and received wisdom of various individuals in different times and within different cultures?

In studying historical sources on the theme of the Knights Templar especially, we become aware very quickly of the problems arising out of the method of research that consists in dogmatically accepting the mainstream version of events and imposing this on future generations.

It is important, today, to be aware that an entire school of historical falsification has arisen in Europe from as far back as the eighth century, if not further, with the aim of suppressing those very impulses that connect human life on Earth to its spiritual sources and goals. Its method was to gain a firm grip on all available written sources, and at the same time to impose the dogmatic view that only such written sources as these are to be deemed reliable.

The tragic end of the Order of the Knights Templar is generally portrayed through a definite will to rewrite history, calling black white and white black. This still proves effective today. The lies the knights were forced to utter under torture are an example of the beginning of an Orwellian culture based on wilful lies. Within this culture real history is rewritten and disseminated by a tyrannical central power with no possibility of revision, except and unless it suits the central power in its diabolic will to suppress individual development—the very opposite of what we call the Parzival way of the present.

It was against this background that Stein's question of moral integrity arose in historical study: of history with a conscience.

In his biography of W.J. Stein, Johannes Tautz wrote that Stein 'now used every conversation with Rudolf Steiner for shedding light about the methods of historical interpretation and presentation'.

> Through this he became aware of the fact that the historian very often arrives at his result not by means of systematic search, but rather through karmic circumstances. That when working in a spiritual-scientific manner he could even learn, through finding certain pieces of evidence, that he was on the right track. Rudolf Steiner said to him: 'You can have a good control over the truth of an inner experience if, at the same as you meet it inwardly, it confronts you outwardly in the form of karma meeting you.'
>
> Stein concluded from this that 'for an anthroposophical method-ology of historical research what is most important is what belongs to the realm of individual destiny'. As far as the portrayal of history during the lessons was concerned, Rudolf Steiner advised him to reproduce

inwardly, as exactly as possible, what often was only an incomplete fragment, and then allow what had been gained this way to ripen until it could present a more complete picture. Steiner told Stein:

'Try to think all historic things in their completeness, even those which are only preserved in fragmentary form. Complete it in your thoughts: make all your concepts concrete with the help of your imagination, but only, of course, after first having taken all historical information into account. Then carry what you have thus acquired into your sleep, and observe how it changes. What has been gained in this way can safely be presented to the children.'

[Steiner] countered [Stein's] suggestion that by using one's imagination one might be in danger of producing inexact results by saying:

'You take into account all that has been handed down and you take with you into your sleep what you have pictorially imagined. It will really undergo a change, for the spiritual world sees to it that the truth becomes known. You will be able to observe, if you continue in this way with the same material, perhaps saying the same thing for several years running, that it undergoes a change. And it changes in such a way that it becomes ever nearer to the truth. It will be much truer than the 'convenient fable' that one calls history.'[4]

It is my conviction that we have here a rich methodological treasure handed down to us through Stein's endeavours to find historical truth beyond the *fable convenue*. It inspires us to follow the traces of those enigmas in history that move our individual hearts and haunt us in our will, that inspire or thrill us into future action together.

Stein strove forward on the path formulated by Rudolf Steiner, most fully in the Foundation Stone Meditation, inasmuch as it can be understood as a kind of lesson for spiritual historical research. Historical research in the end is always karmic research, research that allows the future to become realized in the present moment.

Rudolf Steiner first spoke about this new kind of methodology in September and October 1920 at the opening ceremony of the Goetheanum in Dornach, Switzerland, in a series of lectures entitled *Boundaries of Natural Science*.[5] These lectures culminated in some maxims on a method of modern scientific research going beyond the Kantian 'limits to knowledge' by adhering to a path of becoming conscious within the lower senses: sense of life, movement, balance. (Here again we meet the influence of Capricorn, mentioned above.) These senses, brought to full consciousness, reveal themselves to our higher senses: the sense of *speech* (hearing the word inwardly), the sense of *thought* (noticing thought at the moment of its birth), and the sense of the 'I' (an intuitive meeting of one's ego with that of another person). Thus history becomes social reality.

As touched upon previously, this path of knowledge has its origin in the period of history that Stein dealt with in his first volume of history: *The Ninth Century—World History in the Light of the Holy Grail.*[6] Here he considers the theme of the hidden history behind history. It deals with the biography of that high initiate whose task was to prepare the true spirituality of our modern epoch. This is characterized by awakening through life's experience and developing an empathetic interest in the sufferings of others and learning to overcome our failures—the Parzival path of knowledge and social competence. In a former life, this high initiate was known as Mani,[7] as Rudolf Steiner points out in one of his esoteric studies. In that life one of the qualities that Mani developed was that of the art of painting, showing the movement out of darkness to light through the interactions of colour. Rudolf Steiner indicated how this Parzival path would become the heritage of all mankind.

> This current of Mani's will flow over to the sixth cultural epoch and has been in preparation since the founding of Christianity. It is just at the time of the sixth cultural epoch that Christianity will be expressed in its most complete form. Its time will truly have come. The inner Christian life as such overcomes every form; it is propagated by external Christianity and lives in all forms of the various confessions. Whoever seeks Christian life will always find it. It creates forms and destroys forms in various religious systems. It does not depend on a search for conformity in the outward forms in which it is expressed, but it depends upon experiencing the inner life stream that is always current under the surface. What is still waiting to be made is a form for the life of the sixth cultural epoch. That must be created beforehand; it has to be there so that Christian life can be poured into it. This form has to be prepared by human beings who create an organization, a form so that the true Christian life of the sixth cultural epoch can find its place therein. And this external form of society must derive from the intention, which Mani has fostered, from the small group whom Mani has prepared. That must be the outer form of organization, the congregation in which the spark of Christianity will first be truly kindled.[8]

The abilities that Parzival developed in his ninth-century life had a long preparation, and were fostered afterwards by silent/hidden communities of knighthood. They received a definite form nearly 300 years later in the

Order of the Knights Templar and then in all communities preparing for the sixth epoch. The core of Rudolf Steiner's own teaching and knowledge was this Parzival-inspired living empathy for fellow human beings. This is one of the central virtues of present and future social life that was supposed by Steiner to spring, like a rich fountain, from the life of the Anthroposophical Society into modern civilization everywhere. The Anthroposophical Society is measured more and more by the world in terms of how it is able to realize its commitment to this wellspring of social possibility.

Our theme is the continuation in the modern era of the ideals of the Knights Templar. Let us now consider the shaping of a vessel into which future substance might be poured. Care of this task was taken long ago within the hidden western Mysteries of Hibernia, about which we know very little other than what was given to the world through the activities of the Knights of the Round Table and what is told through Irish mythology. It may come as a surprise that I consider a Celtic origin for future spirituality, as modern civilization tends to look to the Mediterranean world as a sole source of culture. I hope to make clear that we cannot understand our spiritual past and future without earnestly trying to understand this aspect of western spirituality and its metamorphosis. My source for this is Ella Young's *Celtic Wonder Tales*[9] and the German interpretation by the kindred spirit of Maria Christiane Benning. Ella Young was part of a group that included AE—George Russell, W.B. Yeats and Maud Gonne. She spent her youth listening to the tales told by the fishermen of the Aran Islands off the west coast of Ireland. From these she learned of the *Tuatha De Danann*, those gods who, under the guidance of Dana-Brigid, bring to Earth the Four Treasures once Midir of the flaming red hair has destroyed the uncontrolled power of dragons and serpents that threatened to darken the Earth so much that the gods would abandon it as unworthy of their attention. But Dana-Brigid has heard the Earth dreaming of the Light, and takes pity.

Under Dana-Brigid's leadership, the gods bring to Earth the Spear of Victory, the Sword of Light, the Cauldron of Plenty and the Stone of Destiny. In these four images are concealed those cosmic forces that, if kept in true equilibrium, allow the possibility that the Creator Being of the World, the Logos, might incarnate into a human form. This has become a possibility through the activity of the gods working into the etheric geography of Ireland.[10] Through them, Ireland remained protected and aloof from the Fall. Otherwise, there could not have been the earthly balance of substances that would be able to hold the configuration of the *Life Spirit*, the Buddhi of Christ within the Earth's periphery, during the time that His Spirit Self or Manas, incarnated into the body of Jesus of Nazareth during the Baptism in the River Jordan. This gives the true background of the appearance of the Rígh nan Dúl, the Lord of the Elements, as a central notion of Irish Christianity. It came into existence out of the vast lore of traditions of the old Mysteries of Hibernia[11] and kept as a precious trust the secrets of the form of the body and sense organs of the human being through all the vicissitudes of the Atlantean epochs and beyond, right up to the time of Logos-Christ walking on the Earth in a human form, and undergoing death the way only a high god could.

In August 1924, in lectures given in Torquay and London,[12] Rudolf Steiner hinted at higher grades of initiation among the members of the Order of the Round Table. He indicates that this stream bore the etheric image of the Christ and met with souls who later became the Grail stream, who bore Christ's blood in their hearts at the time of the Council of Constantinople in 869. Christ met in the spiritual world what Steiner calls 'the image of His Life Spirit', accompanied as He is by whole groups of souls connected with this image. He is also accompanied by Arthurian souls, who represent the Celtic stream that carried the secret of the Four Treasures in the social sphere and in the life forces of the twelve higher initiates of the Order of the Round Table.

From this we begin to understand afresh all that lies concealed within the images that we form of the Knights of the Round Table. This group of twelve with the thirteenth in the midst is the archetype of the social form for holding a cosmic-human substance of *Life bearing Spirit*. It was able to move, through history, from place to place in company with the higher initiates of that circle. It was able to move away from the etheric geography of Ireland and form itself anew in other regions of Europe: Scotland, Northumberland, Wales, Cornwall, Brittany, and eventually into the South of France, Burgundy, Alsace and beyond, creating, as it were, a new 'Ireland' in many places. And far from the geographical origin the spiritual leaders of Irish life, the Druids, had fostered that from time immemorial.

Thus, inspired by the former Folk Spirit of the Celts, the possibility of the growth of a future spiritual Christianity spread through Europe during early medieval times. Only after that had happened could the spirit of matter-bound Rome arrive on the shores of Ireland. As that took place, the former Folk Spirit of the Celts renounced this task and became the Guardian Spirit of esoteric Christianity for all time, as Rudolf Steiner points out in his lectures on the Folk Spirits of Europe.[13]

The location of the geographical centre for Arthur's circle may well have moved from place to place during prehistory and early history. This is indicated by the number of places that claim to have been Camelot, in Britain, and on the Continent. Meanwhile, all that accepted historical research can tell us is that Arthur was a sixth-century British warrior and all the rest of the stories about him and his circle were no more than flights of fancy.

There has been a spiritual substance, then, intimately connected to the Cosmic Christ and inspired by the Hibernian Mysteries which has had many manifestations throughout long periods of time and in different social forms—such as the groups of twelve Celtic monks on their Christianizing missions throughout Europe. More specifically, it has been what Rudolf Steiner calls the '*Natural Science of the Higher Graduates from Arthur's Round Table*' that has preserved the secret prehistory and history of the Mystery of Golgotha. It was in the realm of the Four Treasures that knighthood could create great common imaginations which would inspire them to redemptive action. This realm contains the more cosmic counterpart to that of the sacred Christ substance dwelling in the blood of the circle of individuals who accompanied Joseph of Arimathaea from Palestine through Europe to Glastonbury.

This substance was later renewed by the high initiate called Titurel in northern Spain,[14] creating the Parzival Mysteries which were carried by that early medieval family out of which the individual later known as Parzival sprang in the early ninth century. It was there that this spirit substance received the name 'The Holy Grail', connecting, through the life work of this initiate, the stream of purified individual *blood* with that older stream of the purified picture-Imagination, living in the *nervous system* in socially developed persons. This is the basis from which a new social order can grow in the future out of the efforts of individuals.

The name Grail, which means a cauldron, occurred within the Celtic imagination many centuries before Grail epics began to haunt the minds of European humanity. We can see how the Cauldron of Plenty is at once part of the Four Treasures, and at the same time finds its apotheosis as an archetype of the Holy Grail. This hidden source of spiritual life forces enables us to find our way as we stumble through the 'stones' of our individual destinies.

It is my conviction that it is this spiritual substance that was brought down to the Earth in a new form as the Order of the Knights Templar, which was founded in the twelfth century. The Order of the Templar Knights aimed to Christianize European soil through using economy, agriculture, architecture and warfare in a way in which personal strivings were subordinate to the needs of the community and the spiritual goal. The Order was guided by a group of twelve knights plus a thirteenth—an order, as it were, within the Order.

The forces of the Sun Demon living in Philip the Fair destroyed this Order of knights.[15] How can it ever come back? Rudolf Steiner points out that it has been present ever since as a constant inspiration, through the development of European society, and springing forth, for instance, in Goethe's fairy tale *The Green Snake and the Beautiful Lily*.[16] This literary gem deals with a group of individuals and each one had the self-knowledge to perceive what his/her specific task could be in the service of a new social living spirit. We may further see how this cosmic Logos-substance searches for communities into which it can incarnate.

It knocks on the door of modern culture in the way that the Theosophical Society and the Anthroposophical Society tried to do. And still it patiently knocks at the doors of people waking up to the innermost language of their conscience in the depths of their hearts. It is my conviction, too, that it lies hidden within the words of the Foundation Stone Meditation as a teaching that leads into karmic awakening inside the spiritual organ of our knees working into our hearts and into our waking consciousness—as when the hidden organs of vision in the knees start to tremble in life crises and go through their metamorphosis, becoming organs of intuitive healing. From there, this organ may grow more and more into an inclusive human quality of health in all forms of social living together on our long path towards the sixth cultural epoch, for which Rudolf Steiner is one who helps us make preparations—starting today.

Alfred Kon was born in Arnhem (Netherlands) in 1950 and studied Philosophy and Theology in Amsterdam and Stuttgart before finding his profession as a curative pedagogical teacher in Saarland. Since 2002 he has run his own centre for cultural healing in Saarbruecken and teaches Art and Humanities in a number of European countries.

His deep interest in the western stream of spirituality stems from experiences on the west coast of Ireland at the age of 19. A few years later this was deepened by finding Rudolf Steiner's lectures on Arthurian Knighthood. He now lives in the 'Celtic part of Germany' and Celtic culture grew into a central interest. This was strongly enhanced by discovering investigations on this theme from a Waldorf teacher with clairvoyant faculties, Maria Christiane Benning (1923–57).

Notes

1. Composite translation by Gil McHattie, mainly using that of Peter Patterson, but see Rudolf Steiner, *Twelve Moods*, tr. G. Karnow and A. Wulsin (Mercury Press, New York 1984) (GA 40).

2. Rudolf Steiner, *From Symptom to Reality in Modern History*, tr. A.H. Parker (Rudolf Steiner Press, London 1976) (GA 185).

3. Rudolf Steiner, *The Foundation Stone Meditation*, tr. D. Aldan (St George Pubs, Spring Valley 1980) (GA 260).

4. Johannes Tautz, *Walter Johannes Stein—A biography* (Temple Lodge Publishing, London 1990).

5. Rudolf Steiner, *The Boundaries of Natural Science*, tr. F. Amrine, K. Oberhuber (Anthroposophic Press, New York 1983) (GA 322).

6. Walter Johannes Stein, *The Ninth Century. World History in the Light of the Holy Grail* (Temple Lodge Publishing, 1991).

7. For further reading on Mani the reader is directed to the article in this volume by Christine Gruwez. On Mani's connection with the figure of Parzival, see an early esoteric lesson in Rudolf Steiner, *From the History and Contents of the First Section of the Esoteric School, 1904–1914*, ed. Hella Wiesberger, tr. J. Wood (Anthroposophic Press, New York 1998).

8. Rudolf Steiner, *The Temple Legend* (Rudolf Steiner Press, London 1997) (GA 93). Lecture of 11.11.1904.

9. Ella Young, *Celtic Wonder-Tales* (Kessinger Publishing LLC, 2008).

10. Rudolf Steiner, *The Wrong and Right Use of Esoteric Knowledge*, tr. C. Davy (Rudolf Steiner Press, London 1966) (GA 178). Lecture of 19.11.1917.

11. Rudolf Steiner, *Mystery Knowledge and Mystery Centres*, tr. E.H. Goddard and D.S. Osmond, revised by P. Wehrle (Rudolf Steiner Press, London 1997) (GA 232).

12. Rudolf Steiner, *Karmic Relationships*, Vol. VIII (Rudolf Steiner Press, London 1975) (GA 240). Lecture 3 (21.08.1924) and Lecture 6 (27.08.1924).

13. Rudolf Steiner, *The Mission of the Individual Folk Souls*, tr. A.H. Parker (Rudolf Steiner Press, London 1970) (GA 121).

14. Rudolf Steiner, *The East in the Light of the West* (Rudolf Steiner Publishing Co. and Anthroposophic Press, London and New York 1940) (GA 113).

15. Rudolf Steiner, *Inner Impulses of Evolution. The Mexican Mysteries and the Knights Templar*, tr. G. Church, F. Kozlik, S.C. Easton (Anthroposophic Press, New York 1984) (GA 171).

16. Johann Wolfgang von Goethe, *Fairy Tale—the Green Snake and the Beautiful Lily*, tr. J. Heuscher, ed. J. deRis Allen (Steiner Books, 2006).
    See also Rudolf Steiner, *Karmic Relationships*, Vol. VI, tr. D.S. Osmond, E.H. Goddard (Rudolf Steiner Press, London 1989) (GA 240). Lecture of 19.07.1924.

Templar Courage Comes of Age—Michaelic Renewal of the Temple, Economy, and Community Life

David Lenker

For nearly two hundred years the Knights Templar healed and transformed Europe with innovative initiatives in such practical fields as agriculture, architecture, medicine, banking, finance and community life. The Poor Knights of Christ won admiration and renown for exemplary courage exhibited on the field of battle. In this contribution we shall consider the far-reaching influence of the Templar Knights as it comes to expression in succeeding centuries as well as in the present third millennium. Specifically, we shall follow the metamorphosis of Templar courage from a quality of soul displayed by valiant knights on the battlefield to cultural impulses 'coming of age' in latter-day social experiments and an economy that serves others. Additionally, we shall consider a Michaelic renewal of the Temple of Solomon—a key for self-transformation in the current age of the consciousness soul with indications for preparing a future form of community life.

Templar courage coming of age—the peaceful conqueror

> William Penn, the great legislator of the Quakers in Pennsylvania, had the success of a conqueror, in establishing and defending his colony among savage tribes without drawing a sword.[1]

On the eve of the 700th Anniversary of the Templars' arrest, an international Conference convened at Camphill Soltane near Philadelphia, USA. On the opening night the significance of Soltane's European namesake was recalled—Soltane was the region where Parzival lived as a youth. The Knights Templar International Conference 2007 convened a stone's throw from Philadelphia and on the very site where, 325 years earlier, in 1682, William Penn extended his hand in peace, brotherhood, and friendship to the Native Americans at Shackamaxson. In this bold and courageous gesture William Penn inaugurated the 'Holy Experiment' as spirit-seed of American freedom and New World cosmopolitanism.

Regrettably, the esoteric significance of Penn's knightly deed is mostly lost on recorded history. Neither American nor Pennsylvania history textbooks draw a clear connection between the Holy Experiment (inaugurated 94 years before the Declaration of Independence) and the spiritual, economic and political forces leading to the American Revolution. We are reminded that spiritual researchers must exercise caution when considering the veracity of external recorded history. In fact, the discrepancy between 'history' and the esoteric realities of recorded events can be so great that 'white is recorded as black and black is written as white'. Too often recorded history does not grasp the role of the driving forces of spiritual powers in world history, the connection between spiritual ideals and their eventual application in civil society.

With the rise of secularism, the American mantra of separation of Church and state obscures the Rosicrucian ideals and the historic significance of the 'Holy Experiment'. In these pages we shall consider the spirit-seed of American freedom as a far-reaching social experiment born of a Templar-like sacrifice. In a lecture on the Knights Templar Rudolf Steiner points out that the Templar Knights were called to stand firm on the field of battle even when the opposing military power was up to three times stronger than their own forces. By standing firm and calmly awaiting their death as a sacrifice, the Knights Templar were able to *establish more firmly in Earth existence the impulse which went forth from the Mystery of Golgotha.*[2] In William Penn, the peaceful conqueror, we see Templar courage, formerly expressed on the field of battle, transmuted into a social impulse which inaugurates a cosmopolitan Michaelic community in the New World. As was the case of the Templar Knights centuries earlier, Penn's bold and peaceful gesture to the Native Americans is born of sacrifice and persecution.

Though of noble birth and well educated, William Penn (1644–1718) spent part of his youth in English prisons. His transgression was to pursue the calling of his soul, Quakerism. In the seventeenth century, the Religious Society of Friends constituted a radical spiritual stream. By way of the Cambridge mystics and the 'Great Theosopher', as Jacob Boehme (1575–1624) was known, the Friends had incorporated into their teachings such esoteric Rosicrucian ideals as the inner light, the voice of conscience, silence and freedom. Penn met Quakerism during his student days at Oxford. Attending Quaker meetings resulted in his arrest on more than one occasion. While thus imprisoned, William Penn had a vision of the 'Holy Experiment'—a place where individuals of different races, ethnicities and spiritual streams might live together side by side in cosmopolitan Michaelic harmony:

> There may be room there for such a Holy Experiment; for the nations want a precedent and my God will make it the seed of a Nation. That an example may be set up to the nations, that we may do the thing that is truly wise and just.[3]

As a youth, William Penn did not have the means to inaugurate this vision, but he continued to inwardly carry the great ideal of spiritual freedom. Today, westerners regard this freedom as a birthright, but in the seventeenth century the ideals of the 'Holy Experiment' were not among the basic rights of Europeans and, by extension, their subjects in the New World. In his native England, William Penn was expected to attend the Church of England. In France, Catholicism was the exclusive spiritual path endorsed by the monarchy, while in Germany, to avoid imprisonment, the populace was required to attend the Protestant Church. Prior to Penn's arrival, English colonies mostly resembled a carbon copy of Europe's patchwork spirituality. Massachusetts Bay Colony welcomed Puritans, but not Quakers or Catholics. In Maryland, Lord Baltimore welcomed Catholics, but not Quakers, Puritans, Presbyterians or others.

Spiritual freedom was the exception rather than the rule of the seventeenth century until William Penn's father, an Admiral in the British Navy, crossed the threshold of death. The elder Penn, Sir William, had been knighted for his naval service to the crown. In settlement of a debt owed by the King of England to Sir William Penn, the son requested—in lieu of cash—land in the New World. Thomas Jefferson, third president of the United States, is reputed to have described William Penn as *the greatest lawgiver the world has ever known*. Prior to embarking on the ship *Welcome*, William Penn drafted the 'First Frame of Government' and later, 'The Great Law'. These statutes were to bring to realization the great spiritual ideals of the 'Holy Experiment'.

In addition to spiritual freedom, 'The Frame of Government' specified treatment of the Native Americans with respect and brotherhood.

Towards this end, in a letter dated 11 July 1681, William Penn conceived a 'Trial by Jury' that invited Native Americans to participate in the workings of the colonial judiciary! Composed of six colonists and six Native Americans, the judicial council would decide any dispute between the cosmopolitan peoples of the 'Holy Experiment'.[4] Recalling his youthful persecution, William Penn also established the first freely elected representative body of government in the New World. Known today as the Pennsylvania General Assembly, the successor of Penn's free assembly currently meets in Harrisburg (third capital of the 'Holy Experiment') on the banks of the Susquehanna River. Penn also established a provincial court which in 1722 became America's first judicial body to function independently of both the legislative and executive branches. The Pennsylvania Supreme Court thus predates the United States Supreme Court by 67 years.

It was an important moment when William Penn, son of a British knight, extended his hand in peace, brotherhood and friendship to the Delaware Indians at Shackamaxson, near Philadelphia. Moreover, Penn's courageous gesture was highly uncharacteristic of his European counterparts in the New World. In Massachusetts Bay, the colonists accepted the help of Native Americans in the early years of the colony, only to subsequently drive them out when colonists could get along without native assistance. In Manhattan, the Dutch swindled Native Americans out of their lands by offering worthless trinkets in exchange. And in Latin America, the lust for gold incited Spanish conquistadors to mow down in cold blood the natives of the Aztec and Inca Empires. By contrast, so long as William Penn was alive, not one drop of blood was spilled between colonists and natives, who were encouraged to live in cosmopolitan Michaelic harmony.

The Susquehannocks and Delawares responded with great affection to William Penn's knightly courtesy. They dubbed him, 'Brother Onas' and promised to live with him in peace for as long as the moon would rise and the stars shine. This historic moment, a coming of age of Templar courage in service of Rosicrucian ideals, has been likened to the Peaceable Kingdom:

The wolf did with the lambkin dwell in peace. His grim carnivorous nature there did cease. The leopard with the harmless kid lied down. And not one savage beast was seen to frown. The lion with the fatling on did move. A little child was leading them in love. [Adapted from Isaiah 11: 6.]

During the early years of the Peaceable Kingdom, there were no forts, garrisons, soldiers or muskets within all the boundaries of Pennsylvania. For their part, the Native Americans, who mixed with the colonists, did not carry bows, arrows or tomahawks. Their 'Brother Onas' had inaugurated a far-reaching social experiment—the spirit-seed of American freedom—without force of arms, but by the power of ideals born of the Sun-initiation of the Knight of the Golden Stone (also known as Christian Rosenkreutz, who in 1459 underwent a third initiation to become the first human being to receive the ego of the Christ from the chalice of the Holy Grail).[5]

A 'Happening Place'—the Silicon Valley of the seventeenth century

News of the 'Holy Experiment' spread like spirit-fire through Europe. Soon the persecuted of the Old World flocked to the spirit refuge afforded them in Philadelphia and Pennsylvania. Moravians, Rosicrucians, Swedenborgians, Quakers, Presbyterians, Catholics, Amish and Mennonites all came to breathe the free air, to cultivate the fertile lands, and experience the shining waters. Established as one of the last of the original 13 British colonies, the influx of spiritual refugees swelled the population of Pennsylvania. As the first capital of the 'Holy Experiment', Philadelphia soon overtook more established settlements to become the largest city in colonial America. As a crucible of culture and spirituality, Philadelphia was soon known as the 'Athens of America'. Born in Boston on Three Kings' Day, 6 January 1706,[6] Benjamin Franklin moved to Philadelphia as a young man in order to be a 'mover and shaker' in this 'happening place'.

The Rosicrucian ideal of freedom, successfully unfolding in the 'Holy Experiment' as a spiritual, social and political impulse, soon spread to neighbouring colonies. Over time, it became the impetus for the 'Spirit of 1776', the political and economic forces culminating in the Declaration of Independence by representatives of the 13 colonies convened at Philadelphia on 4 July 1776. However, freedom would not formally be won from Great Britain until the Treaty of Paris in 1783 and only after Benjamin Franklin secured the aid of the French. With the rise of the Industrial Revolution in the nineteenth century, the cause for spiritual and political freedom was supplanted by a new mantra, 'free enterprise'. During this transition, the cultural and economic epicentre of America shifted from Philadelphia to New York City. The World Trade Centre became the outward symbol of American economic hegemony in the world. Certainly, the events and tragedy of 11 September 2001 cannot be justified in any sense. However, one must ask if this brutal attack was not in some measure an indication or consequence of America having strayed from the Rosicrucian ideals and transformed Templar courage responsible for her founding. If so, the question arises as to how America might find again her true esoteric mission and thereby fulfil her exoteric destiny on the world stage.

Philadelphia—City of Brotherly Love—and the Temple of Solomon

> The anthroposophical wisdom we acquire [today] will become the impulse of love in the sixth age, which is represented by the community expressing itself even in its name as the community of brotherly love, Philadelphia.[7]

Appropriately, William Penn named the first capital of the 'Holy Experiment' after a city in the Book of Revelations. Later, Rudolf Steiner gave the same name—Philadelphia—to the sixth post-Atlantean epoch, which is to follow our current fifth epoch. The Temple of Solomon provides a key to understanding and developing the spirituality of the coming sixth epoch, the next development of human consciousness which we must already begin to prepare for now.

> In the sixth cultural epoch man will understand spiritually what he should become. The ego will have attained a certain stage then, when what Solomon's Temple stands for will be reality in the highest sense ...'[8]

The essential quality of the sixth epoch can be seen as an expression of secrets contained in the Temple of Solomon. The secret of temple life is: *those who live there shall incite the fire of love.*

It is no accident that the *Pauperes Commilitones Christi Templique Solomonici* (Poor Co-Soldiers of Christ and the Temple of Solomon), was founded in Jerusalem near the site of the ancient Temple of Solomon. By founding the order here, the Templar Knights signalled their intent—a renewal of the ancient Mysteries, but in a form appropriate to the consciousness soul of today. The far-spread significance of the Knights Templar becomes apparent when one considers that the brothers penetrated the Mysteries of their own age (the fourth post-Atlantean epoch), became heralds of the new practical, culturally renewing impulse of the fifth epoch, while all the while keeping the eye of their souls focused on the sixth epoch! The Temple of Solomon, which appears on the reverse of the Templar seal, symbolizes the coming of a new living Christianity. The Templars were to prepare an esoteric vessel that would come to full fruition in the sixth epoch when the Rose Cross, as the new symbol of Christianity, recognizes the Temple significance of the Molten Sea and Golden Triangle.[9] The spirit-impulse of the Knights Templar thus stood in opposition to the worldly power and glory of the exoteric Church seated in Rome.

The Templar Brotherhood is founded as twilight begins to set on the fourth post-Atlantean epoch. Through the evolution of consciousness, we understand this period as responsible for the development of the intellectual soul by such leading personalities as Socrates, Plato, and Aristotle. In our own time-period of the fifth epoch, anthroposophy leads one to the *awareness of one's humanity*—an experience typically attained by transforming intellectual thinking into intuitive thinking. Through this process one comes to uncover the individual spirit source of one's thinking and being. To experience the consciousness soul, Steiner calls for the creation of a 'special state' for observing one's own thinking activity: to behold oneself as a free spirit in the act of creating an object (the process of one's own thinking) that is qualitatively identical with the observing subject. The initial division of self and world is then resolved into an inherent but now self-conscious unity. When each individual spirit can relate to every other spirit—I AM to I AM— we rise to the level of the Spirit Self dwelling within a community of free spirits. This is the city of sisterly and brotherly love or the community of Philadelphia.

Today, two phenomena already signify the coming of Philadelphia: the Temple of Solomon and group and branch life. In the *Temple Legend* Rudolf Steiner shows how the proportions of Noah's Ark are in a direct ratio to the proportions of the present physical body. Similarly, the proportions of the Solomonic Temple contain in seed form the proportions of the physical body that shall prevail in the sixth post-Atlantean epoch.[10] On many occasions Rudolf Steiner pointed to group and branch life of the Anthroposophical Society as a new form of sister-brotherhood, one that will come to fruition in the community life of the sixth epoch. When individuals of different destinies, races, ethnicities, genders, professions and applied anthroposophical initiatives come together periodically to study the esoteric truths of spiritual science in a group setting, something can light up through the bonds of soul to soul, namely the spirit of the universally human. This new form of sister-brotherhood, sustained by Michaelic knowledge rather than ties of blood, unleashes the forces of the Spirit Self.

> We must become conscious of a higher form of community founded in the freedom of love between sisters and brothers, as a breath of magic that we breathe into our working groups ... We may therefore picture to ourselves that by uniting in brotherliness in working groups something hovers invisibly over our work, something that is like the child of the forces of the Spirit Self—the Spirit Self that is nurtured by the beings of the higher hierarchies in order that it may stream down into our souls when they are here again on Earth in the sixth epoch of civilization. In our groups we perform work that streams upwards to those forces that are being prepared for the sixth epoch.[11]

The forces of the Spirit Self, signified by Solomon's Temple, arise through the interaction of I AM to I AM. It is in this context that Dr Virginia Sease of the Goetheanum Executive Council observes, 'Group and branch life is the modern School of Initiation'. Through a modern Michaelic renewal of the Temple of Solomon, we prepare for Philadelphia. The renewed Temple arises wherever three attributes hold sway: 1) study of spiritual science, 2) absolute freedom (no confession of dogma), and 3) sister-brotherhood (interest in and service to others). The fundamental building stone and identifier of this Michael Rose Cross Temple is elucidated by Rudolf Steiner in a lecture on the Knights Templar:

> One human being manifests one individuality, a second another, and a third a different one again. All these individualities in their several workings are focused in a point—the point of the ego or 'I'. There we are alike, and through this focus-point where we are alike can pass the spirit-element common to us all. This 'I'-point, where we are alike, gives the possibility for the development in humanity of a community life.[12]

Templar sacrifice anchors brotherly love

Through a deed of sacrifice on the field of battle, the Knights Templar firmly anchored brotherly love—the great ideal of the sixth epoch—into earthly evolution. The following reflections are offered through the spiritual research of the author, as a fruit or a deepening of indications given by Rudolf Steiner.

At the dawn of modern consciousness the Knights Templar unfurled a new spiritual impulse. For nearly two hundred years the Templar Knights healed Europe with innovative initiatives in a variety of practical fields. At the heart of the Order were brothers steeped in mysticism, meditation, prayer and devotion. Through an intensification of the feeling life, many brothers attained a form of Christian initiation. By this initiation they were able to experience at every moment of their life 'Not I, but Christ in me'.

When these 'warrior monks' rode into battle, they did not go in pursuit of earthly fame, honour, glory or the spoils of conquest. Rather, the Templar Knights rode in service of a spiritual mission proclaimed by their motto: *Non nobis Domine, non nobis, sed Nomini Tuo da gloriam* (Not for us, O Lord, not for us, but to Thy Name give the glory). Singing *Non nobis Domine* . . . they experienced 'Christ in me' with such mystical devotion that it was the blood of Christ coursing through their veins. On their souls was the seal of Michael. Templar brothers were called by Michael to stand firm, even when the opposing military power was three times stronger than their own. As we have seen, Rudolf Steiner advises that by standing firm and calmly awaiting their deaths, the Templars were able to 'establish more firmly in Earth existence the impulse which went forth from the Mystery of Golgotha'.[13] How can we understand this? How can a military sacrifice on the field of battle contribute to furthering the greatest mystery of all mysteries; the mystery of birth, death and resurrection—the Mystery of Golgotha?

The greatest mystery is the mystery of how the highest spirit principle in the universe could come to dwell in an earthly body and, through the Crucifixion, overcome death to implant a new, living impulse into the stream of humanity. We know that during the Mystery of Golgotha, the turning point of all past, present and future evolution, a Roman soldier pierced the side of Christ with a spear. In that moment blood and water gushed forth. A portion of this fluid was captured by the same vessel used at the Last Supper and known as the Holy Grail. However, a portion of this blood fell to the earth below. Due to the nature of the Christ as the former being of the Sun, the Son of God, who had become man, His blood was spiritually charged. His blood had the character and quality of the future Atma or Spirit Man. These drops on Golgotha were thereby able to change the nature of the physical Earth, to transmute the decaying Earth-existence and implant into it a spirit-seed such that one day, through the transforming work of humanity, the physical Earth might become a star!

Just over a millennium later, the Soldiers of Christ ride into battle singing the Templar anthem. Standing side by side on the field of battle, the brothers bear within their souls the spiritual fervour of a mystical life. Called to courage by Michael, the Templars are one in the blood of Christ. And when the swords of the infidels pierced the sides of the brothers, their blood fell to the earth below and commingled. In those moments of sacrifice, was the Earth in fact changed again? As the blood of the brothers blended with the earth, was the love of the One imbued with the love of I AM to I AM, that is, brotherly love? In those moments of Templar sacrifice was the Earth not brought one step closer to the New Jerusalem, to Philadelphia, City of Brotherly Love? Surely, this invincible city is more firmly anchored on Earth through the courageous deeds of Templar Knights and, centuries later, inspires Walt Whitman:

> I dreamed in a dream I saw a city invincible to the attacks of the whole of the rest of the Earth. I dreamed it was the new city of friends. Nothing was greater there than the quality of love, it led the rest. It was seen every hour in the actions of the men and women of that city; and in all their looks and words.[14]

Brother, Can You Spare a Dime?

An American contemporary of Whitman, Ralph Waldo Emerson, upholds the primacy of soul and spirit when economic calamity afflicts the young nation. In the spring of 1837, the cultural and economic shift from Philadelphia and the 'Holy Experiment' to New York and the Hudson Valley was already in full swing. The industrial revolution was taking hold in predominantly agrarian America. However, the new mantra of 'free enterprise' had hit a bend: the panic of 1837. Half of the 850 US banks had partly failed or closed. High unemployment, depression and inflation ensued.

Karl Marx was 19 years old and was about to formulate a world-view based purely on materialistic and economic determinants. To eliminate the exploitation of one social class by another, Marx would deny the factors of individual destiny revealed by soul and spirit. To create a social utopia where all were equal, the state would assume the means of production and administer a society humming with all the efficiency of 'cogs in a machine'.

This vision of socialism failed to inspire Emerson, who completed his essay on self-reliance just three years after the 1837 panic. And in the midst of panic, he set matters straight by courageously affirming the unconquered soul and spirit ideals as the driving forces of world history:

I see a good in such emphatic and universal calamity as the times bring, that they dissatisfy me with society. Under common burdens we say there is much virtue in the world, and what evil co-exists is inevitable. I am not aroused to say, 'I have sinned: I am in a gall of bitterness, and a bond of iniquity'; but when these full measures come, it then stands confessed—society has played out its last stake; it is checkmated. Young men have no hope. Adults stand like day labourers, idle on the streets. None calleth us to labour. The old wear no crown of warm life on their gray hairs. The present generation is bankrupt of principles and hope, as of property. I see man is not what man should be. He is the treadle of a wheel. He is a tassel at the apron string of society. He is a money chest. He is the servant of his belly. This is the causal bankruptcy, this is the cruel oppression, that the ideal should serve the actual, that the head should serve the feet. Then first, I am forced to inquire if the ideal might also be tried? Behold the boasted world has come to nothing. Prudence herself is at her wits' end.

Pride, Thrift, and Expediency, who jeered and chirped and were so well pleased with themselves, and made merry with the dream, as they termed it, of Philosophy and Love—behold they are all flat, and here is the Soul erect and unconquered still. What answer is it now to say, 'It has always been so?' I acknowledge that, as far back as I can see the widening procession of humanity, the marchers are lame and blind and deaf; but to the soul that whole past is but one finite series in its infinite scope. Deteriorating ever and now desperate. Let me begin anew. Let me teach the finite to know its master. Let me ascend above my fate and work down upon my world.[15]

Forget the profits!

As the panic of 1837 gave way to the gilded age of robber barons, the industrial age revealed its two-headed demon: the reduction of humanity to 'the treadle of a wheel', and the efficient exploitation (enslavement) of countless factory workers to enrich a few. In this very milieu we find the Grand Master of the Knights Templar reincarnated as a factory owner in Rudolf Steiner's Mystery Drama, *The Soul's Awakening*. However, the reincarnated Grand Master, Hilarius, does not conform to the profit ethic of the industrial era's robber barons. By contrast, Hilarius operates his modern business not primarily to maximize profit and efficiency, but in order that something artistic might infuse the soulless realm of mechanism:

Thomasius, as artist, is to lead the place of work that I shall build for him nearby. What we provide mechanically will take on form through his artistic spirit, and supply for human daily use such things as are both practical, and truly beautiful. Art then and craftsmanship shall work as one to bring real taste into men's daily lives.[16]

In this context we may turn to an example of Templar courage coming of age to renew the economy. We shall see the dragon's industrial behemoth rendered in service of a far-reaching social experiment as living proof of the seminal thoughts later explained in *The Threefold Commonwealth*. It is the inspiring saga of a little-known American industrialist and philanthropist, the rags-to-riches story of perseverance, courage, trial, tribulation and 'can-do' American will. It is an astonishingly clear example as the 'Not I, but Christ in me' principle applied to economics: to use gold not for profit, but for the good of all.

Milton S. Hershey (1857–1945) was born a poor farm boy. The budding American industrialist endured a string of business failures or setbacks in Philadelphia, New York City, Chicago, New Orleans and Denver. Courageously undeterred by the tribulation of failure and setback, he ultimately achieved entrepreneurial success in the region of his birthplace: the bucolic splendour of the Susquehanna Valley, heart of the 'Holy Experiment'. In the year 1900, as the long-standing Kali Yuga comes to a close, he sold the Lancaster Caramel Company for one million dollars. A staggering sum at the time, he committed the proceeds to a far-reaching social experiment. In the same year that supersensible experience is again possible for humanity, this industrialist followed, for the rest of his earthly days, the Templar Rosicrucian

impulse of service to others. As an example of industrial philanthropy unfolded in freedom, this modern Templar social impulse founded a model town, bank, museum, theatre, park, rose garden, school and junior college, as well as later endowing the school for orphans 'in perpetuity'. This industrial philanthropist responded with a familiar saying whenever a business action threatened to negatively impact either his workers or the affairs of the model threefold community, 'Forget the Profits!'

Unlike the Carnegies and Rockefellers, he did not turn philanthropic in the twilight of his life when he was about to meet his Maker. His philanthropy did not arise from a last-ditch pang of conscience as atonement for years of unscrupulous business or fortunes won by breaking the backs of his workers. Throughout his entrepreneurial and philanthropic pursuits, he lived the motto that hung above his desk, 'Business is a matter of human service'. In 2009, we celebrated the centennial of a threefold community established when the King and Queen of Chocolate, Milton and Catherine Hershey, still in the prime of life, executed the Deed of Trust. This legal instrument transferred proceeds of the economic sphere to the cultural sphere in order that the dregs of American youth, orphan boys begging for subsistence on countless city streets, might be given a home and free independent school education in *the sweetest place on Earth*.

In 1903, Milton S. Hershey broke ground for the world's largest chocolate factory. Simultaneous to construction, he laid out a model utopian town known today as Hershey, Pennsylvania. In 1909, Milton and Catherine Hershey—the King and Queen of Chocolate—founded a school for orphan boys on a 12,000 acre farm campus surrounding the town and effectively completed a threefold commonwealth as Rudolf Steiner understood the free beneficial working of the economic, states/ rights and cultural spheres. In 1918, just one year prior to the publication of *The Threefold Commonwealth*, later known as *The Threefold Social Order*, Milton Hershey gifted his entire personal fortune and controlling chocolate company stock to three community trusts. The largest of these was earmarked for the orphans' school, which continues today as America's largest residential school for disadvantaged youth.

The Temple of Chocolate

For Goethe the outer world was experienced as a 'script of the soul'. There are signposts all around us which reveal each individual's unique destiny. One needs merely to be sufficiently spiritually awake to read these signposts, sometimes known as *open secrets*. Ten years before embarking on the far-reaching social experiment in the Susquehanna Valley, Milton Hershey attended the World's Columbian Exposition in Chicago. Commemorating the 400th anniversary of the voyage of Christopher Columbus, the exposition celebrated the marvels and new versions of such inventions as the telephone, phonograph, moving picture machines and electric trains. Among the many halls showcasing electricity, manufacturing, machinery and liberal arts, Hershey was most intrigued by the 'Temple of Chocolate' tucked away beneath the 130 foot high glass dome of the Agricultural Hall. The edible temple stood 38 feet tall and was built by the Stollwerck Brothers of Cologne.

> From a foundation of dark chocolate blocks rose columns topped by Teutonic eagles. The columns were made with swirls of white cocoa butter—a by-product of cocoa manufacturing—to make them resemble marble. They supported a dome with a crown at its highest point. Inside the temple was a larger-than-life chocolate statue of the mythological Germania, complete with sword, standing on a pedestal.[17]

Presumably, Hilarius would be pleased with this most artistic creation of one of Europe's largest confectioners. For the erstwhile poor farm boy, the visit to the Chocolate Temple was a moment of destiny and turning point. Seven years later he sold the Lancaster Caramel Company for a staggering sum and used the proceeds to build the world's largest chocolate factory. The success of the caramel company had enabled Hershey to travel to the Continent and British Isles. He was well aware that Cadbury's had moved their factory out of the slums of Birmingham to a rural site and had plans to build a company town. Not far from the Chocolate Temple, in the nearby Palace of Mechanic Arts, was a full chocolate works operated by the Lehmann Company of Dresden. Before leaving Chicago, Hershey purchased all of Lehman's chocolate producing machines on display. A few days after the exposition closed on 30 October 1893 the machinery was crated and placed on rail cars bound for Lancaster, Pennsylvania.

In the same year that Milton Hershey made a life-altering pilgrimage to the Temple of Chocolate, Rudolf Steiner put the finishing touches on his *Philosophy of Freedom*.[18] Steiner's seminal work was to place esoteric mystery wisdom, previously available only to a few, on a scientific exoteric footing. This milestone of epistemology makes the treasures and secrets of esoteric knowledge accessible to all human beings. In the following year, 1894, Rudolf Steiner published *The Philosophy of Freedom*. Meanwhile, across the Atlantic, Milton Hershey founded the Hershey Chocolate Company. The logo of the new company depicted a babe emerging from a cocoa pod (the risen Christ ascending from the grave of Earth existence). At the time, chocolate was a luxury item in the United

States and within the reach only of an exclusive few. By developing a formula for the mass production and distribution of milk chocolate, Hershey's goal was to make it available to every American. The Great American Chocolate Bar would bring moments of happiness to the common man.

Progressives and reformers began to take notice of the 'Hershey Idea' as a social impulse born of a benevolent, self-regulated business model. Hershey's became the leading manufacturer of confectionery products in North America, demonstrating that business could make a healthy profit *and* provide for the cultural life of the community and region. Workers, townspeople, factory executives, and orphans shared in the vision, loyalty and rewards of a threefold-interlinked community.

The round barn

The Chocolate King considered the school for orphan boys and (later) girls the crown jewel of the community. Bereft of family, the boys here forged ties of brotherhood which are today as much a part of the sacred geography of Hershey as Spring Creek and the lush rolling countryside. The boys lived on farms surrounding the town where they milked cows that provided a key ingredient of the Great American Chocolate Bar. In turn, the profits of the chocolate company provided the boys with all of their needs including, upon graduation, four years of paid tuition to the college of their choice.

One of the barns on the farm school campus had a distinctively round shape. Although it no longer stands, the round design inspired the lasting memorial and tribute to Milton S. Hershey, erected 25 years after the founder crossed the threshold. As administrative hub, dining hall and auditorium of the Milton Hershey School (K-12), Founder's Hall affords a breathtaking silhouette of white arising majestically from the serene Hershey landscape. The immense round hall, built of white granite and marble, supports a dome whose rotunda is the second largest in the world. The design recalls the distinctively round churches of the Knights Templar. In the rotunda of the hall stands a statue of Milton Hershey with an orphan boy. The sculpture group was given to the school by alumni and bears a prominent bronze plaque with the inscription: 'His deeds are

his monument. His life is our inspiration'. Of the three Templar pillars—
wisdom, beauty and strength—it is strength that predominates in this temple
hall of alabaster. Templar courage, reborn as 'can-do' American social
will, achieves the deeds that eluded Hilarius in *The Souls' Awakening*.

Templar courage comes of age—the City of David defeats Goliath

By the early twenty-first century, the controlling stock of the Hershey
Chocolate Company (originally gifted to the school in 1918) had grown
to a trust fund of some seven billion US dollars. The largest independent
school endowment of its kind in the world, it continues to exceed the
endowments of all but the most elite US colleges and universities. By
early 2002 a variety of factors, including the scandalous failure of such
major corporations as Enron and WorldCom, led trust fund managers to
think the unthinkable. No doubt, a contributing factor included whispers
from Wall Street brokers, who salivated at the prospect of lucrative fees
that would accompany any sale of the renowned Hershey Chocolate
Company. Trust board managers voted to investigate a sale of the
chocolate company with the intention of reinvesting windfall profits in
diversified stock holdings. Claiming that diversification would make
school investments more secure, neither Wall Street nor the trust board
publicly addressed what might become of the threefold community if the
new owner of Hershey Chocolate decided to shutter both the factory and
corporate headquarters. In the interest of efficiency it was widely
anticipated that a new owner would consolidate operations in another
state. Moreover, the trust managers decided to conduct the transaction in
secret and only announce to the community when a deal was finalized.

To the chagrin of brokers and trust managers, word leaked out,
headlines blared, and a hue and cry went forth from *the sweetest place on
earth*. While community activists set up an electronic town hall (the
Friends of Hershey website), Wall Street was undeterred. Community
protests inevitably succumb to the right of the stockholder to maximize
return on his or her investment. Reporters began arriving from around
the world to cover the moral battle of the century.

Ultimately, the community and extended region petitioned the judge
of the Orphans' Court of Dauphin County. By Pennsylvania law, the
Orphans' Court held legal jurisdiction over the 1909 Deed of Trust
executed by Milton and Catherine Hershey. As trust managers prepared
to meet in Valley Forge (85 miles east of Hershey) to vote on a proposed
sale to the Wrigley Chewing Gum Company, the Orphans' judge

ordered an injunction against the sale. The judge reasoned that since the Deed of Trust specified that the school must be located in Hershey, a sale of the chocolate company would irrevocably change the character of the community with potentially negative repercussions for the well-being of the disadvantaged youth, whom, by terms of the trust, were tied to the Hershey community. Defying the judge's order and confident of appeal, trust managers proceeded to vote in Valley Forge. The proposed sale was only narrowly defeated. The Michaelic triumph was complete when, two months later, the Orphans' Court judge of Dauphin County removed from the school trust each board member who had voted to sell the Hershey Chocolate Company.

As jubilation broke out on or about Michaelmas Day 2002, one could clearly see the working of all three spheres delineated by Rudolf Steiner's *Threefold Social Order*.[19] The overreaching tentacles of the economic sphere had been beaten back by Christ manifesting through the judicial sphere as the Lord of Karma—a spirit action made possible by both the founder's vision, and the courageous initiative of the diverse elements of the community (rights sphere).

Epilogue

I recently visited Independence Hall in Philadelphia, birthplace of the Declaration of Independence and US Constitution. In the hall where centuries earlier the Continental Congress met and debated the destiny of the 13 colonies, one could discern, as an architectural embellishment high above the Speaker's chair, the crest of a knight's helmet. Further investigation confirmed that the embellishment included William Penn's full coat of arms. Directly below the helmet, engraved on the Speaker's chair was a half Sun. Benjamin Franklin is said to have observed of this half Sun that he could not determine during the deliberations whether it was a *rising* or *setting* Sun.

Purely practical aspects of deliberations weighed heavily against declaring independence. For instance, Congress had no authority to conscript soldiers and had to rely on state 'donations' for military funding. Additionally, delegates who signed for independence would commit treason (subject to hanging). In order to sway the proceedings towards the cause of freedom—a Rosicrucian ideal born of a Sun initiation—the situation called for the presence of an initiate known as the Knight of the Golden Stone. (Focusing on the esoteric aspect of the founders' deliberations vis-à-vis the Declaration of Independence, my earlier research on these matters was clarified and deepened in Vermont by a presentation offered by a member of the Goetheanum Executive Council. That we had come to similar conclusions independently speaks to the spirit efficacy of a Rosicrucian initiate presence at the founding of America).

The knight's helmet at Independence Hall reveals the transformed courage and social deed of the peaceful conqueror, William Penn. *Templar Courage Comes of Age* when Penn's deed serves the consecration of a Rosicrucian ideal—freedom. We close with an excerpt from the words of the peaceful conqueror:

> The Great Spirit rules in the Heavens and the Earth. He knows the innermost thoughts of men and women. He knows that we have come here with a hearty desire to live with you in peace. We use no hostile weapons against our enemies; good faith and good will towards men are our defences. We believe you will deal kindly and justly by us, as we shall deal kindly and justly by you. We meet on the broad pathway of good faith and good will; no advantage shall be taken on either side, but all shall be openness and love ... The friendship between me and you I shall not compare to a chain, for that the rains might rust, or the falling tree might break. We are the same as if one man's body were to be divided into two parts; we are all one.
>
> We shall be brothers, my people and your people, as the children of one father ... We shall transmit this league between us to our children. It shall be made stronger and stronger, and be kept bright and clean, without rust or spot, between our children and our children's children, while the creeks and rivers run, and while the Sun, Moon and stars endure.

William Penn, Shackamaxson, 1682

David Lenker holds a degree in Latin from Dickinson College, USA, and completed anthroposophical studies at Emerson College, England. His special interest is the Temple of Solomon *and the metamorphosis of Templar brotherhood as the social fabric of group and community life both today and in the future.*

To commemorate the 700th anniversary of the Templars' arrest, 13 October 2007, David chaired an initiative group responsible for planning a Knights Templar International Conference near Philadelphia, USA. He now organizes annual Templar conferences in Hershey, Pennsylvania, USA sponsored by Susquehanna Corps de Michael—Anthroposophical Society in Hershey. www.corpsdemichael.org

David also offers classes for the School of Spiritual Science, chairs the Corps de

Michael, runs an organic farm with a partner and serves as a financial advisor for Pennsylvania's largest credit union, PSECU. He lectures on a variety of Templar and related themes in such US locales as Boston, Buffalo, New York, Washington, DC, Michigan, Oregon, Pennsylvania, and Vermont.

Notes

1. Arthur O'Leary, 'Plea for the Liberty of Conscience', cited in *Remember William Penn* (Harrisburg: Commonwealth of Pennsylvania, William Penn Tercentenary Committee, Pennsylvania Historical Commission, 1944).

2. Rudolf Steiner, 'The Templars and the Forces of Evil' (GA 171). Lecture of 02.10.1916, included in Rudolf Steiner, *The Knights Templar*, ed. M. Jonas (Rudolf Steiner Press, 2007).

3. 'Vision of William Penn' inscribed in gold leaf at the base of the Capitol Dome, Palace of Art, Harrisburg, Pennsylvania (completed 1906 as the enduring monument to the 'Holy Experiment').

4. William Penn in a letter dated 11 July 1681 and published in *Remember William Penn*, op. cit.

5. Virginia Sease and Manfred Schmidt-Brabant, *Paths of the Christian Mysteries* (Temple Lodge Publishing, 2003).

6. Born on Three Kings' Day 1706, the subsequent institution of the Gregorian calendar changed Franklin's birthday by eleven days (per Dr Virginia Sease in a lecture at Kimberton Waldorf School, Annual General Meeting of the Anthroposophical Society in America, 2006).

7. Rudolf Steiner, *The Apocalypse of St John* (Rudolf Steiner Press, London 1977) (GA 104).

8. Rudolf Steiner, *The Temple Legend* (Rudolf Steiner Press, 1985) (GA 93).

9. Ibid.

10. Ibid.

11. Rudolf Steiner, *Preparing for the Sixth Epoch* (Anthroposophic Press, Spring Valley, New York 1957) (GA 159).

12. Rudolf Steiner, lecture of 02.10.1916, op. cit.

13. Ibid.

14. Walt Whitman, *Leaves of Grass* (The Modern Library, New York 1921).

15. Ralph Waldo Emerson, quoted in 'Out of Panic, Self Reliance' by Harold Bloom, op-ed contributor, *The New York Times* (*nytimes.com*, 12 October 2008).

16. Rudolf Steiner, *The Four Mystery Plays*, tr. Adam Bittleston (Rudolf Steiner Press, London 1982) (GA 14).

17. Michael D'Antonio, *Hershey: Milton S. Hershey's Extraordinary Life of Wealth, Empire, and Utopian Dreams* (Simon & Schuster, New York 2006).

18. Rudolf Steiner, *The Philosophy of Spiritual Activity. The Philosophy of Freedom*, tr. R. Stebbing. 2nd rev. ed. (Rudolf Steiner Press, Bristol 1992) (GA 4).

19. Rudolf Steiner, *The Threefold Social Order*, tr. F.C. Heckel. 2nd ed. (Anthroposophic Press, New York 1972) (GA 23).

Photos

William Penn in his knightly attire, age 22. Published in *Remember William Penn.*

Milton and Catherine Hershey, watercolour c. 1909 while travelling in Europe.

Founder's Hall, Milton Hershey School, Hershey, Pennsylvania USA (school photo).

ADDITIONAL MATERIAL

Rosslyn Chapel and the Sephirotic Tree

Peter Snow

Rosslyn Chapel lies some eight miles south of Edinburgh. It is a fairly small building currently used by the congregation of the Scottish Episcopalian Church as the Collegiate Church of St Matthew. It is famous, above all, for its remarkable carvings in the stone of the building, both inside and out. So rich is the profusion of these that the chapel is a place of pilgrimage for many people for all sorts of reasons. Legends attach themselves to the place like burrs to a sleeve—some of them intriguing, others less worthy of attention. Dan Brown's book *The Da Vinci Code* and the film based on the book made much of Rosslyn, seeing it as a chapel of the Grail, although interpreting the Grail in a very materialistic and reductive way. Tourists flock to the chapel every year, in all seasons and weathers, to see what it is that is so interesting. Some leave disappointed, others with questions and impressions that linger. Is it really a Grail chapel, and what does that mean? Did the Templar Knights really have anything to do with its construction? Is a priceless treasure concealed somewhere in the building? What is it that gives the chapel its curious dual atmosphere, at once exciting and frightening, intriguing and oppressive, full of both darkness and light?

Dr Tim Wallace-Murphy,[1] a Freemason with a deep interest in esoteric Christianity, informs us that there are five signs by which we can recognize the influence of the Templar Knights in a church building. These are: 1) the Dove in flight, with an olive branch; 2) the *Agnus Dei* (lamb with cross); 3) a disembodied hand; 4) the veil of Veronica; 5) a five-pointed star. Each of these signs is to be found, among the plethora of other images and symbols, in Rosslyn. The anthroposophist and prolific writer on esoteric subjects Sergei Prokofieff, on a visit to Rosslyn Chapel, identified certain mason's marks in the fabric of the building as Templar in origin. The Templar influence in the construction of Rosslyn must be understood as something of a riddle, as the Order of the Knights of the Temple was dissolved about a century and a half before the first stones were laid for the foundations of Rosslyn. No doubt Dr Wallace-Murphy is quite right in that the esoteric nature of the Templars' unique spirituality survived the cruel end of the Order and is to be found in Rosslyn—and, no doubt, elsewhere—where it joins other esoteric streams.

Rosslyn is a building of extraordinary complexity, rich in meaning. No single spiritual stream can claim predominance in the chapel's design, unless we weave together a number of strands into a single entity that we can call esoteric Christianity (though admittedly, for some, even that would be controversial).

The legendary connection with the Grail, and hence with esoteric Christianity, is one of the reasons that it keeps recurring in studies of this subject. Some who believe the Grail to be a thing, an object in space, are ready to credit the notion that it lies somewhere hidden within the fabric of the chapel. Rosslyn does have its secrets, certainly. For example: what lies beneath the nave of the chapel, apart from the bodies of the eldest sons of the Sinclair family, who were laid out there in their armour from the time of the chapel's construction until the Battle of Dunbar in 1650? One of the chapel's functions is as a family mausoleum, but after 1650 other arrangements were made for the funerals of the heads of the family. However, speculation is rife about what else may lie under the floor of Rosslyn, although such speculation misses the artistry of the chapel which for many is its real treasure. But what do these carvings represent? I have written elsewhere about the stories, myths and legends represented in the chapel's carvings.[2] My task in this article is to draw attention to another aspect of the chapel, which is rarely discussed elsewhere in Rosslyn literature. I refer to the influence of Kabbalah, but Kabbalah of a uniquely Christian and esoteric kind.

Kabbalah—the word in Hebrew means 'tradition', or 'that which is received'—is said to be the unwritten tradition that accompanies the destinies of the Children of Israel through all their sufferings and wanderings, although there are books which embody the Kabbalistic relationship to the world, such as the *Zohar* (the *Book of Splendour*). Kabbalah contains mysteries that can only be communicated through symbol and imagery. It is mystical and theosophical in its nature.

One of the most common images of Kabbalistic study is the Sephirotic Tree. Certain spiritual qualities, such as strength, overcoming, wisdom, intelligence, and so on, are brought together and linked in a way that resembles the leaves of a tree (see Fig. 1).

This 'tree' represents the human being in unfallen state, i.e., as he existed in archetype in the spiritual world before the creation of the physical-material world. It also represents the human being as microcosmos, embodying all of creation and bearing within him the informing influences of the cosmos. Finally, it represents the human being in the far distant future as a being of pure spirit, evolved beyond the physical to be

The Traditional Sephirotic Tree

Left Pillar	Centre Pillar	Right Pillar
Justice	*Mildness*	*Mercy*

Kether
Crown
Seraphim

Binah		**Chokhma**
Intelligence		Wisdom
Thrones/Saturn		Cherubim

Geburah/Din		**Chesed/Gedulah**
Strength/Justice		Mercy/Greatness
Principalities/Mars		Dominions/Jupiter

Tiphereth
Beauty
Powers/Sun

Hod		**Netzach**
Splendour		Overcoming
Archangels/Mercury		Virtues/Venus

Yesod
Foundation
Angels/Moon

Malkuth
Realm
Human beings/Earth

Fig. 1

at one again with the Powers who created him. To put it another way, the Sephirotic Tree represents the human being in a perpetual state of transformation. It is entirely consistent with the meaning of the chapel to have the Sephirotic Tree represented. These qualities are considered meditatively by the Kabbalist at different levels of consciousness, from the mundane and everyday to the most rarefied and spiritual. Their inter-connections and interactions are subject to the deepest contemplation.

If we consider the Sephirot as indicating divine qualities, we can relate each quality to members of the celestial hierarchy, mentioned in various places in the Bible but notably in the Epistles of Paul. In this way, the quality *Kether*, or Crown, is related to the Seraphim; *Chokhma*, Wisdom, to the Cherubim; and *Binah*, Intelligence, to the Thrones. In the second level or hierarchy of the Tree, *Chesed*, Mercy, is connected to the Dominions (Kyriotetes); *Geburah*, Strength, or Life, to the Principalities (Dynamis); and *Tiphereth*, Beauty, to the Powers (Exusiai). At the third level, *Netzach*, Victory or Overcoming, is identified with the Virtues (Archai); *Hod*, Splendour, to the Archangels; and *Yesod*, Foundation, to the Angels. The last of the Sephirot, *Malkuth*, Realm or Field of Endeavour, represents the Human Being whose destiny, it is to be hoped, is to become one with the nine hierarchies in the far distant future.

We can also connect the Sephirot to the seven planets, so that in the old, traditional picture, Saturn belongs to *Binah*, Jupiter to *Chesed*, Mars to *Geburah*, the Sun to *Tiphereth*, Venus to *Hod*, Mercury to *Netzach*, the Moon to *Yesod*, and the Earth to *Malkuth*. One can go further, and see how the Ten Commandments of Moses connect with the Sephirot and the planets. Then we see, for instance, that the commandment 'Thou shalt not steal' is in the place of Mercury, god of doctors, merchants and thieves. 'Thou shalt not commit adultery' is found in close connection with Venus. 'Thou shalt not bear false witness', the injunction not to give a false reflection of the truth, is connected with the Moon, whereas the commandment that brings us face to face with the immediate world around us—telling us that it is better not to covet our neighbour's wife, servants, ox, ass and so forth—belongs to *Malkuth*, the world in which we live. One can, in fact, find connections with each commandment and its planetary Sephira (singular of Sephirot).

Study of Kabbalah came to prominence among the Jewish scholars who gathered together in Spain during the thirteenth century. From there it was taken up by, among others, Ramon Llull (*c.* 1232–1315) and Pico della Mirandola (b. 1463) who reinterpreted Kabbalah in a purely Christian way. There is, in Judaic Kabbalah, sometimes an eleventh Sephira, or quality, but this hardly ever appears in the Christian versions of the Sephirotic Tree. Both Llull and della Mirandola, however, claimed to have made Jewish converts to Christianity on the strength of their own Kabbalistic studies.

Looking at the dates of the Christian Kabbalists, however, it seems impossible that they could have had anything to do with the building of Rosslyn. Even Pico della Mirandola who died in 1494, some seven years after the construction work on the chapel was completed, is highly unlikely to have exerted much of an influence over Earl William Sinclair, his wife Elizabeth Douglas and Sir Gilbert de la Haye, the architects and designers of Rosslyn, even though his dates allow for the distant possibility. He died at the age of 31, and would have been too young to have any meaningful connection with Rosslyn. None of the other Renaissance Kabbalists lived at the time of the building of Rosslyn, and yet . . .

When we look at the version of the Sephirotic Tree of the English alchemist and Rosicrucian Robert Fludd (1574–1637) we find that he has turned the tree round into its mirror image. This is not surprising when we compare, for instance, the design of a Christian church with a Jewish temple. We enter a temple from the east, and move towards the Holy of Holies, in the west. In a Christian church we enter from the west and move towards the altar in the east. Just as the temple is reversed, so is the Sephirotic Tree in a Christian context.

However, on 10 May 1924, Rudolf Steiner, the philosopher, educator and founder of the spiritual science anthroposophy, gave a talk to the workers engaged on the reconstruction of the Goetheanum. Situated in Dornach, Switzerland, this is the headquarters of the Anthroposophical Society, containing the offices that take a close interest in anthroposophical endeavours all over the world. The original Goetheanum, a magnificent structure in wood, was destroyed by arson. The new Goetheanum was built in concrete, one of the first buildings to be built of this material on such a scale. It was Steiner's habit to speak to the workers on a wide variety of topics, and on this occasion he gave yet another picture of the Sephirotic Tree in which we notice certain changes (see Fig. 2).

At first one might be tempted to think that Rudolf Steiner simply made a mistake, but he was not given to error in such subjects, and as we place Steiner's Sephirotic Tree over the ground plan of Rosslyn we find something quite unexpected and extraordinary. Like the Christian Kabbalists of the Renaissance such as Fludd, Steiner maintained the mirror image of the traditional Hebrew version but he put some of the spiritual qualities, the Sephirot, in different places. He put *Tiphereth*, Beauty, in the place where traditionally, one would expect to find *Geburah*, Life and Strength. *Geburah* he now connects with the Powers or Elohim, the Spirits of Form, and the life of the Sun, whereas before it was placed under the sign of Mars and the influence of the Principalities.

This seems to me to be a happy adjustment of the more traditional picture: the placement of the spiritual source of life in the central Sephira, which stands for the Sun and the Exusiai or Powers, referred to in the Hebrew version of Genesis as the Elohim. Steiner did the same with *Hod*, Splendour, and *Yesod*, Foundation, reversing the places where one might expect to find them.

Let us now consider Rosslyn and its carvings, and see what is revealed

Rudolf Steiner's Sephirotic Tree (10 May 1924)

Left Pillar	*Centre Pillar*	*Right Pillar*
Mercy	*Mildness*	*Justice*

Kether
Seraphim

Chokhma   **Binah**
Cherubim   Thrones/Saturn

Chesed   **Tiphereth**
Dominions/Jupiter   Principalities/Mars

Geburah
Powers/Sun

Netzach   **Yesod**
Virtues/Venus   Archangels/Mercury

Hod
Angels/Moon

Malkuth
Human beings/Earth

Fig. 2

when we compare Steiner's picture of the Sephirotic Tree with the layout of the chapel.

First, we notice the three pillars in the farthest east of the building. Facing them from the west we see that the south aisle, containing images from the Old Testament including Moses and Abraham, is the one connected to the Pillar of Justice, while the aisle in which Christ's Passion is depicted, the north aisle, is dominated by the Pillar of Mercy. The central aisle is watched over by a representation of the Madonna and Child, and we feel the rightness of seeing this in connection with the quality of Mildness, represented by the central pillar.

In the east of the chapel is represented the Magi of Matthew's Gospel, the Three Kings, as well as the kingly child whom they journeyed to honour with their gifts. Another king, Robert the Bruce, is depicted in the east of Rosslyn. Whether heavenly or earthly, *Kether*, the Crown, belongs to this part of the building. The congregation in the chapel, of course, face eastwards and their attention is drawn again to the Most High God, the Father Ground of Creation. They look to the place of *Kether*.

Moving to the south, we find Abraham, Isaac and Melchizedek shown, although the carving of Abraham and Isaac is severely damaged now. The patriarchs Abraham and Isaac and the priest-king Melchizedek represent the quality of *Binah*, Intelligence, which the Hebrew people were to develop through generations on behalf of humankind. The planetary quality here is that of Saturn, the willingness to sacrifice the world in favour of spirit-becoming. It is well known how Abraham at first saw sacrifice in terms of the blood sacrifice of his own son, Isaac, but heavenly powers intervened to show a new way forward.

Opposite them, in the north aisle, there is a carving of an angelic being holding a book closed against his breast (see Fig. 3). Here we see *Chokhma*, Wisdom, which has committed the contents of the Book to heart and no longer needs to open it to find wisdom.

Fig. 3   The Book held to the heart

We cross back to the south aisle and find a picture of devotion. Another angelic form surrenders a heart to the laws of Moses and his priestly rule. Above Moses and the angel yielding his heart, all nine members of the heavenly hierarchies are represented. Not far from these carvings we see a representation of the figure known as St Veronica who braved the anger of the Pharisees and the wrath of the mob to give what help she could to her beloved teacher on His way to crucifixion, using nothing but her best cloth to wipe His brow. There is beauty in these devotional scenes and we are here in the place of *Tiphereth*. The planetary quality in this place is that of Mars, the ordering force through the strength of the word. The Mars aspect of directed activity is present in the offering of the heart, while opposite this figure, in the same window, Moses holds the rod of Aaron as a symbol of ordering force. In his other hand he holds the tablet of the Commandments showing divine law expressed in human language: the Word (see Fig. 4).

Fig. 4   Moses

In the place opposite them, in the north aisle, we see the *Agnus Dei*, the Lamb of God, symbol of Mercy, and the bearded figure of John the Divine pointing to the page of his Gospel where we find the high priestly prayer. This is the place of Mercy, or *Chesed*, and the quality *Gedulah*, Greatness. John was an artist in his description of spiritual realities in the Apocalypse, and here we are in the place of Jupiter, for the quality of the ensouled gesture and the arts. It is in this part of the chapel, too, that we find carved in the architrave, on one side, the harpist distracted from his art of playing by an unruly dog while, on the other side, the dog is now tamed and on a lead. The soul is no longer distracted and is now in command.

In the centre of the chapel, in the aisle of Mildness, we find the place of Strength of Life, *Geburah*, and above our heads we see the inverted pyramid pointing to the centre of the chapel to mark that place. We are reminded that part of the original mission of the Church was to bring warmth and light into the human sphere and to encourage spiritual striving. These we can recognize as Sun qualities within the human soul.

Returning to the south aisle we find the figure of St Margaret holding the fragment of the True Cross which was her most treasured possession in life, in honour of which she founded the Abbey of Dunfermline. It is no exaggeration to say that the moral life of the ordinary people of Scotland was, for many years, inspired by Queen Margaret's saintly example. Next to her we find a mounted knight, symbol of manly virtue (see Fig. 5). Close to these two we find a couple bound by a scroll of scripture exemplifying the pious life (see Fig. 6). This is the place of *Yesod* or Foundation. The Mercury quality of allowing something new to arise out of meaningful human encounter is here depicted in the carvings of St Margaret and the knight and the reverent couple next to them. In the ceiling above them are depicted the four Archangels of the Seasons, and we bear in mind that the sphere of Mercury is that of the Archangels.

Fig. 5   St Margaret and the True Cross; the knight

Fig. 6   The couple bound by piety

Facing these carvings, in the north aisle, we find a carving showing a mother and child resolutely turning away from a demon with ass's ears, to face an angel bearing a long-stemmed cross. Near to these are representations of the Crucifixion and of the tomb found empty on the Third Day. Here are clear pictures of Overcoming, or *Netzach*, the ordinary person's victory over temptation and Christ's victory over death. The mother depicted here with her child is a reminder of the Venus quality of caring, and her whole gesture and demeanour, rejecting the demon that tempts her, is typical of that higher Venus aspect of discrimination with regard to what is essential (see Fig. 7).

Moving to the west, standing in the west door, we look back into the chapel and see the wealth of carving, the stained-glass windows and the wonderfully decorated ceiling and we feel the splendour of the building. This is the place of *Hod*, or Splendour. This is the place of the Moon and we find that at once we have to arrange our manifold sense-impressions into order, perhaps to preserve the memory of what we have seen in this

Fig. 7   Overcoming the demonic temptation

remarkable edifice. These activities are often connected with the Moon aspect of the human soul.

Leaving the chapel and stepping out into the fresh air we are in the world again, the realm in which we all find ourselves striving together. This is *Malkuth*, the Kingdom, or the realm of human activity.

Looking at the traditional version of the Sephirotic Tree we can find no clear connection between it and Rosslyn. Even turning to Fludd's reversed Tree there are difficulties in seeing connections. Yet with Steiner's picture we find a clear resonance between the Kabbalistic Tree and the interior of Rosslyn Chapel.

Is it possible that Sinclair, Elizabeth Douglas and Gilbert de la Haye had some clear understanding of those esoteric Christian principles underlying the transformed Kabbalah? Certainly, if we accept Rudolf Steiner's version of the Tree of the Sephirot given to the Goetheanum workers in May of 1924, we find a reflection of it in Rosslyn that is as resonant as it is remarkable. Templar principles that some say survived to inform the construction of such places as Rosslyn are clearly identified by such

Fig. 8   The celestial hierarchies

commentators as Dr Tim Wallace-Murphy. Could those Templar principles have arisen out of the same spiritual impulse that made its way through esoteric Judaism to gradually find its shape and meaning in Christian Rosicrucian esotericism? If so, it casts yet another sidelight on the strange spiritual eclecticism that goes to make up Rosslyn Chapel.

Peter Snow writes: 'I first became interested in Rosslyn Chapel when, as an Upper School teacher at the Edinburgh Rudolf Steiner School, I agreed to teach a three-week block to our 16- and 17-year-olds on the theme of the Holy Grail. I had visited Rosslyn Chapel before that, but was now alerted to its connections with the Grail and its alleged links to the Knights Templar, or rather to those who kept the ideas, practices and ideals of the Templars alive. Dr Tim Wallace-Murphy, among many others, has pointed to the Templar influences within the chapel, and these are readily identifiable. Less obvious, however, is the informing presence of Kabbalah. It is said that one of the early Templar Knights, the Comte de Champagne, had a Kabbalistic school at his court. If so, this alone indicates an awareness and respect for Kabbalistic principles among the Templars, who were notably eclectic in their spiritual quest. How important Kabbalah was for the Templars and how much it influenced their approach to the world is, however, a topic for another time and place. This essay is the result of my own interest in the chapel and those spiritual streams that were alive in its building.

Notes
1. Tim Wallace-Murphy, *The Templar Legacy and the Masonic Inheritance within Rosslyn Chapel* (Friends of Rosslyn, Roslin 1994).
2. Peter Snow, *A Rosslyn Treasury* (Floris Books, Edinburgh 2009).

The Contemporary Relevance of the Message of Mani

Christine Gruwez

The Manichaean stream went through many transformations—from the Ismaili and the School of the Ishraqyun and others in the East to the Cathars, Knights Templar and others from the West.

The main question, however, is how to live and practise this impulse today.

More and more every individual from every part of the world is confronted with destabilizing events that belong to our time. We have become 'spectators', not able to manage or take part in the phenomena. What can be done?

The Manichaean path can teach us not only how to overcome this state of inertia or 'spectatorship' but also how, in the course of the process, to redeem the forces of evil that are at work.

In historical terms, Manichaeism is a doctrine that was preached by its founder, the Persian Mani who lived from AD 216 to 276. It was also set down in various writings. At the start of the twentieth century these writings came to light. Although the texts are fragmentary, they make it possible to have an overview of the content and import of Mani's message.

Mani deliberately gave his gospel a universal slant. In the Cologne Mani Codex, discovered in 1967, we read the following: '. . . So at that time I was sent out through the gracious pleasure of my all-blessed Father, to come into the world so that through me the creation should be hallowed and so that He, through me, should reveal the truth of His gnosis in the midst of the peoples and religions . . .'[1]

It is characteristic of Manichaeism that it attempts to integrate its views of the meaning and significance of good and evil in terms of a human image. Cosmogony and anthropology go hand in hand. Evil is not something that just happens to human beings: on the contrary the nature of humanity is made up both of the forces of light and the forces of darkness. These forces are first and foremost cosmic forces—that is to say, they operate from without.

The story of creation as told by Mani in dramatic images says that these forces were mingled together in the very beginning of the creation process. This mingling gave rise to the substance which was to give birth to the creation of the cosmos and the Earth. Humanity was likewise created from these two forces, at which point these become ethical forces in that the human individual becomes aware that both forces are written into his nature in the form of inclinations. Light and darkness are creative principles and both are needed if creation is to be achieved. They become good and evil in humanity, in so far as these inclinations become part of human consciousness.

The history of creation finds its definition in humanity. But this final definition is at the same time the approach to a new creation—a creation in which every human being now has the possibility, at least by tendency, to become a creative ethical agent. All human beings have come into existence from the combination of light and darkness and are able to bring the two into an interactive relationship because they carry both within themselves. The possibility of oneself becoming a creative ethical agent is one to which Manichaeism attributes particular importance. This is because the aim of the process is the gradual redemption of the evil through the action of the good. This is not so much an external struggle as a progressive inner development.

One of the Fathers of the Church, St Augustine (354–430), spent nine years as an adherent of the Manichees who at that time had a large following in Western Europe. It appears from his own recorded dialogues with representatives of the Manichaean community that this very point was one where he found a personal fundamental difficulty.

In his view it is not for human beings to redeem evil. Augustine's thesis that evil is not a substance, but rather a non-ens or non-entity (a force or power which is disembodied, that is, of spiritual substance), became the prevailing doctrine in the Roman Catholic Church.[2]

The increasing relevance of the message of Mani for our own times may be inferred from the importance that is given to evil in the world-wide debate about terrorism. I would like, for instance, to quote the American moral philosopher Susan Neiman, who said in an interview with the Netherlands journal *Nieuwe Rotterdamse Courant*, 'Anyone who wants to get to the crux of the problem of the world is bound at some point to hit upon the problem of evil' (27 November 2004).

Her criticism of the thinking in the Age of Enlightenment is connected to the fact that the thinkers of that period did not manage to reach more than a mere awareness, at most, of the existence of evil. Compared to the refusal of the scholastic tradition even to credit evil with existence, this was nonetheless a first step. But the intellectual recognition of evil is not enough. As Neiman puts it in the same interview: 'The attempt to solve the problem of evil in an intellectual manner would be a kind of betrayal. Having done that, you could dismiss the problems of the world just by shrugging your shoulders. The awareness that things in the world are not as they should be compels us to look for practical solutions.'

A consciousness of the reality of evil is certainly not enough, but it may well be a necessary beginning. After we become conscious of evil as an issue, we may find ourselves faced with certain questions: for example, the question as to whether we are concerned with the *dissolution* or the *redemption* of evil. Is it a matter of preventing evil and extirpating it whenever necessary? Or is it actually the case that evil requires to be redeemed? In the latter case, we are first confronted with the question what our conception of this should be. How do we address a research project of this nature, supposing such a thing to be possible? At the same time a second thematic vista opens up which we can express to ourselves thus: how or in what way can I recognize evil, and how do I get to know it?

In the last resort, all this depends on the question of the essential nature of evil. If I acquire an insight into its nature, I will learn what evil is—just as we only get to understand a person when we have been acquainted with this person over a long period of time. Getting to know evil is not the same as asking where the actual originating cause of evil is to be found, or what the effects of evil are. On the whole, when the term 'evil' is used, the reference is to that which evil has brought about. Our regard is focused on the effects of evil, on what evil does, in relation to oneself and to other human beings.

At this point Neiman introduces a distinction between the evil that is occasioned by natural catastrophes, and similar accidents, and evil that is occasioned by human beings. She bases her argument here on the view that the suffering caused by the earthquake in Lisbon (1755), for example, is in a completely different category from the suffering that was inflicted in Auschwitz. But as long as we do not make a real effort to reach a deeper level in enquiring into the nature of evil, this distinction may perhaps seem somewhat arbitrary. Suffering remains suffering, after all.

On the other hand, it is understandable that increasing attention is being paid to the effects of the origins of evil. Why did a certain catastrophe have to happen? Could we have prevented it? Why does someone try to kill another human being? The German philosopher Rüdiger Safranski posed the burning question of whether the western process of civilization—meaning by this term the emancipation of humanity from nature and God—has become something fundamentally unsalutary, whether it has not become something evil. Safranski writes:

> Now human beings have brought into existence a civilization of science and technology. This is their creation. And perhaps this civilization will be just as free in relation to human beings, as human beings were in relation to God: perhaps civilization will pursue a course of its own. (. . .) And what does it mean, if the wilful determination of civilization is stronger than the intention of human beings?[3]

Still more important than the distinction between natural and moral evil is the distinction between the effects of evil and the being that causes these effects. If we take this last question seriously, it means that evil is not just a principle that works anonymously—rather it has the form of an individual being. Even when we enquire into the origin of evil, we are not by any means, to begin with, looking at evil itself. It forms part and parcel of the Manichaean programme that alongside the usual questions we should also put the question of what or who evil actually is. And besides this we need to ask who represents the good?

The mystery of evil

Can a person be initiated into evil? This is, to put it mildly, a rather shocking question! What kind of initiation could we possibly imagine here? And what do we mean by initiation? It usually means a passage through a rite or a situation by which our own being is changed in a radical way. By this change new insights and new faculties have been integrated in our being, which gives us the experience of being reborn. In many cultures, such as ancient Greece, initiation was organized in the context of religious practices. In our time now, however, life itself organizes it for us. We can say now that life itself is an initiation.

In the lecture series *From Symptom to Reality in Modern History*,[4] the Austrian philosopher Rudolf Steiner investigates what it is that is effective in a certain culture as a creative principle, in such a way that all the facts and products of this culture may be understood from the point of view of this principle. This creative principle acts for the whole of a culture or an age as something that is most intimately its own. This close sense of belonging arises in much the same way as with the ancient Mysteries, when the neophyte acquired an insight into reality in the course of the initiation, an insight that became his or her own. Here we can see a parallel between the initiation event on the personal level, and that of the particular era. In this sense Hellenistic culture was dominated by initiation into the Mystery of Life and Death, and in the same way the modern era can be understood as an initiation into the Mystery of Evil. When we speak of evil in this connection, we are not thinking of evil as an outward effect—in terms, that is, of the way in which it is inflicted. Here it is exclusively a matter of the essential form of evil itself. This may be recognized most readily in one of its most intrinsic gestures, namely the gesture of separation.

So what does it mean to be initiated into the Mystery of Evil? It means that the possibility of separating oneself off has become part of the intimate nature of human beings today. To separate oneself off is not just to seek the tranquillity and solitude of nature or to withdraw for a time to one's own room. To separate is the possibility of closing oneself off against one's own environment, of withdrawing oneself from the context in which one is placed. One phenomenon that is in a quite special sense characteristic of the start of the modern period is the discovery of perspective in the early fifteenth century, and it is grounded in this new human faculty of separation. We no longer experience ourselves as part of a surrounding network of circumstances—on the contrary, we detach ourselves from it, we adopt a standpoint of our own and from this point construct the world. This ability to separate represents a valuable quality in the life of every human being and cannot be valued too highly. This is because it opens the door to the human principle of development, namely the ego which is capable of freedom. But at the same time it opens the door to evil.

Here the link between evil and freedom as 'possibilities' comes into view at a still deeper level. In that the ego exercises its freedom independently, this possibility can lead either to a positive development or to a negative one—namely, to the excessive cultivation of the individual's own ego and so to their becoming egotistic. The possibility of separation allows both phenomena. The one is fundamentally inseparable from the other: the sovereign 'Yes' cannot be without the egotistical 'No', and vice versa. An affirmation is only a true affirmation because a denial of the same intensity is equally possible. If we find that we contain in ourselves the possibility of separating ourselves off, this constitutes the first step on the path of becoming acquainted with evil. The essential form of evil involves separation. We do not need to study evil in the light of the various phenomena that we perceive around us because, first of all, what confronts us is generally only the outer effect of evil. However thorough such a study may be, we will not get to know evil by this method, but only what evil brings about in the way of effects. Secondly, we have a direct field of perception that is constantly available to us—namely that which goes on in oneself between the twin poles of separation and belonging, so that this training ground is not just to be found around us but also within us. And this is the very thing that modern Initiation involves. Steiner expresses it thus: '... These forces of evil rule in the universe. The human being must absorb them. In absorbing them, he plants in himself the germ which first makes it possible for him to experience the spiritual life with his consciousness soul[5] ...'[6]

We must distinguish between the two questions 'Where is the original cause of evil to be found?' and 'What effects are occasioned by evil?' What links these two questions together is a third question, 'Who or what is evil?' Only when we get to grips with this third question can we cast light on the first two. The first two problems may still be the subjects of theoretical study, as considered from the point of view of politics, sociology, psychology or some other specialism. But if we go more deeply into the third question, it leads us through a succession of steps whereby the forces of evil are perceived in such a way that they come to be recognized as something peculiar to ourselves.

These steps along the path of becoming a contemporary may also be seen as a Manichaean training path. The approach of historical Manichaeism has been further updated here, so that it opens itself up to the future. The decision to set out on the Manichaean path in order to become truly contemporary can only be a decision taken freely. As citizens of the twenty-first century, however, we are practically compelled at times to put the first and second questions, whether in reaction to an event or as an outburst of disbelief and anger: *How can it happen that all over the world people become the victims of violent outbreaks? Why do people resort to violence?* Here we will find that any possible answers will only hold good until new events come along and overlay the old ones.

The third question, on the other hand, 'Who or what is evil?' is one that does not permit a direct answer. If there were to be such a thing as an answer, then we could only come closer to it by setting out on a journey. But even when we are on this journey, something can happen that is more than just finding an answer or having an answer supplied. Such a happening is related to the initiation event as has been described above. It makes it possible for a person to become a *contemporary*, in the deepest sense of the word.

A Manichaean path of initiation

The initiation process as practised in the ancient Mysteries can be broken down into five distinct steps. The Manichaean training path, similar to the ancient path of initiation, can be described as a journey of five stages which lead to our becoming a contemporary. The five stages are:

1. The spectator
2. Allowing
3. Meeting
4. Being a witness
5. Becoming a contemporary.

It is also possible to describe the phases of this journey in a different way, so that something comes into view from the experience at each stage, thus:

1. Powerlessness
2. Inwardness
3. Contact
4. Being present
5. Being awake.

The first thing we now need to do is to describe each of these stages or steps. Subsequently we will investigate what the mutual relations are between the various steps.

The Manichaean path towards redemption

Step 1—The Spectator/Powerlessness

If we read a newspaper or see the news only occasionally, or if we were able to cut ourselves off completely in such a way that no news of what is happening in the world could penetrate, we are still *spectators* of world events. On the stage of contemporary reality an uninterrupted drama is going on which may at any moment confront us with circumstances that are irreversible. One thing is common to all these circumstances, namely the fact that we are not able to act on or change them in any way.

This places us in an untenable situation. We respond by trying to make the situation bearable, for example by making all kinds of comments, giving vent to our indignation and astonishment or by wanting others to tell us that their view of these events is similar. In other words, we react.

So to the extent that a certain event touches us more closely or affects us personally, we somehow try to believe this state of affairs has not happened or, at least, try to find a way out or a solution. Another possible reaction consists of coming to terms with the fact that in the last resort we are helpless. It is often just a short step from 'I don't know what I should do' to 'It is impossible to do anything about it'. But even in this case our thoughts continue to revolve obsessively around the bare facts so that we continue asking ourselves: 'How could this thing have ever happened?' 'How could such a thing be possible?' 'What sort of time are we actually living in?'

In a wider context we might say that this was the same question as Job cried out in his despair: 'Lord, why me?' In relation to the catastrophes to which his life was subject, he too found himself in the role of the powerless spectator, only being able in the first instance to see that one misfortune after another kept coming to him. If we follow contemporary events from day to day, we can see that one catastrophe treads hard on the heels of the last. It adds up to an endless sequence, in which the same kinds of horror are repeated from day to day.

Loss of heart (the misery will never end, new misery will repeatedly go on confronting us), despair (I can only look on helplessly), insecurity and anxiety (what will happen to us all in the future?), perplexity (I must find a solution, it can't go on like this)—all these are part of being in the role of a spectator or, more precisely stated, we are compelled into this role whether we like it or not.

Step 2—Allowing/Inwardness

First of all it should be made clear that 'allowing' here means letting stillness enter the heart of our being. It is analogous to the great silence that represented the second stage of the path of initiation in the old Mysteries: it means that we allow a stillness to take possession of our innermost heart. All commentaries and reactions, of whatever kind, should be held back. To allow it to become still within us means nothing other than to be prepared to *listen*, to prick up our ears and listen with an ever greater depth and intensity. It does not mean simply 'allowing something to happen', for this would mean coming to terms with the circumstances or resigning oneself to one's fate.

If we are really to hear, we must take what we hear into ourselves—that is, first of all just absorb it and let it penetrate. In other words, we let the events that are acted out on the world stage penetrate deeply within us, so deeply that it might be said that we make them a part of our own being. In this way we create an inner space in which these events can be heard. So long as we are dominated by the compulsion to react, we hear within us only the echo of our own reactions. But if we hold back this flood of reactions, it creates a resonating chamber in which something may be pronounced, and by the same token perceived.

It goes without saying that what we have here is not a 'neutral' proceeding. If in the first step it was still the case that a great part of the strategy of reaction consisted in preventing the accompanying pain from entering our awareness, in the second step, when such strategies are no longer to be applied, we must admit the pain as well. To create a resonating chamber is a painful and laborious task. One is rarely successful on the first attempt. One penetrates to a deeper level of that which expresses itself on the surface in the form of events. So long as we remain focused on the surface, we will be able to answer the first and second questions to a great extent, but the third question involves moving from the first step of being a spectator towards an inward acceptance. The circumstances are then no longer over there outside me, but become a part of my own being. In the end what is involved is a process of integration. I no longer want just to study what has happened, to consider it and look into it—instead, I aim to allow it to be and to absorb it into myself, completely and unconditionally.

Step 3—Meeting/Contact

This inner stillness, through which a space of listening comes into being, can moreover become a stillness which feels as if we are waiting for something which has yet to be completed. This is the moment at which the transition between allowing and completion takes place. In the phase of allowing I have held myself back in such a way that I have become a point, so to speak, a point that is surrounded by a listening space. In being able to wait I become ready to receive. I become a kind of vessel. The time and the patience that are needed in order to sustain a listening attitude correspond to the time and the patience that are needed for something in me to form this vessel. When this has been done, the phase of completion can begin. This now corresponds to the third phase of the initiation process. I come to be initiated into the essential nature of contemporary history. This essential nature carries the seal of evil: a seal that I have become familiar with to the extent to which it finds expression in all those events which are the effects of the capacity of human beings to separate themselves from the world.

Now, however, I am face to face with contemporary happenings, and all those questions that were still in the air in the spectator phase, that is to say, all 'my' questions and all the answers as well that I have been holding back in the phase of inwardly allowing, have now turned upside down and have become a single burning invitation: *Look at me, redeem me*. This is the request that evil addresses to me!

The acute and chronic distress that I felt in the spectator phase is no longer just my own, it is the distress of the times. Nor is it just the case that I acquire this realization—it completes itself in me as well, it comes true. From now on I have been initiated into the Mysteries of Time.

As a result of my becoming a vessel, by holding myself back completely, something happens to make me capable of absorbing and carrying something other than myself. Out of my willingness to be a carrier of the fate of our times (being a *contemporary*), a power is born which comes to meet me and touches me. Willingness and contact meet, completing the birth of this power that makes it possible for us to be contemporaries (see *Step 5*). This coming together involves the acting out of the mystery of that which I myself accomplish and that which is accomplished in me. These two processes become an indivisible unity, but can nonetheless be distinguished from one another. I look into the face of the time as it really is, while on the other hand, in my willingness to bear it, something comes to be redeemed. That which I let die in myself comes back to life at the same moment, as an active power that enables me to play my part in bearing this burden.

Step 4—Being a witness/Being present

This sustaining power can be recognized in me as an open possibility, a potentiality that may be actualized in any situation whatever. It is enough that I should focus myself on the centre of this sustaining power, and everything that I say and do will happen from this centre. Presence of mind is nothing but a habitual focus on the centre of this power that we find in ourselves. This is what is known as giving testimony.

So it absolutely is not a matter of talking *about this power* that has come to birth within me. That would actually mean the immediate cessation of its effectiveness. It is much rather a matter of speaking *from the centre of this power*. It continues to live, so to speak, and acts through my being and my actions. My being and my actions are the medium through which it has an effect on the outside world. The presence of this power is an abiding fact. As a possibility it cannot cease to exist, so it depends entirely on me to what extent it becomes effective or not.

A misunderstanding could arise at this point. It might be supposed that the presence of this sustaining power would mean that I have now found solutions for those problems which left me feeling helpless in the spectator phase. It is certainly not the case that solutions are offered here. But what, from this time on, forms part of the options at my disposal is that rather than a solution being found redemption takes place. There is an ongoing interchange between this quality of taking up the burden of the world and myself, as well as between myself and that which is happening around me. This interchange may well be compared with a piece of woven material, on which work is continuing all the time. This comes into being between myself and the times I live in, and the patterns that are thereby created bear witness.

Step 5—Becoming a Contemporary/Being awake

What can we do? Is there anyone who can do something? Is it possible to do anything at all? These questions are an integral part of being a spectator, in which one is confronted with events without being able to change them in any way. But as a contemporary who is involved in the process of becoming, I am no longer confronted with circumstances out there, but carry them in myself. Every circumstance is in any case a result; it is always the effect of something else. What I start to carry within myself is not the effect of the event, but the thing or the person that has caused it. This thing or person has become a part of my own being. That which acts out there in the world also acts in me, and in the very same way. As a result of this I recognize that it is not that something like a solution is to be found somewhere out there; rather, it is possible for a redemption to occur.

When we have reached this point, we no longer need to make any distinction between solution and redemption. These two processes can even, if we act with a little skill, occur simultaneously.

Contemporary history has come awake in me. It can speak out at any moment, and what it communicates can be recognized at any moment in the circumstances themselves. In the first phase I happen upon circumstances, and then look for what is trying to speak through them. In the fifth phase the reverse process is acted out: contemporary history speaks, and then I turn my attention to the circumstances. In the first phase there is only the possibility of enduring events. In the last phase I have acquired the willingness to engage with events, to enter into whatever may chance to happen.

Cross-connections

The five steps I have described take place over a certain period of time, rather like the consecutive phases of a metamorphosis sequence. To this extent what we have here is in actual fact a path along which we travel, subject to development in time. Some steps take a lot of time as they are steps that need to be repeatedly resumed and re-attempted. This however does not exclude the possibility that the various training steps may occur in parallel, and become involved in mutual interactivity. They now begin to mesh together, so that in the end a single organism comes into being.

The existence of this kind of mutual interaction can be seen in the fact that a clear reversal takes place between the first step and the fifth. The first training step is dominated by events that impinge on us from without and by the feeling of powerlessness—I do not know what I should do—while the last step is characterized by a completely different attitude—I know what is to be done, never mind what may happen.

Likewise between the second and the fourth steps we find a special connection. The second phase is characterized by the activity of allowing what is outside me to exist within me as I take it into myself. In the fourth phase, that which I have taken in and absorbed in the hidden depths of my inner being now acts through me on the outside world. In a certain sense it is possible to experience the second phase as a kind of darkening of the light. Everything one is aware of in the form of explanations, everything that one has ready in the way of solutions, and even all the past experience that one has accumulated—all this is put to silence. In the depths of our being it becomes very quiet, and with the accompanying drilling sensation of pain we may feel that we have been abandoned. In this phase of pure receptivity we find ourselves alone with contemporary history and with ourselves. In the initial phase it was possible for us to proclaim our unease, disapproval or outrage. The intention to retain it, so as to be able to take events into oneself, is a lonely enterprise. It is not possible to share it with anybody, or we would run the risk of falling back into the state we were in during the first phase. We might at most be able to recognize this quite particular colour of loneliness in a fellow human being by comparing it with the loneliness we have experienced ourselves.

The fourth step, on the other hand, consists of an uninterrupted stream of communication, which does not issue from myself (that would mean falling back into the first phase) but from that which speaks through me. This produces an effect as if a central point in myself were the source of a light that beams outward or, more accurately stated, of a light that beams through this central point to the outside world. The activity is now directed not inwards but outwards, and has an unmistakably rousing quality, calling us to wake up. This consciousness of being awake may well make me feel as if there is an unquenchable spring of profound joy bubbling up within me—a joy that does not need any external occasion, but grows from the sense of 'being touched' in the third phase.

The third step is the point on which this five-stage path hinges. The first and second steps represent the process through which one sets out on the journey that is to lead to the recognition, assimilation and transformation of the phenomena of contemporary history in a conscious self. The fourth and fifth steps lead us back towards the outside world, so that now the phenomena of contemporary history become transparent. That this reversal is possible is essentially connected with the third and central step. When I enter the third phase, I find the strength of resurrection, I rise above the powerlessness, pain and sense of abandonment that marked the preceding phases. What comes to meet me now, what addresses me, is the very being that lives and acts in these contemporary phenomena. It is this being that awakens me to become the voice of the time—that calls me to be a *Contemporary*.

It is possible to find images for each of these phases that reveal, either as an isolated picture or in interrelationship, something of the essence of this training path. The Madonna, as she is presented as a quite definite type in the icon paintings of the Orthodox Church, may be taken as an image of the second step—I am thinking of the Panhagia Plathythera here, or the Madonna extending her arms. The icon shows a standing Madonna, as a rule depicted as far as the waist, with arms spread wide open—an impressive, but at the same time inward gesture. The region of the heart opens up and offers space for that which asks to be taken in. In this picture we hear the voice of the soul's attitude of an unconditional willingness of 'allowing': a receiving of that which is to come.

An image of the third step is the symbol and sign of the cross. The cross is the place of completion *par excellence* and, uniquely, the place where the willingness to die and the life-giving force meet, so that resurrection becomes a reality. On one side of the cross stands Mary, who takes the deeply piercing pain of the event into herself, and on the other stands John, who gives testimony to the Spirit. Christ on the cross refers to the intimate connection between these two when he speaks to them. John can only give testimony to the extent to which Mary becomes one who listens in stillness—that is to say, having gone beyond any kind of reaction.

Here it becomes apparent how far the Manichaean training path is also a path of Christian training. Furthermore, the kind of experience that one goes through on this training path is intimately related to the experience of Saul, who became Paul on the road to Damascus. It has to do with an encounter with the essential nature of the risen Christ, and so involves ourselves coming to share in the living forces of resurrection, which have continued to act in human beings and over the world ever since the Easter event.

Seeing things from the point of view of the anthroposophical under-standing of human nature, the transition from the first to the second step means that we allow the sphere of emotional reaction to become calm so that we can pass through it into the region of the organization of the life forces. The pain that raged on the astral level in the first phase can now be taken into the etheric, with all that the etheric is able to provide in the way of healing and regeneration. The etheric receives the pain that has come into being in the astral. For this purpose, silence is essential, and it must be a form of silence that creates space. The second step involves finding a way of accessing the depths of our life organization. The fourth step is the inversion of the second. The life that repeatedly rises from the dead is now raised to the level of consciousness. This is nothing other than to render testimony to the fact that one is continually in contact with this life-resuscitating power, which recognizes itself in consciousness and in this form proceeds to act on the outside world.

1. Being a spectator
                                 } Astral/Etheric[7]
2. Allowing

3. Completion

4. Being a witness
                                 } Etheric/Astral—Consciousness
5. Becoming a contemporary

The Manichaean training path basically starts between the first and the second phase. The first phase brings with it all kinds of reactions, from indifference to rage, along with all the intermediate emotions. And yet this first phase is necessary. This is because it is not certain that we may awaken as the result of our being shocked. Even if we try with all the resources available to us to dull this wakeful state back into insensibility, the fact that we have once been awake can no longer be undone, and it increases the chance that on the next opportunity we will again come awake. Being shocked gives us a brief window of opportunity, which lasts just as long as the alarm bell continues to sound. Waking up means to abandon the cellar of our constructed and cherished securities for an extended period and to view our surroundings.

What is actually going on here? There are still escape routes avail-able, making it possible for us to avoid the opportunity that is offered by the second phase. We may still, for some time and with great seriousness, go in search of something that might improve the situation, some form or other of healing. We may stake our all on bringing about some change. We may just cut loose or drift into an attitude of protest that becomes increasingly worn out until it finally issues in a litany of lamentation, where all we can do is to complain in such terms as 'What kind of times do we live in?' or 'Who would ever have thought such a thing could be possible?' The need to find someone to blame makes us continue to go round in circles. In this context the term 'they' crops up quite frequently in expressions such as 'What can they be thinking of?' or 'What have they done now?' Depending on the point of view and the associated perspective, this 'they' can in principle include practically anybody. This is a necessary result of the spectator consciousness of the first step.

We are neither the author nor the director of the drama that is being played out on a daily basis. The only option remaining to us is to react to happenings in one way or another.

But actively looking for 'solutions' is also a reaction. And to *react* means that we have allowed something to be done to us. This attitude of passivity, of being on the receiving end, is not something that we can put a stop to by making ourselves master of the situation, as a superficial view might suppose.

The Manichaean training path will lead us to this goal in the end. But it will be in a different way and by following quite other paths than if we were to attempt to gain power over events starting from our original situation of powerlessness. This is the reason why the transition between the first two steps, and everything that happens in the interval between them, is of particular importance. But I would like to point out here that I am in no way pronouncing judgement on the search for a solution in a difficult situation and most certainly am not suggesting that this should be 'forbidden'. I am only making the point that the Manichaean path is a different kind of path. In the Manichaean approach it is not a matter of looking for a solution, or at least that is not the only matter of concern: first and foremost we are looking for redemption. The intention of Manichaeism is directed towards the redemption of evil. Anyone who wants to move in this direction has no other option but to put an end to the pattern of reactions in his or her own being. This results initially in the termination of the reactive pattern but it does not end the feeling of powerlessness. This is actually likely to increase and now shows itself for the first time in all its vehemence. But this is the very thing that gives us the real opportunity of making progress.

Christine Gruwez studied philosophy and linguistics at the Katholieke Universiteit, Louvain, Belgium.

She came into contact with anthroposophy through the Waldorf School in Antwerp, which her four children attended and where she was a teacher from 1976 to 1986. She then taught for another decade in the Waldorf Education Training Programme.

The publication of Bernard Lievegoed's The Battle for the Soul[*] *renewed her contact with the Manichaean impulse. She had studied the language and texts during her time at university. From then on, a major research issue for her has been and continues to be how to actualize what historical Manichaeism has initiated in human history. She is much travelled in the Near and Middle East, particularly in Iran, the culture in which Mani was born.*

Notes

1. From the Cologne Mani Codex (108–110), German translation by Ludwig Koenen and Cornelia Römer. Quoted in *Mani, Auf den Spuren einer verschollenen Religion* (Mani—In Search of a Lost Religion) (Herder Verlag, Freiburg/Basel 1993).
2. Augustine, *De Moribus ecclesiae Catholicae*, Chap. 10 et seq.
3. Rüdiger Safranski, *Das Böse Oder Das Drama der Freiheit* (Evil or the Drama of Freedom) (Herder Verlag, Freiburg/Basel 1997).
4. Rudolf Steiner, *From Symptom to Reality in Modern History*, tr. A.H. Parker (Rudolf Steiner Press, London) (GA 185).
5. The term consciousness soul can be understood as the faculty by which a human being can in an independent way rely on his inner self to give an orientation to his life theme. At the same time, this faculty can lead to egoism and striving for personal profit.
6. Rudolf Steiner, *From Symptom to Reality in Modern History*, op. cit., Chap. 5.
7. The etheric is the organism that regulates and sustains the life processes in all living beings, interconnecting them to each other. The basis for mutual confidence is formed through this interconnection. The astral is the carrier of feelings, emotions, desires and reactive thoughts. It is the organism that facilitates awareness and, in human beings, the aptitude towards self-consciousness.

---

[*] Bernard Lievegoed, *The Battle for the Soul* (Hawthorn Press, 1994).

Pioneers of the Anthroposophical Movement and the Order of the Knights Templar

Frans Lutters

The following contribution was given out of a lifelong connection with the impulses of the pioneers in anthroposophy. It is Frans' deep concern that their impulses are not forgotten but are part of present and future spiritual concerns. In a world that needs direction for the future it is necessary that old friends from across the threshold can find fruitful encounter and their spiritual roots again in working together with us. These words convey the deeper meaning underlying the written article.

It was in the year 1302 that the famous mystic and alchemist Ramon Llull met Jacques de Molay, the last Grand Master of the Order of the Knights Templar. Llull landed on the island of Cyprus in 1299 to convert Muslims and Jews to Christianity. But he was poisoned by a servant, nearly died and is said to have struggled for life for 40 days. It was Jacques de Molay who took him to his castle and treated him until he recovered.[1]

This was an extraordinary situation because the two men had very different opinions on the future of the Order of the Knights Templar. Ramon Llull, who knew Philip the Fair, the young King of France, told the King that it was important that the Order of the Knights Templar and the Order of St John, the Hospitallers, should be united under one single Order of the Holy Spirit. Only then could Jerusalem be regained from the Saracens.

Jacques de Molay, the Grand Master of the Templars, was completely opposed to this plan. He would not relinquish or dilute the existing form of the Order of the Templars, however demanding it might be. After his recovery Ramon left Cyprus but remained faithful to his idea and returned to Paris. The year, 2009, was 700 years after Ramon and Jacques met again but under completely different circumstances. The Knights of the Templar Order were arrested on the dark Friday, 13 October 1307. Jacques was then imprisoned and brought to trial at the Council of Vienne and it was there that Ramon again forwarded his plans for the unification of the knightly orders. He wrote a poem for this occasion which had 1200 verses but, as we can imagine, this was too lengthy for the participants of the council. As a result, he brought only some of his verses and wasn't taken seriously because the King and the Pope had much more important matters to deal with—Jacques de Molay and the Templar Order. Llull was called *Ramon lo Foll* (Ramon the fool).

He ended with the verse:

Holy God,
please bring rain
to drown the evil
oh, the sins are growing![2]

So this second meeting also resolved nothing for Ramon or for Jacques. What would have happened if these two men could have worked together strongly? This remains an open question.

Willem Zeylmans van Emmichoven

Who was Ramon Llull? This became a lifelong question for Willem Zeylmans van Emmichoven, the Dutch psychiatrist and member of the Council of the Anthroposophical Society in Holland. On the eve of 5 January 1924 in Dornach Rudolf Steiner came to him after a lecture and said to him, 'I will speak of your karma in tomorrow's lecture.' At that moment two other people were standing with van Emmichoven. The next day Rudolf Steiner spoke about Ramon Llull and also of two other important personalities in the spiritual history of mankind. He described the initiation of Ramon by a wise old man of the mountain whereby Ramon was taken to the top of the mountain and into the depths of the earth. In his initiation he experienced the heights of the spirit and the depths of the body in his soul.[3]

Willem Zeylmans van Emmichoven thereafter worked on this theme for the rest of his life, although still having doubts about it right up to the end of his life. Zeylmans went to Majorca to visit the place where Ramon Llull founded his language school with twelve other Franciscan monks. They had to learn Arabic and Hebrew, as their intention was to convert Muslims and Jews to Christianity. Just before leaving on a lecture tour to South Africa in 1961, where he died unexpectedly, Zeylmans stated to his son-in-law, Wim Engelbrecht, that he had finally become certain about his karmic connection to Ramon Llull.

With this in mind, we can ask: where is Jacques de Molay to be found in the life of Willem Zeylmans van Emmichoven? Did Llull and de Molay meet again? I have lived with this question for some time and consider it noteworthy that as early as 1924 Willem Zeylmans van Emmichoven was given, as a member of a circle of anthroposophical doctors, a research theme by Rudolf Steiner. The theme that he received was short and clear: Templars and Rosicrucians.

D.N. Dunlop

I would now like to look at another personality from the founding time of the Anthroposophical Society in Britain—Daniel Nicol Dunlop. Dunlop was the founder of the World Energy Conferences, which started in Wembley, London in 1924. Thousands of delegates from all over the world attended the first conference. This organization still exists and in 2010 held its conference in Montreal. Daniel Nicol Dunlop met Rudolf Steiner in person in 1922. It was the Dutch manager Joseph van Leer who brought them together. They sat at the table together—Rudolf Steiner who spoke no English and Daniel N. Dunlop who spoke no German. Joseph van Leer stepped in as translator but what he didn't see was that Rudolf Steiner took the hand of Daniel Dunlop and held it, under the table, during the whole of the conversation. In 1934, during one of his famous summer schools, Dunlop shared the memory of this with his friend Walter Johannes Stein. He made an even more interesting statement, that Rudolf Steiner on this occasion said to him, 'We are brothers.' Eleanor Merry, also an active member of the early British Anthroposophical Society, worked intensely with Dunlop for the last 14 years of his life during which time he told her that Rudolf Steiner gave him an insight into a former life of his where he, Dunlop, had been a member of the innermost circle of the Order of the Knights Templar.[4]

Walter Johannes Stein

To find out more about this inner circle we have to look at the work of Walter Johannes Stein who was a teacher at the first Rudolf Steiner School in Stuttgart. In 1933 he left Germany for England because of the political situation, he being half Jewish. Daniel Dunlop invited Stein to work for his organization on World Economics as Stein had already worked with Dunlop during the first Anthroposophical World Conference in London 1928 when a new publishing house had been founded, the Orient Occident Publishing House based in Stuttgart, The Hague and London.

Many books came out at the 1928 World Conference in London but one book had already been published in 1927. It was a reprint of a long dramatic poem by Zacharias Werner, a contemporary of J.W. von Goethe in Weimar. The book is called *Die Söhne des Tals* (The Sons of the Valley).[5] Goethe was highly critical of the work of Werner because he felt that some of the secrets of Masonic ritual were described in the book. It was Goethe's opinion that what is esoteric should stay esoteric, in other words remain hidden.[6] It could be that Goethe, in this statement, is also referring to the main character of the poem, Robert d'Heredon. The eighteenth grade in the Masonic ritual is called the 'Prince of the Rose Cross' but in Scotland it is also called the 'Knight d'Heredon'.

Stein wrote the introduction and notes to this reprint. He states that the term 'Sons of the Valley' is important because Werner connects it in his book with a hidden valley in Jerusalem called 'Josaphat' and Stein recalls a lecture by Rudolf Steiner (contained in the *The East in the Light of the West*[7]) where he states the name 'Josaphat' derives etymologically from 'Bodhisattva'. This refers to the Spiritual Council of the Twelve Bodhisattvas with Christ in the centre. The Sons of the Valley form the inner circle of the Templar Order and the members of this inner circle experience Christ Jesus himself as their Grand Master. The poem states that there are not only Sons but also Brothers of the Valley which are, according to Stein, the Bodhisattvas themselves. Rudolf Steiner describes this spiritual community as the Council of the Holy Spirit. The Sons of the Valley are on the earthly plane connected to the Spiritual Council of the Holy Spirit, i.e. the Brothers of the Valley.

We can ask here if the Templars stayed in contact with the Master Jesus, who is the Spiritual Master leading esoteric Christianity. Rudolf Steiner refers to Anastasius Grün who states in his poem *Schutt* (Ruins)[8] that every year at Easter it is possible to meet the Master Jesus at Golgotha. Did the first Templar Hughes de Payens and, before him, the leader of the First Crusade, Godfrey de Bouillon, both have the experience of meeting the Master Jesus at Golgotha? The Master Jesus helped to build the temple of the body to receive the Christ, as the Solomonic Jesus, during the baptism by John in the River Jordan.[9]

And Easter was there once again,
When Christ was looking down
Through the valley into town
The cross was broken down from many roofs
Only one remains on his grave ...

Und wieder Ostern war's, vom Ölberg wieder
Sah Christus in das Tal zur Stadt hinab:
Das Kreuz, gestürzt ist's von den Zinnen nieder,
Nur eins steht schüchtern noch ob seinem Grab.

Anastasius Grün, Schutt (Ruins). (*Fünf Ostern 3*)

Walter Johannes Stein was very impressed by the personality and
spiritual abilities of D.N. Dunlop. When he wrote the introduction to the
work of Zacharias Werner, Stein did not know that in Dunlop he was
meeting with someone who, according to Steiner, was connected to this
inner circle of Templars in a former life. In Werner's poem is a central
figure, Robert d'Heredon, who is purported to be the unknown son of
Jacques de Molay. Jacques is concerned about the safety of Robert at the
time he leaves Cyprus around 1305, having been ordered to Paris by King
Philip IV to speak about the future of the Order.

Later Robert d'Heredon returned to Scotland and took with him the
secrets of the Templar Order, having become involved in the secret inner
circle of the Order. Some contemporary researchers claim that a group of
Knights left France just before the Templars were arrested and went to
Scotland. Some also say they landed on the Island of Mull and stayed there
a short time. Many legends say that these Templars fought alongside
Robert the Bruce, although there is no outward historical confirmation of
this, and that they lived around the longest Scottish Lake, Loch Awe in
Argyll.

Daniel Dunlop had been raised by his grandfather on the Isle of Arran,
very near Argyll, on the west coast of Scotland.

One day when he was about ten or eleven years old, it was raining and
very stormy and his clothes were very wet, and as evening drew on the
storm increased. He and his grandfather were in the little house with no
other human being at hand. As he lay in his little bed a great feeling of
eeriness crept over him, so he asked his grandfather to allow him to
come into his bed. There, in the arms of his grandfather he fell asleep.
But that night the old man died, and when the boy awakened he found
himself lying in a pool of blood. He was shocked but not frightened.
He stood up and stirred the fire, dried his wet clothes in front of it and
sat on a little bench in the window looking out to sea. He had fried a
herring and began to eat it, and after this little meal he began to think.

He said to me: 'I was fully conscious that my grandfather was dead
and that I was alone, but I had no feeling of hurry. So I started thinking

and my thoughts turned to dreams, and from dreams to visions. I could see myself riding upon a camel and others joined us, and I saw my grandfather, but with another face, on horseback. He was wearing rich white clothes.'[10]

Dunlop told this to his friend Walter Johannes Stein. Was this a past memory of a time when he lived as a Templar Knight? Stein was deeply impressed by this and it was of crucial importance for his own inner life. In 1924, under the guidance of Rudolf Steiner, Walter Johannes Stein had already discovered a former life of his own. In March of that year Stein was attending a religious service held by Karl Schubert for the children of the Waldorf School in Stuttgart. Stein suddenly lost consciousness and was taken out of the room to recover. When Rudolf Steiner heard of this episode he gave Stein a meditation to work with and said to him that this illness would bring him important spiritual development if he could work and meditate with it. As Stein always did things that Rudolf Steiner advised him, because he felt the utmost regard for him, he carried out the work with great intensity.

Two months later he could say to Rudolf Steiner that he had experienced his death in his previous life and again, at the end of August 1924, he discovered that he had died in a former life as the Portuguese Knight of the Order of Christ, Francisco d'Almeida, on the beach below Table Mountain in South Africa. This happened on 1 March 1510. He asked Rudolf Steiner about this whose answer—which Stein wrote down in his diary—was, 'It could well be so.' After this Stein became very involved researching the knightly orders and their mission in the world. He knew very soon that the Order of Christ was founded by the Portuguese King Dionysus to save the Knights Templar who had escaped into his country. At the time Stein wrote the introduction to *The Sons of the Valley*, he had become very knowledgeable about the history and the inner impulses of the Knights Templar and their ongoing work through the Order of Christ.

Jacques de Molay and Ramon Llull

Now I return to the question stated earlier concerning the connection between Jacques de Molay and Ramon Llull. Did Willem Zeylmans van Emmichoven (Ramon Llull) meet the reincarnated Jacques de Molay again in a modern incarnation? And if he did, was it fruitful for the future?

What I have to offer now is still being researched and so my findings need to be viewed as incomplete and left open-ended. But the subject is too important at this moment in history to be silent about and so I take courage and share here some facts that are generally unknown in the history of the anthroposophical movement.

At the Christmas Conference of 1923/1924 the new Council of the Anthroposophical Society was inaugurated. Rudolf Steiner said some words to every member of the Council and asked the members to show their confidence in each member by way of applause. For most of them the applause was long and loud but for one member the applause was shorter and quieter. This was because she was unknown to many members at that time. However she had done a lot of work within the society for many years. She founded the archives. She was a Doctor in Astronomy. She typed one of the Mystery Play texts for the actors one night in Munich so that they could work on the play the next day. And she had lived for years in the same house as Rudolf and Marie Steiner in Berlin yet still she was unknown. Her name was Elisabeth Vreede.

Elisabeth Vreede

Elisabeth Vreede was born, on 16 July 1879 of Dutch origin. As a young girl she was given by her older brother the popular astronomical books of the Frenchman Camille Flammarion who, as well as being a scientist, was involved in spiritual research. Later she studied at the University of Leiden and in 1904 she heard Rudolf Steiner lecture in Amsterdam on 'Mathematics and Occultism'. Her parents were in the Esoteric School of the Theosophical Society and important theosophical leaders such as Colonel Olcott visited their house in The Hague.

Some years later the whole family became connected to Rudolf Steiner. When Rudolf Steiner stayed at their home he held rituals within the Masonic Misraïm setting, something he did from out of his own personal spiritual responsibility. It was Elisabeth who was asked to walk to the Freemason Lodge to borrow the things that were needed for the ritual. On one such an occasion Rudolf Steiner looked out of the window directly across the road to Park Sorgvliet in front of the house and said, 'The Count of St Germain so often visited the Lodge over there. I love The Hague very much because you can still see the golden traces that go through the cobblestones in the streets where the Count of St Germain used to walk.'[11] The 'Vredespaleis' now stands on the site of this Lodge and could be called 'the International Palace for World Peace'.

So Elisabeth as a young girl was already taken seriously by Rudolf

Steiner. Later she asked him why no one seemed to see her and why she had so few real friends. She could even travel without a ticket because the conductor wouldn't notice her. The answer was unexpected: 'You should not be here. You intended to come (incarnate) at the end of the century, but because of the necessity of working together with me you decided to come to Earth earlier. Therefore many of your karmic connections are not here yet.' On another occasion she wondered why she never had accidents. Rudolf Steiner, standing with some others, replied to them, 'It is good to travel with her; she will never be involved in an accident because in a former life she died in a natural catastrophe and therefore she is free from accidents now.' Later he told her that this catastrophe happened just after the time that Christ was in a physical body on Earth. (Elisabeth Vreede confided these statements to her close friends such as Hilda Verrijn Stuart-Alma.)

After the Christmas Conference of 1923/1924 Elisabeth Vreede led the Section for Astronomy and Mathematics within the newly founded School for Spiritual Science. She made horoscopes for disabled children when Rudolf Steiner gave his course on Curative Education. He told her she had to look at the moment of conception, and that in the ten moon months (i.e. the nine calendar months) of pregnancy, seven of the life-stages of the coming life are built up in a child's body, spirit and soul. It was as though Rudolf Steiner was telling her a secret of the Temple as he often stated that the human body is a Temple.[12]

Who was Elisabeth Vreede and what was her personal destiny that she incarnated at a time which was too early for her? Many of her friends asked themselves this same question. One of them, Willi Sucher, was a pupil of hers whom she trusted very much. She saw in him someone who could finish her work on astronomy and develop it for further use in the world. Willi Sucher also researched the Order of the Knights Templar. He discussed his questions and research with Elisabeth Vreede and, according to Sucher's account, she showed him notes of a conversation Rudolf Steiner had had with her in connection with the last Grand Master of the Order, Jacques de Molay.[13]

So did Ramon Llull meet Jacques de Molay again?[14] I believe that, yes, we can say they did meet—in another incarnation in the twentieth century! But their work and also their working together was still not easy. They were both born in the Netherlands. They were both deeply connected to Rudolf Steiner. They also worked together in the newly founded Rudolf Steiner School in The Hague where Willem Zeylmans was the school doctor and Elisabeth Vreede was the contact person for the central Council of the Anthroposophical Society in Dornach. This also brought problems. In 1926 Willem Zeylmans van Emmichoven took the initiative to found a World School Movement without informing Stuttgart and Dornach, which led to a fierce meeting on the 6 February 1926 in which not only Willem Zeylmans and Elisabeth Vreede but also Walter Johannes Stein were present.

This was the start of the troubles within the Anthroposophical Society that led in 1935 to the expulsion of a group of members from the Society including Willem Zeylmans, Stein and Elisabeth Vreede. Yet during a time when Walter Johannes Stein was strongly attacked he said words that give hope for our time and with these words I will end this exposition of my ongoing research:

> Maybe at the end of the century it will be possible to work in better harmony with those who oppose each other today due to having different impulses of will. Now we stand before the Golgotha of our Movement. The blood that has flowed can transform itself into roses if we truly find each other.[15]

Frans Lutters was born in 1958. He studied theology, Waldorf education and education (MA) at university. He works as a teacher at the Rudolf Steiner School in Zeist in the Netherlands and is well known as a lecturer and author of books such as The Grail Mystery and the Seven Liberal Arts *(Assen, Nearchus CV).*

He also writes articles for VOK, the magazine for Rudolf Steiner pedagogy in the Netherlands and is co-editor of an English internet site dedicated to the work of Walter Johannes Stein and Daniel N. Dunlop: www.thepresentage.net

Notes

1. B. Sánchez-Segura, *Raimundus Lullus und die Templer* (Madrid 2005).
2. Ibid.
3. Frans Lutters, 'Daniel van Bemmelen 1899–1982', *VOK* (2005, 109).
4. Thomas Meyer, *D.N. Dunlop—A Man of our Time* (Temple Lodge Publishing, London 1992).
5. Zacharias Werner, *Die Söhne des Tals* (Stuttgart, Den Haag, London 1927).
6. Zacharias Werner, *Briefen* (Letters, Band II, nr. 210).
7. Rudolf Steiner, *The East in the Light of the West* (Rudolf Steiner Pub. Co. and Anthroposophic Press, London and New York 1940) (GA 113).
8. Anastasius Grün (Anton Alexander Graf von Auersperg), 1806–76, *Schutt* (Ruins), 1835.
9. Rudolf Steiner, *Esoteric Christianity and the Mission of Christian Rosenkreutz*, tr. M. Barton. (Rudolf Steiner Press, London 2000) (GA 130). Lecture of 12.05.1912.
10. Walter Johannes Stein, 'An appreciation of D.N. Dunlop', in *The Present Age,*

Vol. 1 (No. 1, December 1935). Can be found on the website: www.thepresentage.net

11. Elisabeth Vreede, in *Ein Lebensbild*, Natura Verlag, 54 (1976).

12. Per Leo de la Houssaye in conversation with the author.

13. From karmic group work in the Netherlands with Hans Peter van Manen on the karmic connection of Elisabeth Vreede to Jacques de Molay.

14. Elisabeth Vreede carried out her own research on this and travelled to Majorca to find traces of Ramon Llull.

15. From L. Kolisko in *Eugen Kolisko, Ein Lebensbild* (privately printed, 1961), 132.

What is Happening in the World Today?[1] (1931)

Walter Johannes Stein

A mighty process is taking place today in the world of the spirit. It sends its shadows down into the world of earthly happenings and merges here as a world economic crisis. Yet it is of the utmost importance for us to realize that this economic and industrial crisis is but the expression of a mighty spiritual conflict. Those who refer the present crisis to purely material causes are recognizing partial causes quite truly. Some say that trade has always been subject to periodic fluctuations; we are at present suffering from a wave of depression, let us prepare in patience for the ascending wave of prosperity, to carry us up again. Such statements recognize a part of the reality quite truly, but they tend to undermine the initiative of our active will, whereas a full perception of the causes fires our will, creating as it does the necessary insight for right action. Others say that money is the cause of the economic crisis, in view of the prevailing excess of goods. Owing to the decline in gold production, the growing demand for currency (money) cannot be satisfied and as a consequence we have a congestion of unused commodities. This too is true as a partial aspect. Others again say, not unrightly, that the disturbance is due to Russia's artificial severance from the economic life of the rest of the world.

Or we are told that the trouble originated in America, who with her war profits and with the stimulus of an exceptional wave of prosperity swelled her productive capacity beyond all measure and thus brought about in 1929 a crisis in raw materials and shares, of which the present economic crisis is the immediate result. This too is in accordance with the facts. Others say that the age of capitalism and world economy is past. The age of state controlled economy, industry and trade is upon us. 'Autarchy' is the true form of economic life for the future. Last but not least there are some who say that the crisis is spiritual and cultural. There is a regular lapse of 30 years between an invention and its industrial realization on a larger scale. Thirty years elapsed between James Watt's steam engine and the great steam age, 30 years between Stephenson's locomotive and the age of railway building. And so on. But in 1914, these authors say, a period of 30 years was skipped. Aeroplane, wireless telegraphy and telephony found their way into the industrial world at once, without a 30 years' transition period. Therefore the post-war period is lacking in a great undeveloped invention, changing the face of the industrial world and creating wealth and employment as it does so. The creative genius of this generation has been prematurely spent. Therefore the present is in fact a spiritual crisis.

Thus, from the most material to the most spiritual, every conceivable factor is held responsible for the catastrophe. What is the *real* cause? What, in effect, is happening in the world today? I will attempt to set forth the answer.

Two different Time Spirits are battling for the ascendancy. Two different epochs of civilization are with us, superimposed on one another. The one is imbedded in the other. Different in world conception and in mode of life, they correspond to different economic orders. Their styles of life are radically divergent. They disturb each other. Mankind is faced today with the decisive issue: one of the two Time Spirits must be overcome. Either the worldwide view or else the narrow nationalistic view must win the day. Either the growing principle of world economy or that of exclusive national economies, walled in by protective tariffs, must die. They cannot live together. They are in living contradiction to each other. And yet the battle is not merely between two different economic orders; two different ideas of life, two different civilizations are here involved.

Let us have the spiritual courage to call the combatants by their true names. Let us perceive, in the light of history, who and what they are. They both deserve respect and honour. They both are great, and yet they cannot work together, for they are contrary. It is the Latin and the Anglo-Saxon-Germanic spirit which are here involved. It is the conflict between two epochs of civilization: the older one, the Latin, Roman and Romance, the younger one the Anglo-Saxon and Germanic. It finds expression economically, politically and spiritually: economically as the contrast between world economy and national political economy; politically in the contrast between England and France; spiritually in the question of the day—shall the world's economic life be carried on in a common-sense spirit for the satisfaction of the human beings concerned, or is it to be treated as an appendage to the security question or the like? Is economic life itself, or the political power of the State the primary issue?

Let us reply as objectively as we are able. Let history herself bear witness. How did the present world economy come into being? It began with the deeds of Latin peoples. The Portuguese and Spanish were the first great seafarers and traders of modern time. Thereafter, the Dutch and English came to take their place, that is to say, the Anglo-Saxon and Germanic stream took the place of the Latin stream. The process is not yet complete; it still works on, and it forms the present crisis.

We may consider it in detail. Bernard of Clairvaux, in 1147, in Cologne, preached a great sermon summoning men to the Crusade. His words were heard by English, Dutch and German people. They sailed around the west of Europe, landed on the coast of the Pyrenean peninsula and took Lisbon from the Mohammedans. Thus did Portugal as an independent country become separated from the rest of Spain. It was not the national being of Spain which worked on in Portugal. The severance of Portugal signified the entry of a fresh impulse, wherein the Spirit of the new Time was separating off a fragment of a Latin people, not for national but for worldwide purposes. Thus there arose the voyages of the Portuguese to India. I would fain bring this home especially to English people. It is important for them to be aware that the British world empire was prepared for by a new Spirit, severing something off, to begin with, from the Latin element. The voyages of the Portuguese seafarers bore quite another character from the Spanish. The Portuguese went out for spices, the Spanish for gold. Two very different gifts! Under Emmanuel I the Portuguese dominion in the East Indies was developed.

A word about the spiritual impulse that was at work here. Beside the grave of Godfrey de Bouillon, nine of his knights had pledged themselves to carry on his spiritual impulse. Godfrey had wanted to give Christianity another centre than that of Rome. For this reason he had gone to Jerusalem. He wanted to create a Christianity not Roman (using the Latin language) but of the people, living in local dialect and language. He died before his end was achieved. Most interesting are the detailed facts by which his work was frustrated. In the year 1095, Pope Urban II summoned two Councils. The one was on 1 to 7 March at Piacenza, the other in Clermont, from 18 to 26 November. At the former Council, ambassadors appeared from the Greek emperor Alexius, asking for help against the infidels. The Pope and many 1000's promised a campaign of help to Constantinople. On 27 November, at the close of the latter Council, this campaign was to have been inaugurated. Urban gave a wonderful address, preaching the Crusade. 'It is the will of God,' said the Pope. 'It is the will of God,' echoed the assembled people. But, the historians say nobody knows why the Pope thereupon diverted the expedition from Constantinople to Jerusalem: 'The annals do not tell us what was the occasion for this change.' But in fact they do. Godfrey de Bouillon was discussing the plan of the Crusade with twelve of his companions. It was at St Marie de Puy. In the following night the Archangel Gabriel appeared to one of the twelve, whose name is given as Bartholomew, and thus instructed him: *Send Bishop Ademar of Puy to Pope Urban, to tell him to set free the Holy Tomb.* This then was done.

It was at the behest of the Archangel Gabriel that the Pope diverted the Crusade from Constantinople to Jerusalem. Rome made into her own the very impulse, which had been inaugurated against her, and thereby Godfrey's plans were set at naught! For it is known that Godfrey conceived the plan of the Crusade on the walls of Rome and in conflict with the Pope. So an eyewitness tells in the Zimmern Chronicle. Michael, himself, on the other hand, led Godfrey. Michael, the Prince of the Sun, abounds in all the Godfrey legends. See, for example, the visions which are related by Albert of Aix-la-Chapelle. Gabriel, the guiding Spirit of the Latin impulse (are we not told that the lily in the crest of France was given to a hermit for the King, by the Archangel Gabriel himself!), was the real opponent of Godfrey's intentions. But the nine knights of Godfrey—among them a step-uncle of Bernard of Clairvaux—founded the Order of the Knights Templar, who afterwards received their Statutes from St Bernard himself.

It was the Templars who founded the first international bank. They acquired an untold wealth in gold. But the gold belonged to the Order. The individual Knight Templar was poor. You could pay in an amount to the Order of the Knights Templar in one city and draw it out in another. It was a banking system, administering gold in a selfless way—enough to make such bankers worthy to be put to death! Philip IV, Philip le Bel, the founder of French nationalism, the first French king to forbid the export of gold, once at a time of rebellion took refuge in the house of the Knights Templar. While in the outer courtyard the Templars were shedding their blood on his behalf, Philip, intoxicated by the splendour which surrounded him, resolved in his heart to destroy the wealthy Order and to gain power of their gold himself. And so he did. He brought his influence to bear and compassed the annihilation of the Templars, not only in France but in other countries. Only in Hungary was their persecution postponed. In Portugal and Britain, however, the Order lived on, though in another form. The King of Portugal saved the Knights Templar, their property and their Statutes, and carried them over into the newly founded Order of Christ, the Knights of which became the great discoverers. It was the Orders of St Iago di Compostella, of Calatrava, of the Wing of Michael and of Christ who battled to bring in the new Time for the world. Henry the Navigator, who founded the great seafaring school in southern Portugal, was Grand Master of the Order of Christ. The following Portuguese kings were also Grand Masters of this Order. Thus the

Knights Templar, who could not really be destroyed, led by Michael, brought in the new age that was to come. They were the real inaugurators of our modern world economy. And the Dutch inherited their conquests. For at the very moment when Spain seized hold of Portugal and the progressive spirit in Portugal was thus exterminated, the Spirit of the new Time separated Holland out of the Spanish Empire. The Dutch trading companies took over the Portuguese possessions in East India. And in the end, India came into the hands of the English. An all-embracing view of history shows how the worldwide trading spirit of modern time, which is the true basis of England's greatness, arose out of the Latin being. We can trace the process throughout modern history. The Anglo-Saxon, Germanic being wrests itself free from the mother womb of the Latin. Highly significant, for example, was the defeat of the Spanish Armada, accomplished, incidentally, not simply by the hand of man but by the hand of Michael himself. For it is not for nothing that Goethe, in the *Prologue in Heaven* to his *Faust*, lets the Archangel Michael speak these words:

> And rival storms abroad are surging
> From sea to land, from land to sea.
> A chain of deepest action forging
> Round all, in wrathful energy.
> There flames a desolation, blazing
> Before the Thunder's crashing way:
> Yet, Lord, Thy messengers are praising
> The gentle movement of Thy Day.

> [Bayard Taylor's translation]

It was the storm that destroyed the Spanish Armada. Inexorably, the advancing age came on.

And how is it today? The German Reich, founded in Versailles, was destroyed again in Versailles. So on all hands we see the Anglo-Saxon and Germanic being at grips with the Romance and Latin. And so it is in the economic life.

It is the mighty task of the Latin peoples to give form to all that which lets the 'I' of man wax strong in Memory. Hence we can understand the French idea of *Gloire*, the French idea of national honour. Nationalism took its start from France. The ego-feeling of nationhood was indeed born in France. And it was here that the centralizing power of gold was recognized.

England has quite another task. England is really the first colonial power, in the true sense of the word. England created free trade and the freedom of the seas. England's task is not centralized but decentralizing and worldwide.

But England must not fall a prey to the Latin spirit, not even under stress of difficulty. No doubt the world conditions may be such that in spite of being 'free trade' in idea one is obliged to adopt protective tariffs. The welfare of the nation may demand it. But if one does so one should also recognize that the spirit of the nation is thereby endangered. It would be a backward step not only for England but for all the world if the worldwide spirit were suppressed by a narrowing spirit. This, however, is the danger at the present moment, so long as we only see the world economic crisis as an *economic* crisis. It is so indeed, but above and beyond its economic aspect there are two different Spirits of the Times at war, for the habits of life, the very pace of life, and in the last resort for the civilization of mankind as a whole. This may not be forgotten.

We see how for France and England different things are right. Is it not admirable if one nation, France, out of its sanguine temperament creates fashionable things, while another with a more phlegmatic character, England, produces goods of sterling worth and lasting? The world can do with both. But if the concentration of gold in Paris were to compel England to give up her expensive and sterling manufactures, the whole world would be the loser. The transference of a financial centre from the City to Paris would have a spiritual significance, reaching right down into economic matters.

We live, in spite of all, in the age of world economy and must learn to think in a worldwide spirit. A world economy calls for the highest individualization of economic life and industry. Only if this is recognized will cut-throat competition, with its ensuing wars, give place to mutual and friendly aid. Why should not America excel in mass production, England in goods of sterling quality, Germany in artistic productions (the Zeppelin) and France in things of fashion? Must the whole world be Latinized? If England gave way to this, ceasing to champion the true Spirit of the Time, it would be a great disappointment to Germany. I had hoped that England would have freed herself from the gold standard out of free insight and not only under stress of circumstance. Gold is a thing that must either be administered selflessly, which at the present there is no inclination to do, or we must get free of it. World economy requires that the claim of one as against another should be based on genuine economic services. This kind of claim is conveyed by any piece of paper on which it is recorded. Why bring in gold? Gold only serves to introduce might and political power into the economic life, and in the age of world economy this cannot be. There was some meaning in it in the age of national economies, when the Latin spirit, continuing the impulses of ancient Rome, gave form to political states and powers.

England herself, as a political state, was only gradually born out of the Latin mother. It was at the time of Joan of Arc that the guiding Spirit of the new age freed England from her entanglement with France. Two armies faced each other then. St Michael was pictured on the standard of the French, St George on the standard of the English. It is the same Being. St George is but the human and knightly aspect of the Archangel Michael. We can learn much from this. The Spirit of the new age was leading both armies. The French and the English alike were led by St Michael. Why so? Because the new age needed differentiation. The English and the French nation-souls were from thenceforward to evolve apart, for the healing of both peoples and of humanity. Would that as many human beings as possible might recognize how the spiritual guidance of mankind really works, with impartial love for all, who with their diverse faculties rightly separated can work together for the good of all!

England today stands face to face with the mighty question: Is the impending world economic crisis *merely* an economic crisis? There is clearly to be heard in it the inspiring voice: *Look for the way from Gabriel to Michael!*

Walter Johannes Stein was born in Vienna in 1891. He studied mathematics, physics and philosophy at the University of Vienna and during this time met Rudolf Steiner who gave him guidelines for his studies in philosophy. From this moment Stein became his pupil and he said 'the remainder of my life has been lived in the sign of this discipleship'. He was devoted to Christ and to Rudolf Steiner.

Frans Lutters mentions in his article, included in the present volume, that Stein, through intense spiritual practice, became aware of a previous life in which he was a knight of St James of Compostela. In his autobiography Stein said 'I was not a Cistercian but belonged to an Order of Knights which had been founded on Cistercian principles.' He began to research thoroughly into the Orders of Knights and the following article has been included because of references made about Templar Knights that arose from this research. The article was written in 1931, a time of economic decline; the points he makes also have relevance to the economic difficulties experienced today.

Note

1. Published in *Anthroposophy*, Christmas 1931 (vol. 6, no. 4), pp. 339–50.

An Observation/Meditation Exercise

Siegfried Rudel

The picture below is of a wall panel sculpture that is set high into the wall of the south transept in the Church of St Mary at Sompting, West Sussex. The Knights Templar built the south transept in the late twelfth century. It is a sculpture that 'asks' to be used for observation or meditation and this is set out below.

The figure stands firmly but only with his left leg. Or is he sitting? The right leg may only just have joined the left—in other words, he may have just walked to where he is now. The suggested forward movement is also made visible through the capitals of the two pillars.

The upright stance of a bishop's crosier stands behind him on the left

and has an upright 'stature' of its own. The two enshrining pillars also have an upright quality, and so has the stand to which his hands are reaching out. We therefore see five striking uprights of which the central one is the figure itself.

The foliate tops of the two pillars are not the same; they have quite different gestures. On the left we see a series of sharply upward-pointing arrow shapes, which, if we follow their direction, seem to be filling a bowl above them from which a stream issues that rises upwards into an arch and descends to fill a similar bowl on the opposite side. This is met by a capital with the opposite gesture from the one on the left, namely one of receiving. Its opening gestures are rather like the open beaks of young fledglings anxious to be fed. While the first series of sharply pointing upward gestures are next to the top of the crosier standing by them, the second ready-to-receive gestures on the right can be seen as relating to the mysterious central piece.

The central figure and its gestures may hold the most important messages. Peace streams from his radiant halo. His earnest, silent gaze is directed forwards. His activity lies in his hands and arms, both presented in outsized proportions, especially his hands. Is it really just a book that he points to? Or is it more likely a musical stringed instrument that he is playing? The twice seven rings on his arms readily relate to the seven musical steps, from prime to octave.

Here we do well to remember the role of music in education, as made abundantly clear by Rudolf Steiner in a lecture to the first Waldorf School teachers in Stuttgart on 16 September 1920. He quotes Shakespeare in *The Merchant of Venice* (Act V, scene 1) as an echo in modern terms of what was known in ancient Mystery centres.

> Since naught so stockish, hard, and full of rage
> But music for the time doth change his nature.
> The man that hath no music in himself,
> Nor is not moved with concord of sweet sounds,
> Is fit for treasons, stratagems, and spoils . . .
> Let no such man be trusted.

Where can our observations lead us? Can they begin to 'speak' to us?

Firstly, the crosier's position not only points to the fact that the bishop has come into our vision from the left, but also that he has left this symbol of his rank standing—we might even say abandoned—from where he last held it. He is now moving forward without it.

His gaze, and perhaps his gait also, is directed ever further away from his solitary crosier. He has left it behind, both physically and symbolically. If there were any doubt about this 'leaving behind', we might notice that the other distinguishing mark of a bishop, his mitre, is absent altogether.

The reader may have watched the procession of bishops during the Pope's visit to Britain in 2010 on television. What an impressive array of the many bishops, all adorned with crosiers and mitres!

Here, in the sculpted portrait, only the bare head of the bishop is shown and no mitre is visible. But it *is* shown as the head is surrounded from behind by a radiant sun-aura. His eye, oddly positioned, seems divided into two directions at once—one in the overall forward movement towards the right and the other, directed towards us, the viewers. This is where his hands speak eloquently. They are unusually large, as if to draw our attention to what might be seen and heard as he plays. Are we to join him in his gaze ahead, enlivened by the music he plays?

What are we witnessing? Is it the magic of music that can help to uplift the individual soul to the level of partaking in spirit awareness? We can sometimes observe this when watching a musician lovingly stroke the strings of his instrument.

In conclusion this stone carving that the Templar Knights chose to occupy a space in their chapel may be more than just a picture from the dim past but also a renewed call for selfless working in our present time.

Siegfried Rudel was born 1928 in Glatz, Germany, now Klodzko in Poland. His father and most of his siblings died in the war on the eastern front and he and his mother fled westwards, away from the invading Russians, to Dresden. After the British air raids on Dresden they managed to board a refugee train and travel to Stuttgart where Siegfried was able to take one of the last places in the newly reopened Waldorf school which the Nazis had closed.

He then began his lifelong work in special education, working in Camphill, Aberdeen and Sonnenhof, Switzerland before opening his own school in England— Peredur Home School. Other ventures arose from the Home School project, one of which was Peredur Lanthorn Press which published anthroposophical educational books.

Siegfried has just authored a book on the origin and the 60 years of development of the school, the title of which is By the Light of the Lanthorn *(Temple Lodge Publishing 2011).*